Microsoft® SQL Server® 2012

MASTER DATA SERVICES

Second Edition

About the Author

Tyler Graham is Director of Industry Solutions for the Profisee Group. He moved to Profisee after completing the latest release of Master Data Services as a Senior Program Manager for Microsoft. He has spent over ten years in the data management space and is a frequent speaker at conferences. When he is not working on learning new industry, he is skiing, swimming, or hiking with his family.

About the Technical Editor

Lynn Gasch has worked in software development and testing for more than ten years. After completing degrees in computer science and mathematics at Virginia Tech, she hired on at a small Seattle office focused on artificial intelligence research, and tackled projects in diverse areas such as computer-based education, network monitoring and security, data mining, and information retrieval. She joined Microsoft four years ago and is currently a member of the SQL Server Master Data Services test team. When not working, Lynn and her family enjoy the recreational opportunities of the Pacific Northwest, and she will endeavor to stay off crutches next ski season. Lynn's review of this book was based on her own personal opinions, and not in her capacity as a Microsoft employee.

Microsoft® SQL Server® 2012

MASTER DATA SERVICES

Second Edition

Tyler Graham

New York   Chicago   San Francisco
Lisbon   London   Madrid   Mexico City
Milan   New Delhi   San Juan   Seoul
Singapore   Sydney   Toronto

The McGraw·Hill Companies

Cataloging-in-Publication Data is on file with the Library of Congress

McGraw-Hill books are available at special quantity discounts to use as premiums and sales promotions, or for use in corporate training programs. To contact a representative, please e-mail us at bulksales@mcgraw-hill.com.

Microsoft® SQL Server® 2012 Master Data Services, Second Edition

Copyright © 2013 by The McGraw-Hill Companies. All rights reserved. Printed in the United States of America. Except as permitted under the Copyright Act of 1976, no part of this publication may be reproduced or distributed in any form or by any means, or stored in a database or retrieval system, without the prior written permission of publisher, with the exception that the program listings may be entered, stored, and executed in a computer system, but they may not be reproduced for publication.

All trademarks or copyrights mentioned herein are the possession of their respective owners and McGraw-Hill makes no claim of ownership by the mention of products that contain these marks.

1234567890   DOC DOC   1098765432

ISBN   978-0-07-179785-6
MHID   0-07-179785-8

Sponsoring Editor Wendy Rinaldi	**Technical Editor** Lynn Gasch	**Composition** Cenveo Publisher Services
Editorial Supervisor Janet Walden	**Copy Editor** Bill McManus	**Illustration** Cenveo Publisher Services
Project Manager Sandhya Gola, Cenveo Publisher Services	**Proofreader** Madhu Prasher	**Art Director, Cover** Jeff Weeks
Acquisitions Coordinator Ryan Willard	**Indexer** Karin Arrigoni	**Cover Designer** Jeff Weeks
	Production Supervisor Jean Bodeaux	

Information has been obtained by McGraw-Hill from sources believed to be reliable. However, because of the possibility of human or mechanical error by our sources, McGraw-Hill, or others, McGraw-Hill does not guarantee the accuracy, adequacy, or completeness of any information and is not responsible for any errors or omissions or the results obtained from the use of such information.

Dedicated to Tera, who made all of this possible.

Contents at a Glance

Contents

Foreword

In the last few weeks I have received duplicate mailings from my bank. My doctor confused my records with another patient, also "D. Farmer." A carrier delivered a ceiling fan, ordered online, with a remote control that does not match it; and the next day delivered a pair of shoes of the right brand, the right color, the right size, but the wrong model.

I doubt that I am especially unlucky: we have all had similar experiences. The retailers, manufacturers, and service providers on the other side of these mishaps all have something in common—problems with *master data*.

That these problems are so familiar is a sign that they are pervasive. And over the years we, in the world of data management, have tried to solve them in many ways. We created reference data sets, but often ended up with multiple reference sets covering the same field confusingly. We built data warehouses to drive reporting and analytics, and thought to use them as our "single version of the truth." However, the data warehouse was populated and maintained on a different cycle, and for different purposes, than our line-of-business applications, and the data was not a suitable source for operational use.

In recent years, however, a body of practice has emerged that is aptly named "master data management," or MDM. Practitioners don't stop at just compiling a reference data set, but implement architectures, data-driven processes, practices, and policies that oversee the entire lifecycle of data.

Tyler Graham has been at the forefront of this new practice. Tyler has seen the start of the master data management movement as a consultant solving complex issues for enterprise customers. He has also worked on software solutions, with the vendor Stratature, building an agile and effective MDM solution. More recently, Tyler has been at Microsoft building their Master Data Services platform, which brings master data capabilities to every user of the SQL Server database.

So, I don't think you could find a more able author to introduce you to Microsoft SQL Server's Master Data Services. This book covers everything you need to know: identifying systems that source or require master data; handling the data itself; establishing roles and practices for the "data stewards" and others who manage the processes; and naturally there is a wealth of practical advice on the Master Data Services platform itself.

You'll find this book to be an invaluable guide to a challenging subject area, and a fascinating technology.

–Donald Farmer
Product Advocate for QlikView, QlikTech

Acknowledgments

I would like to thank the entire MDS team for a great second release. Let me give a shout out to Val Lovicz, who provided great feedback on Chapter 14. I would like to thank my wife and kids for their patience while I was writing this, as many commitments suffered accordingly.

–Tyler Graham

Introduction

The release of SQL Server 2008 R2 Master Data Services was the beginning of a new, more accessible era for master data management (MDM); SQL Server 2012 Master Data Services is this vision realized. Because of price and complexity, most solutions on the market today are geared toward large corporations and require dedicated consulting teams to implement. MDS, a feature of SQL Server Enterprise Edition, was built to democratize this process, providing MDM capabilities to a larger audience for a fraction of the price. MDS is meant to be rapidly deployed to any size organization and can solve a variety of master data challenges. The MDS Add-in for Microsoft Excel provides a paradigm shift in master data management by bringing it to the Information Worker (IW) tool of choice.

This book is intended for anyone interested in the features of MDS. It is meant to be used as an introduction, a learning tool, a training guide, and a reference manual. Even if you have no experience with MDS, each chapter builds on the previous chapter, so by the end of the book, you should be able to complete a majority of the tasks needed for a working MDS implementation. If you are a consultant with prior experience in the MDM market, you should find value in the product overview and web service examples, which allow you to adapt your existing MDM practice to support MDS.

Master Data Services is composed of some simple-to-understand components that can be used in a variety of ways. In order to provide the clearest understanding for new users, most of the book shows examples of standard, straightforward implementations. Complex examples and edge cases have been omitted from the book to avoid confusing the message. These complex topics are addressed in various resources you can find on the Internet, including the MDS team blog, www.mdsmodeler.com, and www.mdsuser.com.

What You'll Learn in this Book

The intent of this book is to get you up and running with MDS. By reading it, you should become familiar with MDS-specific terminology (models, entities, attributes) and learn how to use MDS to solve your business problems. Each chapter introduces you to basic concepts, shows you how to use the Master Data Manager web application to perform related tasks, and gives you examples to complete the related tasks programmatically by using the web service.

While the book provides advice on how to create a solution specific to your organization, implementing any MDM solution requires buy-in from many people across the organization. Doing the work to create models that will work for you and getting agreement that the MDS system is truly the system of record is more than half the battle. The book hopes to give you the confidence to approach your organization's MDM issues with a solid knowledge of how to implement and manage an MDM solution by using SQL Server 2012 Master Data Services.

Chapter 1: Introduction to Master Data Services

This chapter introduces the field of master data management and discusses its history. It explores the variety of popular MDM solutions and compares them to the Microsoft Master Data Services solution.

Chapter 2: Installation and Configuration

This chapter helps you consider the scope of your MDS implementation, and then gives you the steps to install and configure MDS. This chapter has a list of the Windows features and roles you must install before you can configure the Master Data Manager web application. This chapter also provides information about updating a prior instance of Master Data Services.

Chapter 3: Starting an MDS Project

This chapter gives you more in-depth ideas about how MDS will fit into your organization. Before you begin working with the product, it is important to spend quality time determining your organization's master data management needs. This chapter also includes information about how to deal with duplicate records and data cleansing.

Chapter 4: Creating Your Model

In this chapter, you start building a model. This chapter explains how to deploy the sample models that are included when you install MDS. This chapter also provides a start-to-finish walkthrough for creating the primary model objects. At the end of this chapter, you will have created a complete product model and should be able to understand the relationships between the MDS model objects.

Chapter 5: Integrating Master Data Services with Other Systems

This chapter explains how to load master data into MDS so that users can begin to manage it. This chapter introduces the database staging tables and the format required for importing data into the tables. It presents sample data, as well as procedures for loading the data and initiating the staging process, which imports the data into the correct tables in the MDS database.

Chapter 6: Working with Hierarchies and Collections

This chapter introduces the different types of MDS hierarchies: explicit and derived. After a brief introduction, you are led through the creation of some sample hierarchies. This chapter also shows variations on these hierarchies, which address specific business cases. This chapter also introduces the concept of collections and shows you how to create one. Finally, code samples show you how to use the web service to work with hierarchies.

Chapter 7: Working with Master Data

This chapter is intended for users who need to work with master data on a daily basis. It details the new Explorer UI in SQL Server 2012 and new features for data exploration and update. This chapter shows you how to filter data to find what you need, how to edit your data, and how to work with data in hierarchies. In addition, you learn how to review and reverse the transactions that are recorded whenever a user changes data. You also learn how to annotate transactions and data, which can be useful for change tracking. Finally, this chapter includes samples for using the web service to retrieve and update data.

Chapter 8: Using Business Rules

This chapter shows you how to create and configure business rules, and then how to publish them and apply them to data. You are shown how to configure e-mail notifications, how to use business rules to create internal workflows, and how to use business rules to trigger external workflows. Finally, code samples show how to use web services to interact with business rules.

Chapter 9: Creating Versions of Data

In this chapter, you learn how to change a version name and description. You learn about saving versions of your data (rather than your model structure), and about what it means to lock and commit a version. This chapter explains how to validate a version against business rules, how to flag a version of your data for subscribing systems or users, and how to determine where a version of data came from. And like all chapters, web service examples are provided.

Chapter 10: SQL Server 2012 MDS Add-in for Excel

This chapter introduces the new SQL Server 2012 "killer app" for Master Data Services, the MDS Add-in for Microsoft Excel. This utility will change the way companies approach master data. This chapter explains how to leverage Excel to make batch updates to existing MDS data and how to create new entities from data stored in regular Excel spreadsheets.

Chapter 11: Implementing Security

This chapter covers how to configure the granular level of security provided by MDS. There have been a number of simplifications made to the MDS security model in the latest release. This chapter explains how to add users and groups, how to configure administrators to have more permissions than the average user, and how to test permissions to ensure you've configured them correctly. This chapter explains the difference between functional area permissions, model object permissions, and hierarchy member permissions. It also explains which permissions apply when overlapping assignments are made. Finally, web service examples show how to set security.

Chapter 12: Publishing Data to External Systems

This chapter explains the concept of subscription views, which are standard SQL views that you create from within MDS. This chapter shows how to use these SQL views to export data to systems outside of MDS.

Chapter 13: Extending MDS with Web Services

This chapter shows you how to enable the web service. It includes a summary of all operations and gives you a basic idea of the use of each. It also includes additional code samples that weren't provided in other chapters, including how to search for members, return member counts, validate data, get and reverse transactions, and handle errors.

Chapter 14: Advanced Modeling

This chapter discusses some advanced modeling techniques to help users get more out of their Master Data Services application. Working with the field, I have seen a number of common errors occur when people build their MDS models. This chapter is labeled advanced to indicate not all users may be able to fully utilize the information in this chapter.

About the Sample Company

Throughout this book we use a fictional company called "Main Street Clothing Company." We envision this company to be a small clothing retailer, just large enough to have a corporate office and manage its own IT. We thought that using one single continuous example would be the most successful way to demonstrate MDS concepts to the uninitiated. MDS was built and priced to provide a solution that can truly solve MDM issues for companies of all sizes, and we wanted to provide a complete example for this new emerging market. No matter the size of your business, many if not all of the concepts explained using Main Street Clothing Company should be applicable to your situation.

About the Sample Data

In many chapters of the book, we mention www.mdsuser.com. We created this site to give you sample data to use as you go through the chapters in the book. Our intention was to give you two common models—Product and Finance—that you could experiment with while reading the book, and then modify in any way you want. These models are not meant to be taken too seriously—they are samples that we put together with the hope that it is easier to learn something when you can see a real-world example. MDS can be used for any domain you care to manage; it's not restricted to lists of customers or products, but these domains provide you with a frame of reference.

You should always feel free to deploy these models, update them to your heart's content, and then delete them and start over. In the writing of this book, we've created and deleted our model dozens of times, and the only recourse is that we lost track of what we were doing from time to time. Until you've seriously solidified your MDS solution, you should feel free to push MDS to its limits and seek help when you're stuck. There is a community of committed users on the MDS forums on MSDN; the forums are often a good place to start when you're troubleshooting.

In this book we also provide code samples that illustrate the more common procedures described in each chapter. Chapter 13 is devoted completely to how to programmatically interact with MDS. All of the code samples in the book are available electronically at www.MHProfessional.com/computingdownload and at www.mdsmodeler.com. These samples are free and are meant to be used in support of the book. We truly hope you find the samples and this book useful and that you achieve success with your MDM implementation.

Chapter 1

Introduction to Master Data Services

In This Chapter

Master Data Services (MDS) is Microsoft's solution for managing master data. In the past, master data management (MDM) has been a highly problematic area for database administrators. To help you understand better how MDS addresses the inherent challenges of MDM, this chapter begins by explaining what MDM encompasses and how it has been handled historically. It then introduces you to MDM solutions other than MDS and explains their shortcomings so that you can fully appreciate the features and functionality of MDS, which is introduced in the latter half of the chapter. The chapter wraps up by introducing you to the sample company we'll be using throughout the rest of the book and describing some of its business problems that a master data management solution is meant to solve.

What Is Master Data Management?

Master data management (MDM) is the management of the nontransactional data within an organization. Throughout the book we will use the terms organization, business, and company interchangeably. The definition of "master" data varies by organization, but can be loosely defined as the nouns that describe all business processes. These nouns might be organization-specific data, like your organization's list of products or list of employees. Or the nouns might be common reference data provided by an external service provider or government agency, like address information or a Dunn & Bradstreet (D-U-N-S®) number. Although customer and product are the two most commonly managed domains, many businesses find value in managing additional domains, such as wells and fields at big oil companies and recipes at food manufacturers.

NOTE

When we discuss MDM, we often use the word domain. *We use this overloaded word to mean a group of related business data that is an area of focus for an MDM solution—for example, accounts or customers.*

In most businesses, customers buy products or services. Because customer relationships are essential, each time a customer buys a product or service, the transaction is recorded. After the transaction is recorded and coded properly, the details of the transaction will never change. MDM is about managing the relationships between these static transactions, rather than the transactions themselves. For example, for a retail chain, each store has a certain group of products in its inventory and a database of registered customers. The list of products available to sell and the list of customer addresses are master data. That Sally bought four shirts on Friday is a transaction.

The more often this data is required for a transaction, the greater its importance to your organization. Central management of this data helps identify data discrepancies between multiple transactional systems and helps your organization run more efficiently.

Master data management is composed of the following:

▶ The business policies (who owns the data, where the data lives, and so forth)

▶ The processes (how the data is updated)

▶ The technological tools that facilitate these processes

By definition, all companies must utilize some form of MDM, although the term generally refers to the implementation of formalized processes and specifically designed tools.

History of Master Data Management

When companies began using computer applications to manage information, in order to perform tasks and generate results, all pertinent data had to be loaded into each application directly. Over time, companies adopted more applications and had to enter the same dataset into each of them. As a response to this, developers began to employ the technique of creating master files that stored key, reusable data for use within each application. These initial master files were the first MDM systems.

Once the master data was loaded into each application, new records would be added in the application or to the master list, the result of which was that the two sets of data were no longer in sync. Early data reconciliation efforts were time consuming and costly. Very few tools existed that could identify differences and manage duplicate records.

Enterprise resource planning (ERP) systems were then created to help combine the data in these systems and to solve the constant need for integration between systems. ERP systems were meant to be single software suites that managed standard business processes within an organization. Each module in an ERP system could leverage the common master data tables required for the associated business process. Many organizations today consider the master data tables within their ERP systems to be the "master" data within their organization.

As more and more organizations adopted ERP systems, they realized that using these single systems in isolation was an unrealistic solution. They then adopted multiple ERP systems, and their master data problems re-emerged. Specialized systems designed to manage the most problematic domains became major implementations in larger organizations. Now there is a push in the industry to provide solutions that can solve MDM issues across a wide variety of domains.

Overview of Other Master Data Management Solutions

All organizations must deal with their MDM issues. Whether managing domains in Excel spreadsheets or managing them with a specialized solution, a key role of the IT department in any size organization today is to provide processes for managing master data and integrating it across all systems. Various solutions other than MDS are available, but each has weaknesses that are addressed by MDS.

As explained in the following sections, ERP solutions have several drawbacks as MDM solutions; other specialized solutions can prove to be too specialized; and MDM solutions typically cater to only the biggest organizations. As you will read later in the chapter, in MDS, Microsoft hopes to provide an adaptable solution that can cater to organizations of all sizes.

ERP Systems as MDM Solutions

While ERP systems are a significant consumer of master data, using these systems by themselves to manage master data has major drawbacks. Also, the initial vision that a single ERP system would handle all of the computing needs of an organization was shortsighted.

ERP Systems Are Not Specialized or Innovative

While many ERP systems contain modules for most common business processes, a specific industry need or the need for more innovative software leads businesses to implement additional systems. Integration of these new systems with current IT infrastructure and business processes becomes a major implementation cost of any new system.

ERP Systems Do Not Play Well with Others

When a company merges with or acquires another company, it inherits additional ERP systems. Since these systems are highly customized and not initially designed for easy integration, additional processes must be created to ensure that these systems are synchronized across the organization. The complexities of these software systems and the underlying data models make successful integration, or even effective synchronization, extremely difficult for large organizations. When Tyler moved across the country for work, it was impossible for his electronic bank accounts at a nationwide bank to move with him because each of the bank's regions was on its own system. Imagine, it was easier to move the contents of a house 3000 miles than to move a set of data and transactions that would fit on a thumb drive.

ERP Systems Do Not Manage Analytical Dimensions Effectively

The need for complex modeling and analysis of transactional data to determine statistics and trends has led companies to create advanced online analytical processing (OLAP) systems and associated data warehouses to go along with them. These systems have added new, complex data modeling needs that simply are not supported in legacy applications. Hierarchies and other consolidations are not natively managed by ERP systems.

ERP Systems Are Not Designed to Manage Attributes

Many ERP system vendors realize that users will want to store additional attributes in their master tables. To accommodate this, they provide a few custom fields for customers to use as they see fit. These custom fields get overloaded with information without providing any validation of appropriate use.

Specialized Master Data Management Solutions

As you would suspect, the most common domains for management are those domains most troublesome to large organizations. Specialized systems have been created to manage these domains, with many features designed directly for them. These systems are designed to manage a single domain and don't translate well to other master data problems. The two most common types of specialized solutions for managing master data are customer data integration and product information management.

Customer Data Integration

Customer data integration (CDI) solutions are designed to provide a standard view of customers across an organization. Some CDI solutions accomplish this as a single system that centralizes customer data across an enterprise. Other solutions manage the integration of multiple ERP systems and additional systems through a registry approach. These solutions manage customer IDs from multiple systems to ensure synchronization and to provide a consistent view of each customer.

A central feature of CDI solutions is the ability to identify and manage duplicate customer records. Other common features include address correction and standardization and the ability to integrate with service organizations to further enrich business-specific customer knowledge. CDI implementations tend to incorporate most systems within an enterprise and focus on a relatively small subset of attributes.

Companies with customer management problems will certainly benefit from a CDI implementation. Unfortunately, these features do not translate well to managing other domains across the enterprise such as organization or product.

Product Information Management

Product information management (PIM) solutions are designed for the product domain. There are fewer PIM solutions than CDI solutions, and PIM solutions tend to focus on specific industries. Most PIM solutions centralize product data management and provide integration to many distribution systems. These solutions tend to be implemented in large retailers and wholesalers that need to manage multiple sales channels for large product catalogs. Management of online catalogs and integration with standardized product channels are some specialized features of PIM solutions.

Again, these systems are highly effective to solve a narrow band of problems. These systems do not translate well to additional domains. Very few providers have solutions in both the CDI and PIM spaces.

Catering to the Titans

Historically, vendors of MDM solutions have catered to the needs of Fortune 500 companies. Until recently, the MDM market was dominated by complex and expensive applications that generate large amounts of consulting dollars to trained implementers. These companies generally have the means and the budget to pay for the consulting time and tools that comprise an MDM solution. These solutions are tied to either a specific domain or a feature set that supports one domain better than others. These solutions are expensive and are built to solve a unique set of issues in large organizations. The size and complexity of these engagements has led many of these projects to end in failure.

The MDM market's focus on Fortune 500 companies doesn't mean that small and midsize companies don't face similar issues with managing their data. Any organization that's attempting to store critical data in multiple systems or spreadsheets and having trouble determining a true version of its master data is in need of an MDM solution.

The costs associated with MDM solutions and the high risk of failure in self-deploying such solutions leave a large portion of the small and midsize business market underserved. Out of necessity, many of these businesses are using Excel spreadsheets or internally designed systems to manage master data. These systems typically neglect the need for security, central management, and versioning.

Microsoft's Solution to Master Data Management

Microsoft first shipped Master Data Services with SQL Server 2008 R2. That release was largely about Microsoft entering the MDM market and beginning to shape the discussion around MDM. It also provided an opportunity for Microsoft to begin building channels for partners that both implement the solution and create additional applications on top of MDS. In effect, the first release was about getting into the game. The second release is about changing the rules. In SQL Server 2012, MDS looks to redefine the MDM market, expanding the types of data stored and easing the barriers to managing that data. This section provides a quick overview of the new MDS features in SQL Server 2012 as well as the features carried forward from SQL Server 2008 R2.

New Features of MDS in SQL Server 2012

Microsoft has added a number of new features to increase the usability and applicability of MDS.

MDS Add-In for Microsoft Excel

Well before the original version of MDS shipped with SQL Server 2008 R2, Microsoft had the most widely used MDM tool in the market: Excel. More master data is stored within Excel worksheets than any other tool on the market. The new SQL Server Master Data Services Add-in for Microsoft Excel will enable owners of this data to continue to leverage all of the features of Excel that they know and love as they move their data from the desktop to the server. Chapter 10 provides a tutorial on the new Add-in for Excel.

Entity-Based Staging

While the original MDS staging process is available in this release, a new staging schema will contain a new staging table for each created entity. These tables provide a far more intuitive process for loading bulk data into MDS. This new process will be described in Chapter 5.

What Master Data Services Still Delivers

MDS provides a number of features that facilitate central management of master data while providing greater access to the editors and consumers of this information.

Domain Agnostic

MDS is not designed for a specific domain. Any data type and virtually any data schema can be supported by the MDS system. Chapter 3 discusses how to map your organization's systems and determine how MDS might best suit your needs. Chapter 4 shows you how to create your models, entities, and attributes, which are the core MDS objects.

Hierarchy Management

Excel- and IT-developed applications are notoriously bad at representing hierarchical data. Specialized controls and multiple hierarchy types in MDS provide effective and flexible management of business hierarchies. Chapter 6 shows you how to create hierarchies and collections.

Web-Based UI

A web-based user interface (UI) provides access to a large user base without the need for installing software on numerous machines. As intranet access becomes more portable, mobile device access can be integrated into the MDM story. Chapter 7 provides instructions for business users to help them work with data in the Master Data Manager web application, which is the primary place where business users will interact with the data.

Transaction Logging

Even with a robust security model, it is essential to provide an audit trail of changes. MDS provides a filterable transaction log to ensure a manageable history of changes. Chapter 7 explains how to view and reverse transactions. It also explains how to annotate transactions so users can explain why they made changes to the master data.

Data Validation

Many master data lists require additional validation to ensure certain fields are populated in specific cases. Business Rules can provide users with a proactive monitoring process to ensure data validity before these lists are used in process systems. Chapter 8 shows you how to create business rules and set up notifications to users of Master Data Services.

Versioning

Many domains require snapshots of different points in time to be maintained. With MDS, each model can be versioned, which allows users to tag specific versions for subscribing systems. Chapter 9 shows you how to create versions of a model and how to flag versions for subscribing systems.

Security

The ability to control access at the entity, attribute, and record levels allows IT to empower business stewards to update data in a single centralized tool without risking unauthorized changes. Chapter 11 shows you how to implement security.

The Value Proposition

The MDS system is built to be rapidly deployed for any domain within an organization. Once deployed, all models support additional customization without complex coding or reconfiguration. The intent is to make MDM software more accessible to small and midsize businesses, and to aid departments of large companies in creating solutions for themselves. While MDS provides a rich web services platform for system integration, enabling you to use web services to create your own custom user interface, you do not need to use web services to take advantage of what MDS has to offer. An MDS implementation can be completed successfully by business users with no programming knowledge.

About the Sample Company

In an effort to provide context to the features of MDS, all of our examples are based on a fictitious children's clothing company called Main Street Clothing Company. This company is a regional retailer with stores in three states.

For the past ten years the company has been in an expansion phase; it has a novel store layout and, with the bankruptcy of a competitor, it has grown to 13 locations. As the economic environment has cooled, the company is looking to manage costs and understand its business better.

An IT study early in the year determined that a new ERP implementation would be cost prohibitive and that the company would be best served by committing to its current IT infrastructure for a minimum of five years. Figure 1-1 shows the overall IT infrastructure.

In the ERP study, a number of inefficiencies and poor business processes were identified:

▶ While the purchasing department was able to track merchandise purchases through purchase orders added to the financial system, contacts and specifics were being managed in a number of Excel spreadsheets. When the purchasing manager was in the hospital unexpectedly for two weeks, the employees who filled in didn't understand much of the process.

▶ The addition of a new website sales channel in 2007 led to a rapid expansion in both product and customer lists that were not managed well. Customer information was inconsistent and difficult to manage. Many products online were drop shipped, leading to some confusion with the current warehouse process because logistics personnel could not readily identify these items and thus spent time looking for the items or attempting to request additional inventory from the purchasing department.

Figure 1-1 *System architecture for Main Street Clothing Company*

▶ Management has been complaining about the speed at which reports have been provided at month end. Complexity of the organization and the constant changes to its hierarchies has led to almost a week of cleanup and reconciliation effort with each month's end.

By implementing Master Data Services in Main Street Clothing Company, we hope to provide continuity to the procedures and give context to the business problems and processes being solved in our implementation.

Summary

Master data management issues are pervasive within organizations and have existed since the beginning of the electronic age. Solutions have evolved over time to address these issues, and Master Data Services is another phase of that evolution. Traditionally, MDM solutions have tended to cater to larger corporations that can afford customized solutions for specific domains. MDS provides an accessible and affordable solution for organizations of all sizes. Throughout this book, we will incorporate samples designed for a small company that is tackling common MDM challenges.

Chapter 2

Installation and Configuration

In This Chapter

- ▶ **Determining the Initial Scope of Your Project**
- ▶ **Preparing the Web Server**
- ▶ **Installing Master Data Services**
- ▶ **Creating an MDS Database**
- ▶ **Creating the Master Data Manager Web Application**
- ▶ **Securing Your Web Application**
- ▶ **Getting the Latest Version of MDS**
- ▶ **Upgrading 2008 R2 MDS**
- ▶ **Repairing the MDS Database**

T he first step in any software application is to deploy the software, and Master Data Services is no exception. In this chapter, we begin with a quick discussion of project size and scope. This should help you determine your needs, including whether you need any external assistance. We then discuss installing the application to a server. As MDS is a web-based application, the deployment and configuration can be extensive. Many users may be upgrading MDS from 2008 R2, we will discuss this process as well as the new repair feature. At the end of the chapter, we discuss options to ecure your data and some steps to extend the application.

Determining the Initial Scope of Your Project

Before installing Master Data Services, it is important to determine your short- and medium-term goals for the application. MDS was designed as a web application to provide a simple deployment model for a wide range of organizations. This is also a good time to make sure you have the necessary information to deploy and configure the application successfully, and to determine whether your project requires external expertise. There are a number of questions to consider before installing MDS:

▶ *Which domains will I manage in MDS?* While this book addresses how to organize this data in later chapters, it is important to take an initial assessment of what data must be stored to create a functional MDS solution.

▶ *How many attributes will I need to manage?* For each domain that will be managed in MDS, it is valuable to understand the number of attributes that are relevant to the organization. A central benefit of MDS is the ability to modify your model at any time, so a complete list is not essential. A rough estimate of the number of attributes provides one of the best metrics of the scope of the management problem and can provide insight into the owners, editors, and consumers of the records to be managed.

▶ *How many employees will edit the data?* To provide an effective long-term solution and to see the largest return on investment (ROI) for any master data management solution, it is imperative to empower the owners of the data to make changes directly within the system. Whether this is accomplished directly in the Master Data Manager web application or in some external entry system that is integrated with MDS, empowering the business owners reduces IT effort and eliminates the communication breakdowns that occur when routing data changes through IT.

▶ *How many employees will consume the data?* Ideally, completed implementations should give everyone with a business need in the organization the access to the cleanest and most accurate data at all times. In most MDM projects, reaching this ideal state is a work in progress and data consumers should be prioritized based on business need and the costs associated with providing access.

▶ *How many systems do I need to integrate?* Depending on the size of the organization, identifying all systems that rely on a specific domain may not be feasible this early in a project. Most small and medium-sized businesses should identify all systems that consume the domain to be mastered and determine the primary owner of each system.

Based on the preliminary data that you discover from answering the preceding questions, you can determine the relative complexity of your MDM project. The table shown in Figure 2-1 should help you to enumerate the complexity of your project.

The complexity of your project should affect both the scope of the implementation and the amount of ongoing effort required to maintain the MDS project. Small projects should be manageable by novice individuals with sufficient business knowledge and the aid of this book. These projects should be functional and productive within a week's worth of effort.

	Small	**Medium**	**Large**
Entities	Fewer than 20	Fewer than 50 per model	More than 50 per model
Attributes	Fewer than 20	Fewer than 50 per model	More than 50 per model
Hierarchies	Fewer than 5	Fewer than 4 per model	More than 4 per model
Source Systems	Fewer than 3	Fewer than 3 per model	More than 3 per model
Subscribing Systems	Fewer than 5	Fewer than 5 per model	More than 5 per model
Simple Workflows	Fewer than 5	Fewer than 5 per model	More than 5 per model
Complex Workflows	0	Fewer than 3 per model	More than 3 per model

Simple   Complex

Figure 2-1 *Project scope*

Many small projects revolve around finding a home for "homeless" data within the organization. This data is critical to regular business processes, but not important enough to be managed in any standard process system. Much of this homeless data tends to live in unmanaged Excel spreadsheets. The transition of this homeless data into MDS can provide structure and control over it. If IT personnel were previously responsible for managing changes provided by business users, they can now provide users with access to the appropriate data directly. No formal roles or duties need to be created.

A wide range of projects fall into the intermediate range. These projects can be handled internally, but require resources to be fully committed to the implementation effort. Most small and medium-sized business implementations will be intermediate-sized projects. As these projects become more complex, bringing in outside expertise for the implementation should be considered seriously. Making the decision to do so does not diminish the need for internal knowledge and education; although these consultants will aid in the implementation of the solution initially, internal staff will be needed to maintain the MDM system and processes going forward. Most of these projects can be managed in a single phase, requiring approximately 30 to 200 hours to be successfully implemented. Identification of at least one data steward within the organization is essential to long-term success.

Data steward is a common role found in MDM projects. These individuals tend to be technically savvy while still understanding the nuances of the business domains. A data steward must be a champion of data governance and must help create sustainable data maintenance processes within the organization. Many times, data stewards find themselves acting as referees in how data is maintained, caught between competing business processes and applications. Systems may maintain different rules regarding the quality and timeliness of data that must be managed by the data steward. The ability to find efficient compromises will determine how effective a data steward is for an organization.

Once projects reach a certain level of complexity, they become too large to manage in a single phase. The cost and complexity of these large projects requires engaging external expertise that can provide the guidance and resources necessary to implement enterprise-wide MDM solutions. These large projects may span multiple years and locations, and breaking these projects into multiple milestones and ROI checkpoints is advisable. If these projects can be broken down into more manageable intermediate projects, lessons learned from preceding projects can be applied to later implementations.

About the Main Street Clothing Company Implementation

Main Street Clothing Company will be managing two models within MDS, Finance and Product. Within these models, the company plans to maintain fewer than ten entities. Initially, the number of systems to integrate will be limited to three process systems. Based on this information, IT feels comfortable providing a single internal resource to build and deploy MDS. Billy Jean, an IT-savvy assistant to the controller, has been identified to manage the Finance model. The Product model will be managed by a designee of the VP of Purchasing. This person has not yet been identified.

Preparing the Web Server

Master Data Services requires a 64-bit machine and runs only on the following operating systems:

- ▶ Windows Server 2008
- ▶ Windows Server 2008 R2
- ▶ Windows Vista Business, Enterprise, and Ultimate
- ▶ Windows 7 Professional, Enterprise, and Ultimate

While MDS needs to create (or attach) a backend database to either a SQL Server 2008 R2 instance or a SQL Server 2012 instance, this instance does not need to be located on the same machine. MDS does not support SQL Server Standard or Express editions for the database backend.

In preparation for installing the MDS application, you must enable a number of Windows features to support the web-based UI.

Windows 7 Web Application Requirements

Figure 2-2 identifies the minimum Windows features that must be enabled for MDS to function properly in Windows 7. To turn on these features, open Control Panel, click Programs, click "Turn Windows features on or off," select the check box for each of the features highlighted in Figure 2-2, and then click OK.

Figure 2-2 *Windows features (highlighted) required in Windows 7 for MDS*

Windows Server 2008 R2 Web Application Requirements

In Windows Server 2008 R2, use Server Manager to configure the following role services and features.

First, install the Application Server role services by completing the following steps:

1. Open Server Manager.
2. In the left pane, expand Roles.
3. Click Application Server.
4. In the Summary section, Role Services subsection, click Add Role Services on the right.
5. Select the following role services:

   ▶ NET Framework 3.5.1

   ▶ Web Server (IIS) Support

   ▶ HTTP Activation (under Windows Process Activation Service Support)
6. Click Install.

Now, install the Web Server role services by completing the following steps:

1. Open Server Manager.
2. In the left pane, expand Roles.
3. Click Web Server (IIS).
4. In the Summary section, Role Services subsection, click Add Role Services on the right. Select the following role services:

Role Service	Setting
Common HTTP Features	Static Content Default Document Directory Browsing HTTP Errors
Application Development	ASP.NET .NET Extensibility ISAPI Extensions ISAPI Filters
Health and Diagnostics	HTTP Logging Request Monitor

Role Service	Setting
Security	Windows Authentication
	Request Filtering
Performance	Static Content Compression
Management Tools	IIS Management Console

Now install the following features by completing the following steps:

1. Open Server Manager.
2. In the left pane, click Features.
3. In the right pane, click Add Features. Select the following features:

Feature	Setting
.NET Framework 3.5.1 Features	.NET Framework 3.5.1
	WCF Activation
	HTTP Activation
	Non-HTTP Activation
Windows PowerShell Integrated Scripting Environment	
Windows Process Activation Service	Process Model
	.NET Environment
	Configuration APIs

Installing Master Data Services

Installing MDS is a relatively simple process and is only responsible for dropping the bits onto the machine. Any machine that will implement the Master Data Manager web application or the web services needs to run the installation package. In SQL Server 2012, the MDS feature is now a shared feature of the standard SQL Server setup.

Procedure: How to Install Master Data Services

To install Master Data Services, complete the following steps:

1. Run the BI or Enterprise Edition SQL Server Install, as MDS is now a part of the main install process as a shared feature.

2. On the Installation Type page, shown here, select a 2012 server instance or install a new instance. Since MDS is a shared feature, this will have no effect on the installation.

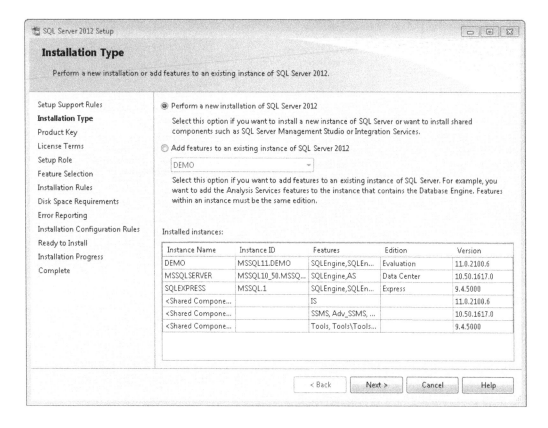

3. Click Next.
4. On the Feature Selection page, select the Master Data Services check box at the bottom of the Features list.

5. Click Next.
6. Depending on the other features you have selected, additional setup pages may appear. No settings chosen on these pages affect your Master Data Services implementation.
7. The last setup screen shows a summary of your installation selections.
8. When the installation completes, click Finish.

   After successful installation, you must open Master Data Services Configuration Manager. You can now use it to create your database and website and to enable web services.

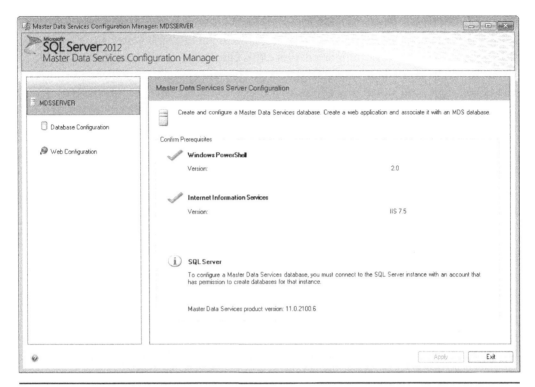

Figure 2-3   *Master Data Services Configuration Manager*

About MDS Configuration Manager

Once the bits are installed, MDS Configuration Manager will assist you in the process of configuring MDS for first use. MDS Configuration Manager, shown in Figure 2-3, is divided into two sections: Database Configuration and Web Configuration. The initial screen indicates whether or not the prerequisites, valid versions of Windows PowerShell and Internet Information Services, can be found. If not, you will need to resolve these issues before continuing with configuration of MDS.

Creating an MDS Database

The initial step in configuring Master Data Services is to create a new MDS database. You can create the database on either a SQL Server 2008 R2 database server or a SQL Server 2012 database server. Whether this is a local instance or an instance that exists on another database server, MDS Configuration Manager will perform a check to ensure that the database server is Enterprise, Developer, or DataCenter. In SQL Server 2012, the BI edition is also supported. Once this check is successful, an "empty" MDS database will be created on the database server. This empty database will contain all of the tables, views, and stored procedures that make up the architecture of MDS.

You must first determine whether to install the MDS database locally or on another machine. There are two major factors that should influence this decision:

▶ *Do you already have access to a database farm or server running SQL Server 2008 R2 or 2012?* Although not always available, this would provide the most economical way to split the two roles of MDS onto separate machines. Please be aware that MDS licensing requires that all machines that have any component of MDS installed must be licensed for the SQL Server 2012 BI edition or higher. The only exception to this is a database server supporting SQL Server 2008 R2.

▶ *Does your organization have any restrictions about having the database server and web server roles on the same machine?* Although this is an antiquated philosophy born in older, less secure versions of both products, some companies still insist that the database server and web server not be on the same box.

A lesser concern for most companies should be the application's performance. Although it is true that MDS will use processor capacity for both stored procedures on the database server and handling requests on the web server, in most implementations these burdens should be handled by standard hardware that is available on the market today. Microsoft does not provide minimum hardware requirements for MDS, but due to the cost of the license, we suggest a minimum of 8GB of RAM on a quad-core machine. With this configuration, an implementation that must support 20 concurrent users would be fine.

Procedure: How to Create an MDS Database

The Master Data Services database is where your master data will be stored. To create an MDS database, complete the following steps:

1. If Master Data Services Configuration Manager is not open, launch it from Programs | Microsoft SQL Server 2012 | Master Data Services | Configuration Manager.

NOTE

Master Data Services 2012 can be installed concurrently with MDS 2008 R2, so be careful that you open the correct Configuration Manager.

2. In the left pane, click Database Configuration.
3. In the right pane, click the Create Database button.

Click to create the database.

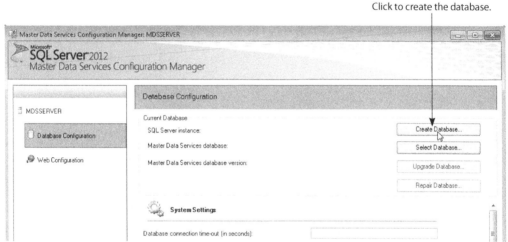

The Create Database Wizard is launched.

4. Click Next.
5. On the Database Server page, leave the defaults unless you want to connect to a remote instance of SQL Server or use a different type of authentication. If you choose Integrated Security, you must use the credentials of the logged-in user.

NOTE

In this example we specify a local account, but you can use a domain account instead.

6. Click Test Connection to ensure you can connect successfully.

7. Click OK to close the dialog box.
8. Click Next.
9. On the Database page, enter a name for your database. Depending on the collation and regional settings for your database, searches you do in the Master Data Manager web application may or may not be case sensitive. I would not change default collations without a good reason within your organization.

10. Click Next.
11. On the Service Account page, type the name of the account that the websites use to connect to the database. Later, you will designate the same account if you create an associated website.
12. Click Next.

13. On the Administrator Account page, type the name of a user who you want to have the ability to edit all data and to view and update all models. This user is more likely to be a business owner than to be an IT person.

14. Click Next.

15. On the Summary page, click Next.

16. A progress message is displayed while the database is created. When it's done, you should see a success message.

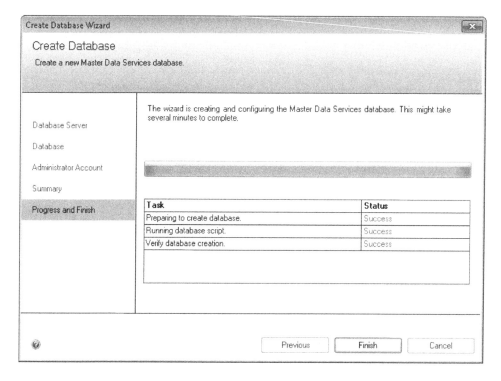

17. Click Finish to close the wizard.

MDS Configuration Manager opens and displays the default settings.

About System Settings

System settings displayed on the Database Configuration page of MDS Configuration Manager are stored in your MDS database in the tblSystemSetting table. These settings apply to the database, the website, and web services. Many of the system settings are self-explanatory, but we will discuss them in the chapters that explain the features they apply to. For now, you can leave the default values.

Creating the Master Data Manager Web Application

Throughout much of this book, we will talk about Master Data Services as a platform. MDM applications need the capability to integrate with all of the systems and business processes within an organization. Unlike other platforms that Microsoft creates, MDS comes with a complete user-facing, web-based UI. Configuring this web application on a web server will allow any user to access MDS through their browser.

NOTE

MDS officially supports Internet Explorer 7 and 8. While users can access the site using other browsers, those other browsers may display screens incorrectly, with menus that behave poorly or not at all. Unless you are extremely adventurous and vehemently opposed to IE, always access MDS with IE 7, 8, or 9.

When creating the Master Data Manager web application, there are two possible workflows: either you select the default website and create the web application, or you create a new website and the web application is automatically created. Later in this chapter, we discuss how to secure your website. If you plan to secure MDS to require Secure Sockets Layer (SSL) connections, it is advisable to create a new site now.

Changes to any of this web configuration information at any time will not affect the underlying MDS implementation. All MDS implementation-specific data is stored in the database. This allows you to back up and restore MDS on any number of servers or configurations without any potential for loss of data. The same database could potentially be used by multiple websites or servers configured instead of the same database server. If your server is part of a server farm where the default site has been removed or you cannot use it, you can create a site now. Otherwise, you can skip this procedure, select the default website, and go straight to creating your application.

Procedure: How to Create a Master Data Manager Website (Optional)

To create a Master Data Manager website, complete the following steps:

NOTE

If you create a new site, the web application is automatically created. You can skip the procedure for creating a web application and continue with associating the site to the database.

1. Open Master Data Services Configuration Manager.
2. In the left pane, click Web Configuration.
3. In the right pane, select "Create new website" from the Website drop-down menu.

A new website is now an option in the Website drop-down list.

4. In the Create Website dialog box, enter a name for your website.

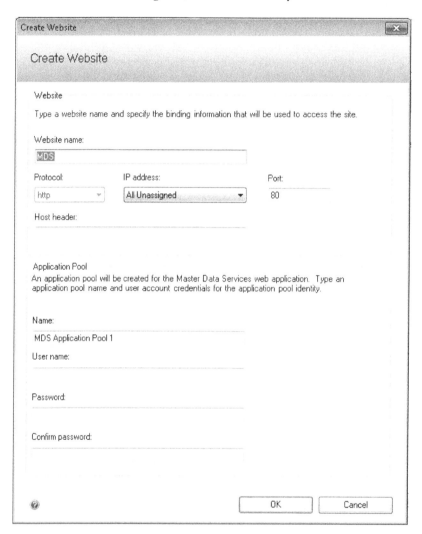

5. The Protocol setting is now locked down for HTTP. If you need to use HTTPS, you will have to use IIS to configure the site after it is installed.

6. In the IP address and Port fields, leave the default values or enter new values. A default installation in Windows 7 already uses port 80, so you must select a different port, like 8080, or you will get an error.

7. For the Host header field, if your site is going to be on an intranet, leave it blank. If your site will be available on the Internet or you want to create multiple host names for your site, enter the host name.

8. In the Application Pool section, leave the name of the site or enter your own. An application pool with this name will be created in IIS.

9. In the User name field, enter the same username you used as the service account when you created the database.

10. In the Password and Confirm password fields, enter the user account password.

11. Click OK.

12. A note about HTTPS is displayed. Click OK.

For more information about securing your website, see the "Securing Your Web Application" section later in this chapter.

Procedure: How to Create a Master Data Manager Web Application

If you chose to use the default website, you can create the Master Data Manager web application by completing the following steps:

1. In the Website drop-down list, select Default Web Site and then click the Create Application button.

Click to create a web application.

2. In the Create Web Application dialog box, you can change the default alias or application pool names or leave them alone. The alias determines your URL. In this example, the URL will be http://MDSServer/MDS.

3. In the User name field, type the name of the user you used for the service account when creating the MDS database. This user is the application pool identity in IIS.

4. Click OK to save.

Procedure: How to Associate the MDS Database with the Web Application

You must now associate a database with the web application you just created.

1. On the Web Configuration screen, in the Associate Application with Database section, click the Select button.

2.   In the Connect to a Master Data Services Database dialog box, click Connect.

3. In the Master Data Services Database list, your database is automatically selected. Click OK to close the window. You can now view the association between your website and its database.

The SQL Server instance associated with your web application is displayed.

4. Click Apply to save your changes.

After you associate your web application with your MDS database, you are prompted to launch the web application. If you can successfully open the Master Data Manager home page from the local machine and from other machines on the intranet, your installation has been successful.

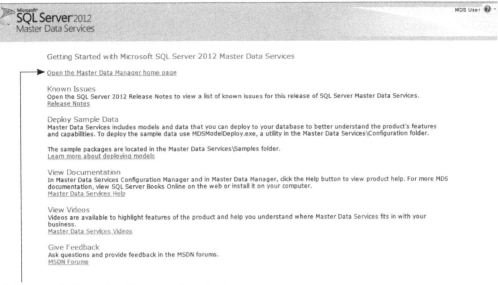

Click to open the Master Data Manager web application.

If Internet Explorer prompts you for your username and password, enter the credentials you used for the Administrator Account when creating the database. Other users do not have permission to access the Master Data Manager web application until the administrator gives them permission.

Securing Your Web Application

MDS Configuration Manager will create an unsecured website only. This means that data traveling over the wire (between the web server and the client's browser) is unencrypted and readable by anyone. Since this site will not be publicly available and the master data stored is not highly sensitive, these settings should be fine for most organizations. If you are concerned about the security of your master data or if sensitive internal information is stored in MDS, you can require SSL for your website.

This requires completing three steps: create or download a certificate, apply the certificate to the default website, and require SSL.

First, you must download a certificate for your website. To do so, complete the following steps:

1. Open Internet Information Services (IIS). You can locate it by clicking Start, right-clicking Computer, and choosing Manage. IIS is listed under Services and Applications.
2. In the Connections pane, click the server name.
3. In the center pane, double-click Server Certificates.
4. In the Actions pane, click the action preferred by your organization. Since every company has a different policy for getting and managing certificates, we will leave the acquisition of your certificate up to you.

After you have a valid certificate, you must apply the certificate to the website. To do so, complete the following steps:

1. In IIS, click Default Web Site (or other site you created).
2. In the Actions pane, click Bindings.
3. Click the Add button.
4. From the Type list, select https.
5. Select the SSL certificate you created.
6. Click OK.
7. Click Close.

Now require SSL by completing the following steps:

1. In the Connections pane, click the website.
2. In the center pane, double-click SSL Settings.
3. Select the Require SSL check box and indicate whether you want to ignore, accept, or require client certificates.
4. In the Actions pane, click Apply.

Getting the Latest Version of MDS

Microsoft issues hotfixes in response to customer requests. These hotfixes are periodically compiled into cumulative updates. And eventually, these cumulative updates are released as service packs, roughly a year after the initial release.

In the case of the latest release of Master Data Services, the initial version release is a far more stable product and you can expect fewer updates to be required with this SQL Server 2012 release.

Upgrading 2008 R2 MDS

All of the moving parts within the SQL Server box can make upgrading from 2008 R2 MDS difficult to understand. Before we discuss upgrade, make sure that you understand the components that make up your 2008 R2 implementation:

▶ **Database Engine**   This is the Microsoft service that shipped with 2008 R2 that mounts and controls SQL Server database files. MDS does not require you to upgrade the Database Engine, as MDS 2012 is compatible with both 2008 R2 and 2012 engines.

▶ **MDS database**   This is the database that you created earlier in the chapter. All information stored in your Master Data Services implementation resides in this database. This database has two versions that you need to concern yourself with. The *database version* is the version of the engine that the database is compatible with. You cannot restore database backups from a previous version of SQL Server (2008 R2, for instance) to a new version (2012). To upgrade the database version, you must upgrade the database instance and all the attached databases. The *schema version* is MDS specific. Just as you were required to update the schema version with some cumulative updates that you installed in the prior release, MDS 2012 requires you to upgrade the schema version, as shown next. The Upgrade Database button is available in MDS Configuration Manager after you select a database. This button is only active if the schema version is not compatible with the current installed version of MDS 2012.

This is the schema version. Click this button to upgrade selected database.

You may need to upgrade your MDS 2008 R2 instance to Service Pack 1 in order to upgrade the schema. Before you upgrade the MDS database schema to 2012, ensure you have made a backup of the database. If you want to keep your 2008 R2 and 2012 implementations running side by side, you will need to back up and restore the database as a different name. Once you upgrade the database schema to 2012, the 2008 R2 web components will no longer work with that database.

Repairing the MDS Database

When you restore an MDS database file to a new database server or a new filename, it may become necessary to "repair" the database. In the past, the required running a number of server changes from script. MDS Configuration Manager now has a Repair Database button that you can click to have these tasks performed automatically. Select the MDS database in question, and if a repair is required, a message will display and the Repair Database button will be enabled.

Summary

In this chapter, we have successfully installed and configured Master Data Services. After determining the scope of our application, we were able to determine the best architecture for our system. We explored the configuration options available in MDS and deployed the web application. The end of the chapter discussed upgrade processes and described the boundaries of the MDS system.

Chapter 3

Starting an MDS Project

In This Chapter

- ► How Do I Know Master Data When I See It?
- ► Business Process Models
- ► System Roles
- ► Mapping the Data
- ► The Main Street Clothing Company Example

- ► Determining System Types
- ► Cleansing Data for Initial Import into MDS
- ► Leveraging the MDS Excel Add-In to Manage Your Project

Before you build a model in MDS or any other master data management (MDM) system, it is essential to have a basic understanding of your data and current processes. In this chapter, we provide deeper insight into what is and what is not master data, and we provide some simple labels for your current business systems. Toward the end of the chapter, we discuss some tips and tricks for modeling your data, with the goal of helping you to free your enterprise from many of the data restrictions that have plagued it for so long. We then apply these lessons to the Main Street Clothing Company example. In this chapter we will discuss system types and data cleansing processes. With the release of the Excel Add-In, implementing an MDS system has become significantly easier.

How Do I Know Master Data When I See It?

Over the past year, one of the questions most commonly asked by customers has been, "Is there a definitive line between master data and other important data in my company?" The truth is, there isn't one and there shouldn't be. In most companies, master data management is used only for business-critical domains like product or customer because the implementation of MDM solutions throughout these organizations would be prohibitively expensive. If an accessible solution with a rapid time to value were available, other important domains could benefit from MDM tools as well.

We've already talked about a couple of the key differentiators between master data and transactional data within an enterprise, but they are worth repeating: Data that you wish to store in MDS should not relate to a single event in time because that is transactional data. In MDS, you should store information that has a state or continues to have a state for some specific period of time. This information is master data.

Business Process Models

Before you build your model in MDS or any other MDM system, it is imperative to understand the flow of data through your enterprise. Where do new accounts, customers, or products originate? What is the process that turns a concept into a product? What is the process to onboard a new customer? How does the data flow from inception to all systems across the organization?

Business process modeling can provide decision makers with the information that they need to prioritize and plan the creation of their MDS implementation. Modeling relevant processes related to the creation and maintenance of domains you are interested in managing is the most logical place to start. Although you could employ skilled business process managers to interview employees and provide detailed designs of their findings, most projects can get by with a do-it-yourself approach.

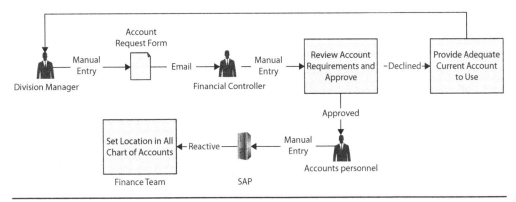

Figure 3-1   *Diagram of sample business process model*

Your first step should be a quick inventory of any existing documentation of current processes, like the example shown in Figure 3-1. Much of what you require might already exist. Be sure to review any existing documents with current employees in the modeled roles. It is astounding how quickly reality can diverge from the documentation given a little bit of time. The more manual the processes, the more easily these processes can change or be abandoned.

When you conduct the interviews required to create a business process model yourself, you should complete the following two steps in sequence. Each step provides insight into the investigated domain. Make sure to record the actors, activity, and length of time required for each business process.

1. Determine how new data members are created in the organization. Make sure to investigate any alternative methods that may lead to the creation of a new member. Lead the interview with questions like "How does this system interact with other systems?" or "Are there any emergency processes?" These can lead to important discoveries. As you begin to integrate systems across organizations, it may be pertinent to ask about any automated systems that may generate new members.

2. For each of the methods discovered in the previous step, drill into any workflow or process to enrich the data member before you consider it complete and ready for use in any systems within the scope of the project. Each system that depends on this information may have different requirements, so it is best to address each system's needs. This step is also the best time to identify the primary owner for each business process or system. Primary owners have a vested interest in their processes and will require assurances that most if not all of their current domain needs will be addressed in any business refactoring.

All of the information you collect will result in a diagram or set of diagrams similar to Figure 3-1. These diagrams will help you to determine the most palatable flow of master data through the organization. You will need to review each system within the scope of the project to decide what type of role it will play for data of each domain type. Determining the role played by each system is the next step in determining how MDS fits into your organization.

System Roles

Systems can be categorized into three different roles. As different domains have significantly different origination points, it is common for the same system to perform separate roles for different domains within a company.

System of Entry

A system of entry (SOE) is a system where data is first entered in a business. These systems typically include all of the users who are able to create new data. Generally, these are the systems that are used daily by the owners of the type of data being investigated. Many systems of entry require that rules be enforced before data can fully be entered. Oftentimes these rules force much of the accumulated information about the member record to be managed outside of the system.

Think of a new product being created. Often, the inception of a new product is scribbled on a napkin or sketched on a whiteboard. Many of the details of the product will be discussed and decided via e-mail format. It is important to capture and manage this process, because creating a workflow and roles around product creation can provide many benefits, like online collaboration and a tracked history of the creative process. The lack of resources to manage this process often impedes the implementation of a new product.

System of Record

A system of record (SOR) is any system within the organization that is considered the source for other systems. Typically, the enterprise resource planning (ERP) system is the system of record within an organization, but oftentimes many other systems can be considered sources for downstream systems. Many data inconsistencies are created on multiple SORs within an organization. While MDS strives to be an adequate SOE for organizations, it is imperative that many if not all of the SORs are moved onto the MDS platform. This is where much of the value of master data management is derived.

Subscribing System

As your MDS implementation matures, the most common type of system should be a subscribing system. Subscribing systems are those systems that consume data from another system with no direct user changes to the managed domain. Some larger companies use an intermediate store to pass data to multiple systems. As long as direct changes are not made in any of these systems, all these systems can be considered downstream subscribing systems.

Mapping the Data

The next phase in the project plan is to determine data sizes and types within the Master Data Services system. Analysis of all source systems' main tables and their columns to determine the best data type for storing that data can provide an initial roadmap for MDS. There are two main questions that must be asked during this phase: What kinds of internal constraints are placed on this column? Are there any downstream constraints in the organization that require further data cleansing to be performed?

You should start the mapping process by identifying those columns within the source system that you will manage in MDS. For each of these columns, determine a rudimentary data type. In Chapter 4, we discuss the different data types available in MDS, but for now just identify data as date, number, or string.

If you identify a date field, be very careful that this field provides information across multiple systems and is a state of the mapped domain. Oftentimes, date fields are red flags that you have mistaken a system-specific field such as "entry date" for a more important field like "start date" or "discontinued date." You should be extra wary of any column that requires the storage of a specific date or time. These fields generally signal that the information stored is most likely transactional in nature.

Columns that you identify as numeric should be reviewed as well. Is this column storing a valid state on a record? We have seen many projects in which the designers have been tempted to map in fields such as account balances or sales figures. These numbers are subject to daily change and are best handled as part of a business intelligence (BI) solution. Master Data Services does not support simple math functions or consolidations, in an effort to dissuade users from storing inappropriate data. This does not mean all numbers should not be stored. MSRP, safety stock levels, standard terms, and credit limits are all valid information for MDS. When identifying numeric columns, you should log the precision, or number of decimal places, each column will require. While many systems may not limit this on the backend, the actual required precision should be easy to determine for the primary system owner.

When mapping a source system to MDS, it may be advisable to create additional tables to store choices for certain fields. Some of these relationships are easy to see. If there is a foreign key relationship within the source system that displays options for one field to another, you should continue to preserve this relationship. For instance, if a customer has a relationship to an address table that stores addresses available to the customer, this relationship can be modeled in MDS.

Some relationships are not quite as evident, though. For instance, a source system may only store specific attributes as text fields, yet valid values for those text fields may be constrained by the business process. If those values are better managed in a separate table, and a foreign key relationship between those tables would be advisable, you want to highlight those relationships now. Determine if any of these relationships may be reused. For instance, within many data sources, there will be a number of fields that map to a choice of either Yes or No. In these cases, you may want to create a single entity to store those valid choices.

Determining What to Do with Duplicate Records

Data quality is a major concern for corporations, and the identification and management of duplicate records is a central task in the effort to ensure data quality. Duplicate records exist within organizations for a variety of reasons. One of the biggest reasons employees duplicate records is that they are unaware that records already exist in a separate system, because the systems are not integrated effectively. These records should be merged wherever possible.

Some companies intentionally duplicate records within systems for a specific purpose, typically to work around limitations within current applications to support necessary business processes. In most cases, these duplicates must remain within the business application to continue to provide the workaround they were designed for. Systems that required duplicate member records should never be considered for Systems of Record. When connecting these subscribing systems to the MDS repository, master data attributes should be updated in all downstream attributes.

Determining Which Attributes to Manage

To determine whether an attribute should be managed in MDS, data stewards must decide on the nature of the attribute. Is this a state of the domain? Is this information useful for multiple systems? All numeric and date fields should be evaluated closely. Tracking information should not be managed if it is specific to an application in the organization. Calculated values or balances should not be managed in an MDS system because these values will change over time. Make sure that attributes that store a product's age are not managed as such but that you manage the product's date of creation instead.

The Main Street Clothing Company Example

Before the Main Street Clothing Company attempts to build anything in Master Data Services, it is critical that it examine its current processes. All of the following chapters of this book will leverage information collected in the following pages. Although building an MDM solution can be an iterative process, early understanding of the problem space and employees' roles in the process can lead to rapid satisfaction and effective adoption of the new system. An early successful implementation can lead to additional requests for new domains.

Finding a Data Steward

Once Main Street Clothing Company had determined that an MDS implementation would be beneficial to its organization, it needed to find a project manager. Since there were a number of important sets of data to manage and some amount of ongoing responsibility would be required post-implementation, Anthony Green was identified as the best candidate for the position. Anthony has been with Main Street Clothing Company for a number of years in a business analyst role. He has some limited database experience and was involved in a number of prior system implementations. Main Street plans to have Anthony remain as the owner of the MDS server and serve as the *de facto* data steward for the organization.

Leveraging the Business Process Models

During the implementation of SAP, the implementation team created detailed maps of the business process for creating new products and accounts. Anthony can use these maps to determine the best way to integrate MDS into the current process. One of these maps is shown in Figure 3-2.

Anthony is able to leverage this information to investigate how much time is required to create a new account, and he finds very little inefficiency in this process. The major issue with accounts is the difficulty the accounting department has when managing multiple consolidations for the chart of accounts. This issue tends to be related to legal and taxation requirements. Figure 3-3 shows Main Street Clothing Company's process for processing accounts.

Figure 3-2 *Product business process map*

Despite his best efforts, Anthony was unable to find any process maps that detailed the location data for the company. Although it has been over a year since Main Street Clothing Company has opened a new store location, everyone agrees that the workflow for opening a new store is disorganized and reactive.

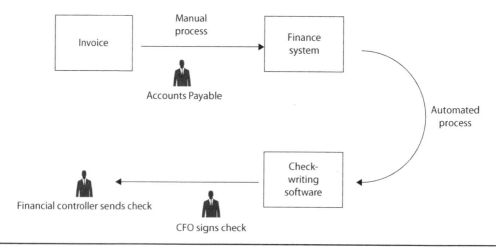

Figure 3-3 *Account business process map*

Filling in the Gaps

In reviewing the existing business process models, Anthony determined that the system of entry for products in his company was first created in a custom Access database run by the product acquisition team. This team consists of a manager and two buyers who work with a number of manufacturers and suppliers.

The product acquisition team enters the products that they wish to purchase into their homegrown system. They also use this system to keep track of notes such as expected demand and types of offers they are considering. After the manager has agreed with their findings, the buyers e-mail a spreadsheet of new product purchases to the accounts team.

The accounts team then manually codes new products into the system and ties them to a supplier code. When an invoice arrives from the supplier, new product inventory is added into the ERP system for those products. Any products that are absent on the initial entry must be entered at this time. An attempt will be made to contact the appropriate buyer to determine whether the new product is accurate, but if the buyer is unavailable, much of the product information will be left blank for later input. Many of these inconsistencies are not found until month-end reports are run and data is blank. Sometimes, additional merchandise is accepted and placed in the store even though it was not intended to be purchased by the buyer. In these cases, the product acquisition team must scramble to determine if this is a fortuitous mistake or if they need to pull the inventory from the shelves. The product acquisition team estimates that this happens two to three times each year.

Anthony then reviews the business process models for location. He determines that much of the information in the SAP system is in one large entry as the location is conceived. Because the creation of a new store is a long process with many people involved, there is no standard process for collecting all the required information, such as square footage, lease type, and other information that is negotiated or decided upon. Anthony determines a larger problem for location is that the parties responsible for managing renewal of leases or other location management do not have access to the system where this data is stored. They are managing this information in files and folders and have very few electronic warnings before these things require attention. This creates the unwelcome situation where lease negotiations or other decisions are triggered by third parties who call headquarters.

Investigation of the employee process shows Anthony that, in many cases, starting dates and ending dates are incorrect in the source system because the accounts team has been incorrectly coding the hire date as the start date for the last six months. One store manager was aware of the issue but had been unable to get the accounting department to fix the problem. The accounts team, which was in the middle of month- and year-end close, felt this problem could wait to be resolved and just forgot to return to the problem once those times of high stress had concluded. Anthony would like to address these inconsistencies as part of the MDS implementation.

Determining System Types

Now that Anthony has reviewed the current processes, he needs to determine the role each system will play when MDS is added into the process. As each business process treats systems differently, he recognizes that he should look at the matrix of each system for each domain within the organization.

Domain	Product Mgmt. System	ERP	Data Warehouse	Warehouse Tracking System
Product	SOE	SOR	Subscribing	Subscribing
Location	No data	SOR	Subscribing	Subscribing
Employee	Subscribing	SOR	Subscribing	Subscribing
Account	No data	SOR	Subscribing	Subscribing

Once MDS is implemented in the organization, many of the systems will perform a different role within the organization. The following table shows the revised system model.

Domain	MDS	ERP	Data Warehouse	Warehouse Tracking System
Product	SOE, SOR	Subscribing	Subscribing	Subscribing
Location	SOE,SOR	Subscribing	Subscribing	Subscribing
Employee	SOE	SOR	Subscribing	Subscribing
Account	SOE and SOR (for hierarchy only)	SOE, SOR	Subscribing	Subscribing

For each domain to be managed in MDS, Anthony builds a new business process model to show what the proposed process will look like once his implementation is complete. He will use these diagrams to socialize the new process and ensure that all participants feel their interests will be met. It is important that all stakeholders feel that the implementation team is aware of their specific needs and that the new process will not be an obstacle to their daily jobs.

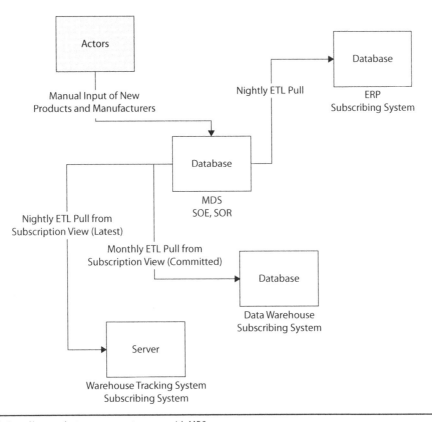

Figure 3-4   *New product management process with MDS*

In the model shown in Figure 3-4, Anthony proposes that the product management database be replaced with a model that includes MDS. All of the functionality that was supported in this system can be replicated within MDS.

Anthony suspects that the distributed nature of locations management makes MDS a natural place to manage this domain. In the model shown in Figure 3-5, Anthony shows the location management process where MDS will now be used to manage the location workflow process.

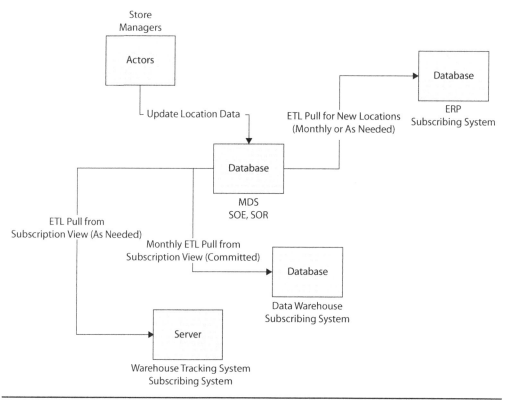

Figure 3-5   *New location process where MDS manages location creation process*

Cleansing Data for Initial Import into MDS

Now that Anthony has socialized the proposed process for managing products in MDS, he must create a clean list of products to initially load into MDS. In many organizations, producing a clean list of products can be a large project; due to the size of Main Street Clothing Company, Anthony will take an export from the product management database as a starting point. He will enhance this export by adding any products that exist in the ERP system. These additional products may have been added if they were part of an invoice received from a supplier.

Very little de-duplication will be required for managing any domains at Main Street Clothing Company. One of the benefits of implementing an MDM solution while a company is small is that you can get a handle on your data before the complexity and size of the processes and data make cleansing a major project for the organization. For each domain, Anthony will create an Excel spreadsheet listing all of the records and their managed attributes.

Leveraging the MDS Excel Add-In to Manage Your Project

With the addition of the Add-in for Excel in SQL Server 2012, Master Data Services is providing a potential game-changing tool when it comes to MDM project management. Excel provides the perfect interface to rapidly build and then hone your model with the end-user base. While none of the preceding steps are removed, the ability to grab data out of any tool using Excel and create an entity within minutes will give modelers the ability to quickly iterate over and refine their models. This approach will be discussed further in Chapter 10.

Summary

It is important to understand the flow of data within an organization before implementing an MDM system. Any MDM system that does not match the natural flow of data through an organization is doomed to fail, as busy users work in the easiest, most natural manner. Analysis of business processes can provide insight into the flow of related data through the enterprise. All systems within an organization can be classified as either systems of entry, systems of record, or subscribing systems.

Many systems within the organization will have data-cleansing needs. It is important to determine what remediation will be acceptable if duplicate records are found. If history must be maintained for duplicate members, a mapping between the MDS source and the system should be maintained. In the next chapter, we discuss how to create our models in MDS.

Chapter 4

Creating Your Model

In This Chapter

I n this chapter, we discuss the creation and customization of MDS models. In MDS, models are the central work surface that will be exposed to the master data editors and consumers once your project goes live. The success of your project will depend mainly on how well you design your model.

We begin with a discussion of modeling concepts. Then we examine how to deploy prebuilt models. We load the sample company's Finance model and then spend the remainder of the chapter creating a Product model from scratch. Finally, we look at examples of how to use web services to perform some of the procedures we've already performed in the web UI. (From now on, "Master Data Manager web application" and "web UI" are used synonymously.)

MDS Modeling Concepts

Master Data Services is made up of a relatively simple group of concepts. These concepts are encapsulated as data containers and services exposed in MDS. While these concepts are simple to understand by themselves, it is the varied and complex data schemas that these concepts support that provide both the power and complexity of MDS. Before we delve into the implementation of the model objects, let's review general definitions of these MDS concepts. Each of these concepts is described in more detail later in the chapter.

▶ **Models**   Models are the highest level of organization within MDS. Models are nothing but containers of related entities. Only entities within the same model can be related within MDS. Models are the first concept discussed in this chapter.

▶ **Entities**   Entities are the base containers for data in MDS. In their simplest form, entities can be thought of as tables in a database. Users control the attributes (columns) that are managed for each entity. If explicit hierarchies are enabled for an entity, the entity becomes far more complex, managing parent members and their consolidations as well as collections, their attributes, and the members associated with those collections. Most of this chapter is devoted to discussing how to create the structures of entities.

▶ **Members**   Members are the records that populate all the entities created in MDS. Members can be either leaf or consolidated. Leaf members are the primary members of an entity. If an entity is enabled for explicit hierarchies and collections, then consolidated members can be created, and can have their own attributes. Members will be discussed in this chapter as well as in Chapter 7.

▶ **Attributes**   Attributes describe members. Attributes can be loosely thought of as columns in a table. Entities contain members and their attribute values. Attributes can be free-form or domain-based.

▶ **Domain-based attributes** Domain-based attributes are attributes in which the available values are restricted to the members stored in a related entity. This is similar to selecting from a predefined list, but in MDS all lists are entities themselves.

▶ **Hierarchies** Hierarchies are consolidations or groupings of members that aid in reporting and analysis. There are two management types for hierarchies in MDS: explicit and derived. Hierarchies enforce rules for member inclusion to ensure consolidations do not lose or double count values in connected applications. Hierarchies will be discussed in detail in Chapter 6.

▶ **Collections** Collections provide member grouping flexibility that is not supported in hierarchies. Collections will be discussed in detail in Chapter 6.

Building a Model

Master Data Services begins as a blank canvas, allowing you to create your data models within the product in any way you choose. The model structure is created in the System Administration functional area of the Master Data Manager web application, or by using the web services. As you create the structure, you can open the Explorer functional area of the web UI to see the results of your work. The Explorer functional area is where users will go day to day to manage their master data.

Opening the System Administration area of the Master Data Manager web UI for the first time can be a daunting experience. In the latest release, System Administration defaults to the model creation screen if you have not loaded any models. When you first create an MDS database, only the Metadata model is created. Figure 4-1 shows this first model open in the Model View screen. This is the only system model within MDS and has been marked for deprecation in a future release. While this model can still be accessed from System Administration or Explorer as its own model, all access to the Metadata features from your own models has been eliminated through the web UI. Access to these features will need to be completed through the web services for Metadata.

If you are a new user of MDS, you have two avenues for creating your first useful model within the product. You can load a sample model deployment package into your database and modify the model from there, or you can build your model from scratch.

Starting with a predefined model can be the easiest way to get started with SQL Server MDS. Over the course of this book, we are going to work with Finance and Product models for our fictional company, Main Street Clothing Company. In this chapter, we are going to deploy the Finance model and create the Product model from scratch. You can find the complete packages of our models, both with and without sample data, at our web site: www.mdsuser.com.

MDS also includes three sample models in the installation. These samples are very basic Customer, Product, and Account models, located in Program Files\Microsoft

Model View

```
⊟ Models
   ⊟ 🔧 Metadata
      ⊞ 🔧 Attribute Group Metadata Definition
      ⊞ 🔧 Attribute Metadata Definition
      ⊞ 🔧 Entity Metadata Definition
      ⊞ 🔧 Hierarchy Metadata Definition
      ⊞ 🔧 Model Metadata Definition
```

Figure 4-1   *The default Metadata model that is created during installation*

SQL Server\110\Master Data Services\Samples\Packages. You can take a look at them
to get a better idea of some of the more common features of the application.

While these model deployment packages provide some data and attributes and
support the documentation provided in Microsoft Books Online for SQL Server 2012,
they are relatively limited in their functionality and do not provide adequate coverage
for the exercises listed in this book. However, these models include sample data,
hierarchies, business rules, and versioning, so you can see what the end result of all your
upcoming work might look like.

In the next exercise, we will walk through how to deploy our sample Finance model.

Deploying a Model

A model deployment package is an XML file saved with a .pkg extension. It includes
the model structure, the business rules (Chapter 8), and version flags (Chapter 9) and
subscription views (Chapter 12). It does not include file attributes (Chapter 4) or user
and group permissions (Chapter 11). Model packages can contain the data from a version
of the model when created from the ModelDeploy.exe command-line executable. Only
the model structure can be created or deployed from the web UI in the SQL Server 2012
version of Master Data Services. The new utility and the limitations on data in the web UI
were added in response to the inability to support all model sizes through the web services.

Model deployment in MDS was designed to provide organizations with two very
important capabilities related to managing data models in MDS. The first is the
capability to develop, test, and deploy a model within three separate implementations
of MDS, while limiting the number of objects that need to be re-created in each

environment. This enables IT management to roll out changes en masse and to ensure that the production environment remains operational throughout the process.

The second capability enables organizations to share their model schemas with others. There are a number of efforts across a host of industries to standardize object models. Previously, most organizations would develop data models in a vacuum, creating schemas that solved their current problem most efficiently. They integrated only those applications owned by the organization and central to the solution. IT departments at all of their competitors were doing the same. This led to a wide variety of data models among competitors in the same industry. Some organizations built data models that were flexible, stable, and scalable, but many did not. When consolidation within an industry occurred, acquiring companies discovered similar business processes were hard to integrate due to the vastly different data models that had been developed in isolation.

Following are a couple of advantages to employing common data models within an industry:

▶ **Benefit of experience** Civilization wouldn't get very far if each new generation needed to reinvent the wheel. By leveraging a common data model developed by industry experts, companies are able to avoid issues that they might otherwise experience personally.

▶ **Standardization** Standards help companies and software providers by limiting the amount of variation that must be managed. Standards allow companies to better manage acquisitions and new integration projects. Software can focus on enhancing business value as opposed to compatibility.

MDS supports these efforts in two ways. By not enforcing its own model, MDS ensures there is one less data model to be managed. Model deployment empowers industry leaders to quickly build master data–centric versions of these industry models, providing efficient deployment across their industry. Any customization that needs to be made to these standardized models is still supported in MDS.

Procedure: How to Deploy a Model Using ModelDeploy.exe

To deploy a sample model using ModelDeploy.exe, complete the following steps:

NOTE

If you want to deploy the sample Finance model we refer to in this book, get it from www.mdsuser.com before you start this procedure.

1. Copy the Finance package file to the Program Files\Microsoft SQL Server\110\ Master Data Services\Configuration directory.

2. Open a command prompt from the Start menu. It is advisable to run the command prompt as administrator to ensure access to the file location.

3. Using the cd command, change the directory to Program Files\Microsoft SQL Server\110\Master Data Services\Configuration.

4. Run mdsmodeldeploy.exe deploynew -model Finance -package finance.pkg.

5. If successful, you should see the message "MDSModelDeploy operation completed successfully" and the elapsed time for the call displayed.

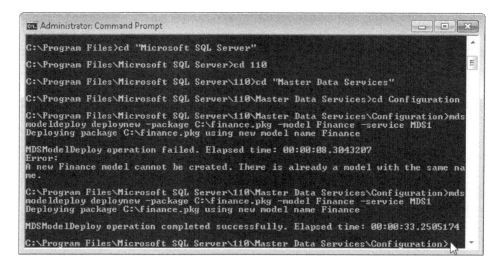

You can confirm that the model was deployed successfully by going to the home page and looking in the drop-down list of available models, as shown next. If you were already viewing the web UI, you may need to click the "Refresh cached information" link on the MDS home page.

To view the Finance model in more detail, select VERSION_1 from the Version list and then click Explorer. Your business users will manage master data in the Explorer functional area. When you configure security, you will be able to give users access to specific data within the Explorer functional area.

All other functional areas of the web UI are intended for administrators. Let's take a moment to discuss the other four functional areas.

▶ **Version Management**   Use this area to validate full versions of your model against business rules. You can also create versions of your models and their data, and assign version flags, which indicate to subscribing systems which version of a model to use. More details about versioning can be found in Chapter 9.

▶ **Integration Management**   Use this area to import data into the proper MDS database tables. You can also use this area to create subscription views, which are SQL views used by subscribing systems to retrieve data from MDS. More information about staging data can be found in Chapter 5. See Chapter 12 for information on exporting data by using subscription views.

▶ **System Administration**   Use this area to build your models, entities, attributes, attribute groups, and derived hierarchies. You also use this area to manage business rules and create and deploy models. You will use System Administration extensively in this chapter and in Chapter 8 when we discuss business rules.

▶   **User and Group Permissions**   Use this area to give users access to specific functional areas and to specific data within those areas. More information about security is provided in Chapter 11.

About Models

As discussed previously, models are the highest level of organization within Master Data Services. Models are nothing but containers of related entities. Only entities within the same model can be related within MDS. This supports a simplified versioning model where all entities within a model are versioned simultaneously. Although many models revolve around a single domain such as customer or product, this is not a requirement. You can combine major entities into a single model if this makes business sense.

When determining whether or not to include an entity in a model, there are a number of factors to consider:

▶   Do the entities in the model have a relationship to one another?

▶   If so, is this relationship master data? Many entities have relationships that are transactional in nature. Only those relationships that are states that change over time and are not discreet instances should be managed in the MDS system.

▶   Do the entities change on similar schedules? If two entities have a natural affinity to be versioned at separate times, you may need to manage them in separate models.

▶   Does an entity relate only to a subset of another entity? If only a subset of the members participate in the relationship between the two entities, ensuring accurate selection may be compromised. Business rules can be used to ensure only the valid members are selected; business rules will be discussed in greater detail in Chapter 8.

About Main Street Clothing Company's Models

After performing all of the analysis discussed in Chapter 3, Anthony Green has determined that he needs to create two models in the organization's Master Data Services instance. The Product model will revolve around a central Product entity. This entity will not require an explicit hierarchy, so Anthony will create only product leaf members to begin. Due to the interconnected nature of all other managed entities, Anthony will create an additional model called Finance. Since there is no finance entity or entities to add, he will create the model only.

Procedure: How to Create a Model

To create a model, complete the following steps:

1. On the Master Data Manager home page, click System Administration.
2. On the menu bar, choose Manage | Models.
3. On the Model Maintenance page, click the Add model button (the green plus sign).

4. On the Add Model page, in the Model name field, type a name for your model. For this example, we'll call the model **Product**.

The three check boxes on this page can be confusing if you've never done this before:

▶ **Create entity with same name as model**   Leave this box selected. This check box does just what it says—it creates an entity called Product. This option is here because, in many cases, a model revolves around a central entity.

▶ **Create explicit hierarchy with same name as model**   Briefly, an explicit hierarchy is a free-form hierarchy in which you can specify any number of levels, with a leaf member being allowed at any level and consolidated members being used for grouping. If you think you might want a hierarchy like this, you can select this check box. Because we don't discuss explicit hierarchies until Chapter 6, clear this check box for now. You can always enable this later.

▶ **Include all leaf members in mandatory hierarchy**   When you clear the preceding "Create explicit hierarchy" check box, this option is disabled.

5. Click Save.

The Product model is now displayed in a tree view in System Administration, as shown in Figure 4-2. If it's not displayed already, click Model View on the menu bar in System Administration to view it.

The hierarchical structure that is displayed here is meant to give you a quick look at the models you have permission to view and to the entities in each. This structure is not meant to represent levels of importance the way a typical hierarchy would. As you learn more about entities and attributes, we will provide more details about this structure.

Figure 4-2   *Models in the System Administration functional area*

Viewing the Results in Explorer

Now let's look at the model in the Explorer functional area. Go back to the Master Data Manager home page by clicking the logo.

TIP

If you are running Internet Explorer 8, you should choose Compatibility Mode before viewing data in the Explorer functional area of Master Data Manager. From the IE Tools menu, choose Compatibility Mode.

Select the Product model from the list. Select the version, which was automatically created as VERSION_1. Now click Explorer.

The first base entity Silverlight Explorer grid will be displayed when you open the Explorer functional area. In the latest release, the old Explorer screen is no longer the initial screen loaded for users. This screen is still available from the menu at the top of the screen.

The top *base entity* is the entity that is displayed by default when you open the Explorer functional area of the web UI. After you create more entities, you will be able to drag-and-drop items in the hierarchy to move a different entity into the "base" position. More than one entity can be listed as a base entity within a model. If multiple entities are listed as base entities, the first base entity will display when Explorer opens. The Explorer screen will still show all base entities for the model. You do not need to have a base entity in your model, though. If you don't, when Explorer opens, the first entity listed alphabetically will be displayed; all entities are available from the menu bar.

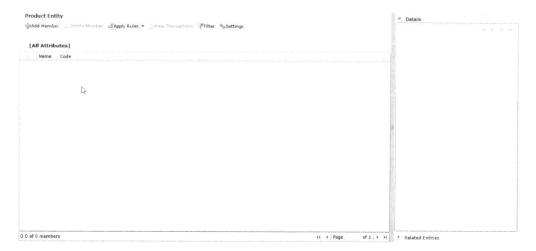

Now you're ready to learn more about entities and practice creating a few.

About Entities

In MDS, all data that is managed by the system is stored in entities. Entities can be loosely thought of as tables in SQL. The data within entities are called members.

MDS's entities can also support explicit hierarchies. Once explicit hierarchies have been enabled for an entity, an entity becomes far more than a single table. The entity can then support parent and collection members, as well as hierarchy and collection relationships. Hierarchies and collections are discussed in detail in Chapter 6.

About Main Street Clothing Company's Entities

Within the Product model, the Product entity has already been created. We now need to create all of the supporting entities that will be used as options for attributes of members in the Product entity. While most of these entities will be used to populate a single domain-based attribute only, some entities can be used to populate multiple entities within the model. Entities such as Neck Style, Color, and Size can only be used for a single purpose, but multiple entities can use attributes with constraints such as "Yes" and "No."

First we will create the Yes No Picklist entity; then we will create all other entities needed in the Product model.

Procedure: How to Create an Entity

To create the Yes No Picklist entity, complete the following steps:

1. On the Master Data Manager home page, click System Administration.
2. On the menu bar, choose Manage | Entities.
3. On the Entity Maintenance page, click Add entity.

4. On the Add Entity page, in the Entity name box, type **Yes No Picklist**.

SQL Server 2012
Master Data Services

Model View	Manage	System

Add Entity
Entity Maintenance

Entity name:
Yes No Picklist

Name for staging tables (optional):

If you do not complete this field, the entity name will be used.

☐ Create Code values automatically

Enable explicit hierarchies and collections:
No   ▼

5. In the "Name for Staging tables (optional)" box, you can type a unique name for the staging table created specifically for this entity. The entity name will be used if no value is provided. This value cannot be changed in the web UI once the entity is saved. See Chapter 5 for more information on staging.

6. You can check the "Create Code values automatically" check box to automatically assign a new integer value to newly created members. See Chapter 8 for more details on this process.

7. In the "Enable explicit hierarchies and collections" drop-down list, select No. Again, you can enable this later if you need to.

8. Click Save.

NOTE

Sometimes when you save an entity, you have to wait a long time for the page to refresh. You know the entity has been created when the Add Entity page closes and you're returned to the Entity Maintenance page.

The Yes No Picklist entity is now displayed on the Entity Maintenance page.

To continue following along with the examples in this chapter, create the following entities: Type, Fabric, Neck Style, Gender, Color, and Size. These entities will contain lists of values that will be used to describe products, as you will soon learn. When you are done, your Entity Maintenance page should look like Figure 4-3. Your entities are automatically alphabetized here.

Viewing the Results in Explorer

Now let's look at the entities in Explorer. Go back to the home page by clicking the logo in the top left or by clicking the Home link.

1. Select the Product model, VERSION1, and click Explorer.
2. Choose Entities on the menu bar, and you see a list of available entities.

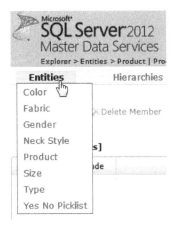

Microsoft®
SQL Server 2012
Master Data Services

Model View   **Manage**   System

Entity Maintenance

Model:
Product

Entity
Color
Fabric
Gender
Neck Style
Product
Size
Type
Yes No Picklist

Figure 4-3 *Completed Entity Maintenance page*

If you select an entity to view it in more detail, you can see that there is no master data in the entity yet. If there were, a grid would be displayed.

After you add master data, a grid is displayed here.

Let's stop creating the model for a moment and talk about the members that will populate the grid.

About Members

Members are the individual records stored in Master Data Services. Members are uniquely identified by the required Code attribute. There are two types of members in MDS: leaf members and consolidated members.

Leaf members are the most granular level of records in an entity and usually represent physical objects within your business. For example, in a Product entity, a leaf member might be Men's Shirt #602. A leaf member in an Employee entity might be John Smith. A leaf member in a Warehouse entity might be Warehouse-98101.

One notable exception to this rule of thumb applies to any entities managed within the Finance domain. When managing entities associated with Finance, leaf members typically represent those low-level identifiers that transactions can be coded to. If transactions are coded with a store, account, employee, and product, you can be assured that the available values for each of these attributes should be stored as leaf member records in the associated entities.

Consolidated members are used only in explicit hierarchies, and will be discussed in more detail in Chapter 6.

About Main Street Clothing Company's Members

When implementing MDS, most entities will need to be populated from an initial data source. In Chapter 3 we retrieved and cleansed an extract file of the current products. In Chapter 5 we will discuss how to use staging tables to populate all of the current members into the proper entities. Before this staging can be completed, Main Street Clothing Company must ensure that all of the entity containers have been properly configured to accept the staged data.

Some entities that are used as domain-based attributes have so many members that loading them through staging at the same time as the product members makes the most sense. In the case of simple entities with very few members, however, the effort to stage the members would exceed the effort needed to create them through the web UI. These members need to be created before we attempt to stage any product data.

Procedure: How to Add a Member

To add a leaf member, complete the following steps:

1. On the Master Data Manager home page, select the Product model and VERSION_1 from the drop-down lists.
2. Click Explorer.
3. On the menu bar, choose Entities | Product.

4. Under Product Entity, click Add Member.

Product Entity

[⊞Add Member] ✕Delete Member ⚙Apply Rules | ▼ ↻View Transactions ▽Filter ⚙Settings

Add a new member

[All Attributes]

Name	Code

5. In this release, all new members are created on the same screen. A new member can be added in the right pane. In this pane, enter a name and code for your product. When we use the staging process to import the majority of our products, the name will be a concatenation of many fields. If you want to continue using our example, complete the fields as follows:

⌄ Details

|◄ ◄ ► ►|

Name	M Red Shirt 3 V Neck
Code	1000

Annotations [ ]

View Annotations

[OK] [Cancel]

Now add a few members to the Yes No Picklist entity:

1. On the menu bar, choose Entities | Yes No Picklist.
2. Above the grid, click Add Member.
3. In the right pane, populate the Name and Code fields, entering **Yes** for the name and **Y** for the code.

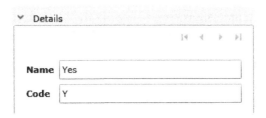

4. Click the OK button at the bottom of the pane.
5. Click Add Member again.
6. In the right pane, enter **No** for the name and **N** for the code.
7. Click the OK button at the bottom of the pane. The members are now displayed in the grid.

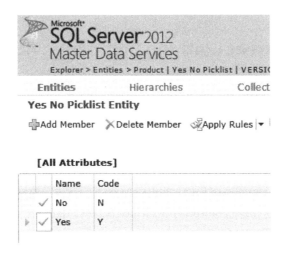

After you learn more about attributes, you will create a domain-based attribute that will use the Yes No Picklist values as the source.

About Attributes

All entities within Master Data Services can be enriched by the creation of additional attributes. MDS supports a subset of the attributes supported in SQL Server. MDS supports four specific types of free-form attributes for leaf and consolidated entity members: text, datetime, number, and link. Text and link are essentially string fields, with link providing one-click support for hypertext links. Number supports as many as seven decimals, and datetime allows you to specify the mask for how the data will be input.

In order to relate two entities and ensure that values are constrained to specific values, MDS gives users the ability to create domain-based attributes. These attributes limit available values to the list of active members within the related entity.

The last type of attribute available to entities is the file attribute. Within a master data entity, it may be advisable to manage some files associated with each member. For instance, there may be instruction documents, specifications, blueprints, or photos that need to be associated with a Product entity within an organization. However, the file attribute has a number of limitations that make it less attractive to use for file management than SharePoint. First, to limit database sizes of MDS, file attributes will not be versioned. Only the last loaded file will be available within the MDS system. The transaction log will display information related to new files that have been loaded, but these will not be reversible.

About Main Street Clothing Company's Attributes

In order for Anthony to successfully load all of the current products into Master Data Services, he must complete the creation of a Product entity. This includes creation of all free-form attributes to the proper specifications identified in Chapter 3. All product attributes that have currently been identified need to be created in MDS.

It is quite possible that during the attribute creation process or subsequent data loads, new information will be uncovered that changes the shape or type of attribute in MDS. Creating models in MDS should be an organic process. As new column needs are discovered at Main Street Clothing Company, Anthony will determine the best process for integrating these columns into Main Street's daily processes, ensuring that no process requirements are overlooked.

Procedure: How to Create an Attribute

Let's start by creating a free-form attribute. To create a free-form attribute, complete the following steps:

1. On the Master Data Manager home page, click System Administration.
2. On the menu bar, choose Manage | Entities.
3. On the Entity Maintenance page, select Product from the list of entities.
4. On the toolbar that is displayed, click the "Edit selected entity" button.

NOTE

The button does not appear until after you click the entity in the list.

On the Edit Entity page, you can see that two attributes are listed: Name and Code. When you create an entity, these attributes are automatically created. You cannot delete them.

5.   Click the "Add leaf attribute" button.

6. On the Add Attribute page, select the Free-form option and complete the fields as shown here:

-   ▶ The value of the "Display pixel width" field determines how wide the column will be when it's displayed in the Explorer area of the web UI.

-   ▶ The "Input mask" field lets you decide whether to show negative numbers in parentheses or show a minus sign instead.

-   ▶ For now, don't enable change tracking. You will use this later, along with business rules, to notify someone when an attribute value changes.

7. Click Save.

On the Edit Entity page, the new attribute is displayed.

Model View   **Manage**   System

Edit Entity: Product
Entity Maintenance

Entity name:
Product

Name for staging tables (optional):
Product_
If you do not complete this field, the entity name will be used.

☐ Create Code values automatically

Enable explicit hierarchies and collections:
No

Leaf member attributes:

Name
Code
Cost

You can click either Save or Cancel to leave this page. Either way, your attribute is saved.

NOTE

To continue following along with the examples in this chapter, create the following free-form attributes: Retail Price (number with two decimal places), Safety Stock Level (number with no decimal places), Reorder Point (number, also with no decimal places), and Design (text).

If you make a mistake, you can delete the attribute and create a new one, or you can edit the attribute and change the editable fields. At this point you might also want to edit the Name and Code attributes to set the "Display pixel width" field to a smaller number.

TIP

If you want to hide an attribute without using security, set the "Display pixel width" field to 0.

Procedure: How to Create a Domain-Based Attribute

Each domain-based attribute has two parts:

▶ The entity that contains the members that will be used as a picklist

▶ The attribute that refers to the entity

You have already created an entity called Yes No Picklist and populated it with two members. Now you need to create a domain-based attribute that uses the members from the entity as attribute values.

To create a domain-based attribute, complete the following steps:

1. On the Master Data Manager home page, click System Administration.
2. On the menu bar, choose Manage | Entities.
3. On the Entity Maintenance page, select Product from the list of entities.
4. On the toolbar that is displayed, click the "Edit selected entity" button.

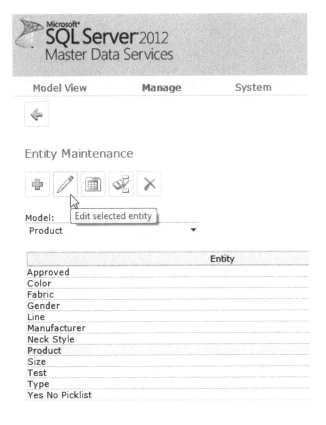

5. On the Edit Entity page, in the Leaf attributes section, click the "Add leaf attribute" button.

6. On the Add Attribute page, select the Domain-based option and complete the fields as shown here:

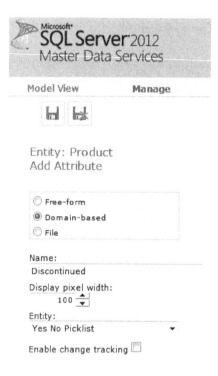

The attribute is going to be called "Discontinued." For each product, we want to know whether or not it has been discontinued. So type **Discontinued** as the attribute name and select Yes No Picklist as the entity that provides the members to use as attribute values.

7. Click Save.

Viewing the Results in Explorer

Now let's go back to Explorer and look at the Discontinued attribute:

1. On the Master Data Manager home page, select Product and VERSION_1 from the lists and then click Explorer.

2. On the menu bar, choose Entities | Product.

3. Select the first member in the grid.

4. Scroll to the bottom of the right pane. You can now select a value from the Discontinued drop-down list.

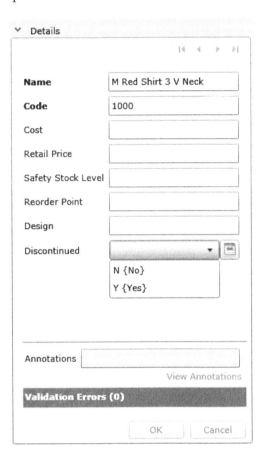

5. Select N {No} for the attribute value.
6. Click the OK button at the bottom of the pane to save the new values.

TIP

You can select the Setting button above the grid to show the name and code of each attribute value, or to show the code only.

Now create other domain-based attributes:

1. Based on the entity Yes No Picklist, create a domain-based attribute named **Available to Outlet**.

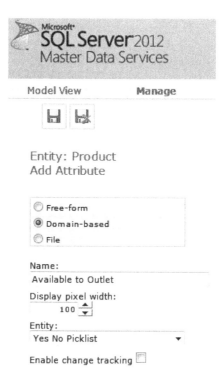

2. Based on the entity named Type, create a domain-based attribute named **Type**.

    You can use the same name for the domain-based attribute that you already used for the entity.

3. Do the same for the Fabric, Neck Style, Gender, Size, and Color entities, using the same name for the domain-based attribute.

Viewing the Results in System Administration

If you go back into the System Administration functional area (or if you are in System Administration already and on the menu bar you click Model View), you can view your model structure in a hierarchical format, as shown in Figure 4-4.

The domain-based attributes can be expanded to show that they are entities with their own Name and Code attributes. The free-form attributes do not have attributes; they are just attributes of the Product model.

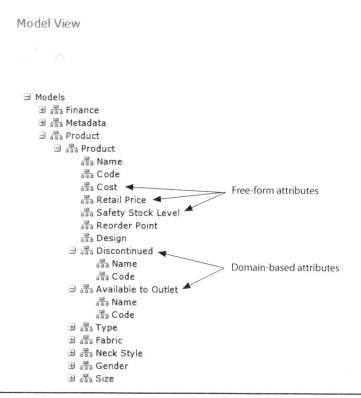

Model View

- Models
  - ⊞ 🔧 Finance
  - ⊞ 🔧 Metadata
  - ⊟ 🔧 Product
    - ⊟ 🔧 Product
      - 🔧 Name
      - 🔧 Code
      - 🔧 Cost ◄────────────┐
      - 🔧 Retail Price ◄───── Free-form attributes
      - 🔧 Safety Stock Level
      - 🔧 Reorder Point
      - 🔧 Design
      - ⊟ 🔧 Discontinued ◄────┐
        - 🔧 Name
        - 🔧 Code ◄──────── Domain-based attributes
      - ⊟ 🔧 Available to Outlet ◄
        - 🔧 Name
        - 🔧 Code
      - ⊞ 🔧 Type
      - ⊞ 🔧 Fabric
      - ⊞ 🔧 Neck Style
      - ⊞ 🔧 Gender
      - ⊞ 🔧 Size

Figure 4-4   *The Product model structure*

About Attribute Groups

Master Data Services can contain every attribute associated with an entity in a business. Because of this, some entities can become unwieldy when viewed as a single table in the web UI. In a large organization, it is not uncommon for a major entity to contain over 400 attributes. Very few, if any, system users are interested in viewing all attributes simultaneously. Most users are interested in viewing only specific, related attributes at any one time. MDS provides the ability to group attributes into multiple tabs in the Master Data Manager web application. MDS calls these groupings *attribute groups*. Any attribute can be added to any attribute group.

Typically attribute groups are created for each role consuming data within an entity. Different functional areas of the organization will be concerned with different groups of attributes for each entity stored in the application. Access to attribute groups can be managed by applying security for different users or groups at the attribute group level. This will be covered in more detail in Chapter 11.

About Main Street Clothing Company's Attribute Groups

Main Street Clothing Company has determined that the best approach to grouping attributes in Master Data Services is to group attributes by role. Because multiple roles are interested in the same attribute values, some attributes will appear in multiple attribute groups. In many cases, the same individuals perform the duties of multiple roles. Managers of these groups saw value in splitting these roles early in the design phase in an effort to prepare for future employee growth. Anthony reviewed all proposed consumers of MDS and determined the following roles:

▶ **Logistics**   In the past year, the company has leased warehouse space in two central locations to manage back inventory and take advantage of bulk discounts. To manage these warehouses, information related to reordering stock and product status is provided in a single group.

▶ **Marketing**   The Marketing role includes the VP of marketing and the individual store managers. All of these individuals need access to information about the variety of products and their costs in order to make informed decisions about incentives and discounts.

▶ **Pricing**   Within the company, multiple groups are interested in pricing. To aid in the management of these attributes, a separate attribute group was created to display only the cost and suggested retail price of each product.

In this chapter, we have shown you a very manual way to create entities, the goal being to explain all of the components of MDS entity creation. In SQL Server 2012, we encourage you to check out the entity creation functionality available in the MDS Add-In for Excel. This functionality quickly creates new entities in MDS with very minimal input from the user required. More information on this process can be found in Chapter 10.

Procedure: How to Create an Attribute Group

CAUTION

In SQL Server 2012, the system-created All Attributes attribute group is always available for users. Attribute groups are no longer a method to hide or secure attributes from users.

1. On the Master Data Manager home page, click System Administration.
2. On the menu bar, choose Manage | Attribute Groups.

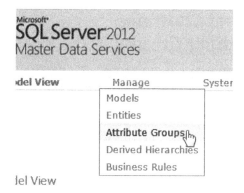

3. Select a model and entity from the lists and click Leaf Groups.

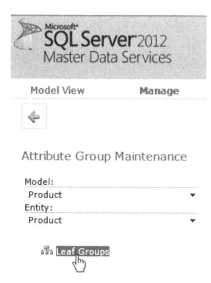

4. Click the "Add attribute group" button that is now displayed.

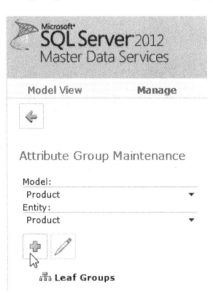

5. In the "Leaf group name" box, type **Logistics**. This will be the first tab displayed in Explorer on the grid that displays members in the Product entity.

6. Click Save. The group is displayed as a folder on the Attribute Group Maintenance page.

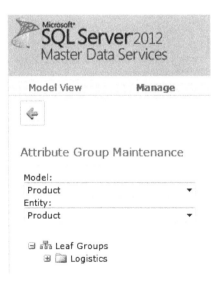

7. Expand the Logistics folder by clicking the plus sign to the left of it.

8. Click the Attributes label. The "Edit selected item" button is displayed.

9. Click the "Edit selected item" button.

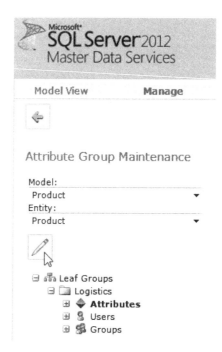

10. A list of available attributes is displayed. Assign attributes to the group by selecting them and then clicking the right-pointing arrow. In this example, we're going to add Safety Stock Level, Reorder Point, Discontinued, and Available to Outlet.

TIP

You can use CTRL-click to select multiple attributes and then add them all at the same time by clicking the arrow. The double arrows will add or remove all attributes to the group.

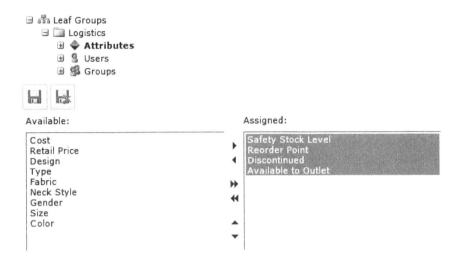

11. Click Save. The attributes are now displayed beneath the Logistics group.

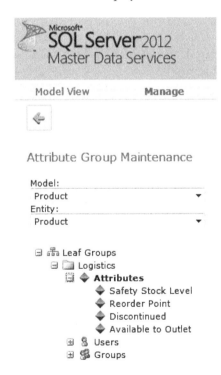

Before looking at the results in Explorer, create a few more groups:

Group	Attributes
Marketing	Color, Type, Fabric, Design, Gender, Size, Neck Style
Pricing	Cost, Retail Price

You can include attributes in multiple groups, or in none. Name and Code are automatically included in all groups.

NOTE

To rename a group, click the name of the group and then click the "Edit selected item" button.

Viewing the Results in Explorer

Let's take a few minutes to view the attribute groups in Explorer.

On the Master Data Manager home page, ensure that the Product model and VERSION_1 are selected. Click Explorer. Then, on the menu bar, choose Entities | Product. The tabs are displayed, and each tab has the columns you selected, in addition to the Name and Code columns.

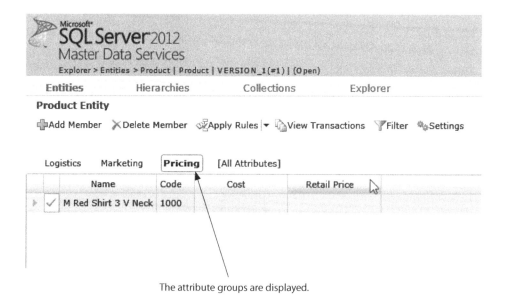

The attribute groups are displayed.

If you decide you want to change the order of your tabs, complete the next procedure.

Procedure: How to Reorder Attribute Groups

You can change the order of your tabs by completing the following steps:

1. On the Master Data Manager home page, click System Administration.
2. On the menu bar, choose Manage | Attribute Groups.
3. Click the Leaf Groups label.
4. Click the "Edit selected item" button.

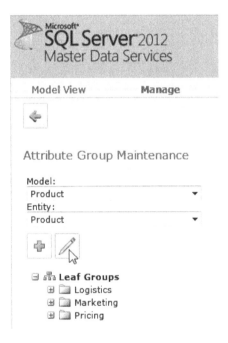

The list of attributes in the group is displayed.

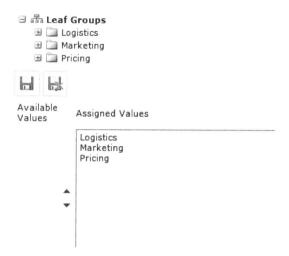

5. Click the attribute group you want to move and use the arrows to move it up or down. The topmost group will be the leftmost tab in Explorer.
6. When you're done, click Save.

Using Web Services

Creating and retrieving any of the Master Data Services objects explored in this chapter are completed using the same MDS web service operations, MetadataCreate and MetadataGet, respectively. While these two calls can be extremely powerful, they require users to create an array of different objects to successfully create and get data from the web service. In the examples in this section, the encapsulation allows developers using these calls to ignore internal IDs and work with only common object names when coding against the MDS web service. Throughout the rest of the book, we will provide examples of calls to encapsulate common coding scenarios.

Creating a Model

The first object that must be created in the Master Data Services system is a model. We can create a new model with a minimum of information from the user.

```
public void CreateModel(string newModelName)
{

    // Create the request object
    MetadataCreateRequest request = new MetadataCreateRequest();
```

```
    //Create new model container and give it a name
    Model newModel = new Model();
    newModel.Identifier = new Identifier { Name = newModelName };

    //Create Metadata container on the request object and
    //add model to models collection
    request.Metadata = new Metadata();
    request.Metadata.Models = new Collection<Model>();
    request.Metadata.Models.Add(newModel);

    // Make the service request to create
    MetadataCreateResponse response = mds_Proxy.MetadataCreate(request);

    //Error handling will be discussed in Chapter 13
    HandleErrors(response.OperationResult);
}
```

Creating an Entity

In this example, we encapsulate the call to create a new entity for a given model. This example only creates an entity that is not hierarchy enabled. The web service requires us to create the model objects to hold the new entity object. More complex examples can be found in Chapter 13.

```
public void CreateLeafEntity(string ModelName, string newEntityName)
{

    // Create the request and response objects
    MetadataCreateRequest request = new MetadataCreateRequest();

    //Create Metadata container on the request object
    request.Metadata = new Metadata();

    //Initialize the entities collection
    request.Metadata.Entities = new Collection<Entity>();

    //Create new entity in the Metadata and set model
    request.Metadata.Entities.Add(new Entity
    {
        IsFlat = true,
        Identifier = new ModelContextIdentifier
```

```
        {
            Name = newEntityName,
            ModelId = new Identifier { Name = ModelName }
        }

    });

    // Make the service request to create
    MetadataCreateResponse response =
mds_Proxy.MetadataCreate(request);
    HandleErrors(response.OperationResult);
}
```

Creating an Attribute

Attributes can be created on a variety of object types in MDS. Attributes can be created
on leaf and consolidated entities, as well as collections. The following example creates
a new attribute of a specified type on the entity and model that has been passed in.
Similar to the entity creation example, this procedure builds on the creation of an entity
object and adds the attribute.

```
        public void CreateFreeFormAttribute(string ModelName,
string EntityName, string newAttributeName, MemberType pMemberType,
AttributeDataType pAttrType, int DisplayWidth)
{
    // Create the request and response objects
    MetadataCreateRequest request = new MetadataCreateRequest();

    //Create the Metadata object
    request.Metadata = new Metadata();

    //Initialize the attributes collection
    request.Metadata.Attributes = new Collection<MetadataAttribute>();

    //Add the new attribute (all of the attribute property settings
    //are included inside required identifier)
    request.Metadata.Attributes.Add(new MetadataAttribute
    {
        Identifier = new MemberTypeContextIdentifier
        {
            Name = newAttributeName,
            MemberType = pMemberType,
            ModelId = new Identifier { Name = ModelName },
```

```
            EntityId = new Identifier{ Name = EntityName }

        },
        DataType = pAttrType,
        DisplayWidth = DisplayWidth
    });
        MetadataCreateResponse response = mds_proxy.
MetadataCreate(request);
        HandleErrors(response.OperationResult);
}
```

Summary

In this chapter we created the initial structure of our Master Data Services solution. We created models, entities, and attributes. Attribute groups provide the ability to display attributes for each role or process that consumes the data stored. Unlike the example in this book, implementing a model in MDS at your company can and should be an iterative process. The customizability and speed of structural changes in this application allows organizations to quickly react to changing business processes or discovered inefficiencies. Often, changes to the data model are identified as we load data into the model, which will be the focus of the next chapter.

Chapter 5

Integrating Master Data Services with Other Systems

In This Chapter

- ▶ Staging Architecture
- ▶ Loading Relationships
- ▶ Importing Data into the Staging Tables
- ▶ Initiating the Staging Process

- ▶ Using Web Services to Stage Data
- ▶ Errors That Occur During Staging
- ▶ Viewing the Staging Batch Table

W hile master data management requires extensive integration with other systems within your enterprise, Master Data Services does not provide any features to perform extract, transform, and load (ETL). MDS is designed to leverage SQL Server Integration Services (SSIS), but it also works well with other ETL solutions such as Informatica, InfoSphere DataStage, or any other product in this space.

To get data into and out of the system and communicate with other applications, Master Data Services uses staging tables for the incoming data flow and uses subscription views for the outgoing data flow. In SQL Server 2012, Microsoft has completely re-architected the staging process in MDS, creating new tables for each entity created in the system. In this chapter, we describe these staging areas of the application and discuss common methods to integrate systems with MDS. We also discuss some tips and tricks for integrating using SSIS and T-SQL jobs. This chapter is not meant to be a substitute for other SSIS books that may be available; for more complex operations, such as complex data flows and manipulations, you should consult *Hands-On Microsoft SQL Server 2008 Integration Services, Second Edition* by Ashwani Nanda for assistance.

Staging Architecture

The new staging architecture of Master Data Services creates a separate staging table for each entity created in the system. These tables are dynamic, adding or deleting columns as new attributes are managed in the entity. As attributes can differ between leaf members and consolidated members, two additional tables are created if the entity supports explicit hierarchies. The _Consolidated table supports loading consolidated members for any explicit hierarchy created for the entity, and the _Relationship table loads the structure of the hierarchy. Hierarchies are discussed in greater detail in Chapter 6.

All of these tables are located in the new staging (stg) schema. This new schema is provided to better delineate between system objects that should be avoided and the tables and stored procedures users are encouraged to work with directly.

Benefits of Entity-Based Staging

This new staging model has the following significant benefits over the three-common-table structure of the previous MDS release:

- ▶ **Strongly typed columns**   Now that each attribute in the entity has a corresponding column in the table, these staging columns can match the type and length of the defined attribute. This can provide rapid feedback about any truncation or data type issues when loading the staging table.

- ▶ **Increased performance**   Using common tables meant that all SQL statements in the underlying code needed to be dynamic. This limited SQL Server's innate ability to create query plans, extremely limiting performance.

▶ **Securable tables**   Using common tables to load data into MDS meant that security was an all-or-none alternative. Users who had the right to load members into one entity or attribute could also load new entity members or update information in entities they had restricted access to. Unique tables for each entity allow database administrators to leverage SQL Server security to lock down access on a per-entity and per-type basis.

▶ **Better integration**   By modeling the MDS entity table structure in the staging tables, integrators are able to better leverage SSIS and other ETL solutions to load data into MDS without significant data manipulation.

Batch Tags

In the previous release of MDS, users were required to navigate a combination of user columns and sweeping procedures in order to manage batches within the system. Many people modified the tblStgBatch table directly in order to control batch IDs effectively. SQL Server 2012 introduces a new batch tag concept to manage data loads. Batch tags add the ability to uniquely tag their data with any character combination up to 50 characters. This tag can then be passed in the load process. For instance, if there is a nightly load of SAP data into MDS, each ETL process could tag the loaded data with a SAP *<Load Date>* batch tag combination, as shown next. This tag would be stored along with the system-assigned batch ID to provide direct history of what data was loaded into each entity each night.

ID	Batch Tag	Version	Entity	Type	Started	Completed	Records	Status	Errors
39	SAP 1/04/2012	Version 3	Product	Leaf			0	QueuedToRun	0
40	SAP 1/04/2012		Product	Leaf			5	QueuedToRun	0
	SAP 1/05/2012		Fabric	Leaf			1	NotRunning	0
	SAP 1/05/2012		Product	Leaf			8	NotRunning	0
	SAP 1/05/2012		Color	Leaf			2	NotRunning	0
	SAP 1/06/2012		Product	Leaf			5	NotRunning	0
	SAP 1/06/2012		Color	Leaf			1	NotRunning	0
	SAP 1/10/2012		Product	Leaf			6	NotRunning	0
	SAP 1/10/2012		Color	Leaf			2	NotRunning	0
38	SAP 1/04/2012	Version 3	Color	Leaf	4/9/2012 3:31:	4/9/2012 3:31:	1	Completed	0
37	SAP 1/04/2012	Version 3	Fabric	Leaf	4/9/2012 3:31:	4/9/2012 3:31:	1	Completed	0
36	SAP 1/03/2012	Version 3	Color	Leaf	4/9/2012 3:31:	4/9/2012 3:31:	1	Completed	0
35	SAP 1/03/2012	Version 3	Product	Leaf	4/9/2012 3:31:	4/9/2012 3:31:	5	Completed	0
34	SAP 1/03/2012	Version 3	Fabric	Leaf	4/9/2012 3:31:	4/9/2012 3:31:	2	Completed	0

Security in Staging

While MDS is a feature of SQL Server, MDS does not rely on the SQL Server security model to secure data within the system. In Chapter 11 we will go into the details of the MDS security model, but in this chapter it is important to be aware that giving access to SQL objects within the MDS database must be handled with care. In SQL Server 2012, securable objects have been broken out into the stg schema. You can secure each of these objects for users who will use staging.

Staging and subscription views are separate from the web-based security model that is enforced in the web UI. Subscription views are SQL views used by subscribing systems to get data from MDS. These views are described in detail in Chapter 12.

The use of the staging tables and the consumption of subscription views are intended for advanced system batch integration. To ensure that these processes can be completed as quickly as possible, database objects lie outside of the security model and rely on database administrators to restrict access using SQL Server security roles to limit access to any sensitive information stored in MDS. We will discuss the securing of these database objects in Chapter 11.

System Settings

Before you load data into the staging tables, confirm the following staging system settings that are set in Master Data Services Configuration Manager, which you launch from Programs | Microsoft SQL Server 2012 | Master Data Services | Configuration Manager.

▶ **Log all staging transactions**   Set this to On to have transactions logged when the staged records are loaded into the appropriate Master Data Services database tables.

▶ **Staging batch interval**   When you set the staging process to start, this setting determines the number of seconds afterward that your batch is processed. The default setting is 60 seconds (1 minute).

About Main Street Clothing Company's Staging Process

Main Street Clothing Company has created what it believes to be a basic, functional model structure. Now Anthony Green needs to ensure that all the requisite information is loaded, to ensure that all products can be staged into the system.

Anthony determines that the best method for addressing new attribute values will be a manual process managed by the Product Procurement team. This process will be managed through the use of business rules, as discussed in Chapter 8.

Anthony compiles a summary of the attribute values that need to be loaded before the company's current product list can be loaded. He reviews each attribute to determine if there is any additional data associated with these values that should be managed as well. For each attribute, he will need to create or load several members to be used as domain-based attribute values.

Attribute	Number of Distinct Attribute Values
Color	15
Gender	2
Neck Style	4
Type	7
Fabric	4
Size	14

Since none of these attribute values requires advanced management nor has over 15 values, Anthony determines that loading these records manually is the most efficient method. A few of the more technical manufacturers have discussed system integrations to provide electronic access to new product lines. As these systems become available, Anthony will review the necessary ETL processes to automatically load new products and their requisite domain-based values.

If Anthony had decided to use the staging process, he could have created a spreadsheet similar to those available at www.mdsuser.com.

Standard Leaf and Parent Staging Fields

A staging table will be added to the stg schema in the MDS database for each entity that is created. This initial table will be named using the Name for Staging Tables input provided when you create the entity. This name cannot be changed using the UI once you have created the entity.

The following table describes the common columns in each leaf and parent staging table.

Column Name	Required?	Description
ImportType	No	This is the type of staging for this member row. You can mix and match ImportType records in the same batch. See the table in the following section for accepted values.
ImportStatus_ID	Yes	The status of the import process. Enter 0 for records that are ready for staging. The system updates this value to 1 if the record is successfully loaded and to 2 if the record is not successfully loaded. This column is required.
Batch_ID	No	Leave this field blank. When the batch is processed, an ID for the batch will populate this field. *Note: This value is also added to the ID field in the mdm.tblStgBatch table when the batch is processed.*
BatchTag	Yes	This is the tag provided by the staging user or system to mark all records in the batch. Staging uses this tag to assign a common Batch_ID to all records at the start of the staging process. This is the tag you provide to the system when you trigger staging from the stored procedure or web UI. The BatchTag will be added to tblStgBatch to help identify the batch in the future.
ErrorCode	Yes	This error code is a bit mask for all the errors that occurred on the member. This can be complicated to decipher. To review errors, open the stg.viw_*<entity>*_MemberErrorDetails view described later in this chapter.
Code	Maybe	The code of the member to create or update. If the entity supports code creation, then this field should not be populated. *Note: Members with duplicate codes will not be imported.*
Name	No	A name for the member. This field is optional.
NewCode	No	Give staging users the ability to update the code attribute of the member. The code provided in the row will change to the new code and will need to be provided in any future staging attempts.

Staging Import Types

Because entity-based staging loads all attributes for a given entity's members simultaneously, a number of import options had to be created. These options load the data provided into MDS based on the import type provided for each member record. Since different import types can be loaded simultaneously and the results of each type can affect data drastically, it is imperative to ensure the correct import type is passed with each member record.

Import Type	Type Name	Description
0	Merge Optimistic	Inserts and updates records with only values that are provided. Ignores any columns with NULL values.
1	Insert	Inserts any new records into the entity. If the code already exists, an error is given for the member record.
2	Merge Overwrite	Inserts and updates records with all values in the table. All NULL values in staging will be updated into the MDS entity. Only used for entire record update.
3	Delete	Performs standard soft delete of the member in MDS. History for the member is retained and the member delete can be reversed in the transaction log.
4	Purge	New! Purges the record completely from the selected version.
5	Delete Automatic	Performs new soft delete process that removes any domain-based attribute dependencies for the member to allow a soft delete of the member from the system.
6	Purge Automatic	Extended purge functionality that removes any domain based attribute dependencies for the member to allow immediate removal of the member from the system.

Member Staging Examples

You can populate the tblStgMember table by using T-SQL statements or by using SQL Server Integration Services. In our SSIS examples, we'll import a CSV file, but there are a variety of options available, including SQL Server, Access, Excel, and others.

The examples in this section are meant to illustrate the staging process, but they do not necessarily build on the Product model that we've laid out so far. You can visit www.mdsuser.com to download the CSV files you need to stage in all of the members, attributes, and collections for the Product and Finance models. You can get those files now and compare them to the examples, or try creating your own sample products.

Use the following examples to create a new leaf member, update a leaf member, delete a leaf member, purge a leaf member, create a consolidated member (needed only for explicit hierarchies), and create a collection (a different type of grouping that your organization may or may not use). When using a CSV file to stage members, the first row in the file should contain the column names. Collection member management will use the prior version staging tables to add or update collection members into the system through staging.

Create a Leaf Member

In this example, we are going to specify the member code required to create a leaf member. We are not going to specify the member name, because the name is not required. In Chapter 8, we'll show you how to use business rules to create a concatenated member name. Since the new staging table schema can load attributes with the members, all attributes could have been added to this example. To ensure readability and brevity, only a few attributes have been added to the following examples unless otherwise specified.

Also in these examples, we no longer need to provide a username with each member record, as was required in the prior MDS release. This process has been replaced with the batch tag. Batch tags can be used to separate loads of data into the system, and SQL Server security can be used to control access to each staging table, stored procedure, and error view.

T-SQL	`INSERT INTO stg.Product_Leaf`
	`(ImportType, ImportStatus_ID, BatchTag, Code, Name, Fabric,`
	`Gender, Size) VALUES`
	`(1,0, N'New Member Load', N'1001', 'Men's Shirt', 'Cotton', 'M', 'L')`

CSV File	ImportType, ImportStatus_ID, BatchTag, Code, Name, Fabric, Gender, Size 1,0, 'New Member Load', 1001, 'Men's Shirt', 'Cotton','M',1000

Update a Leaf Member

Following are two import examples that show you how to update a leaf member with the name _ and the code 1001. In the first example, we only want to update certain attributes and do not need to update any attributes to NULL. In the second example, we want the member record to exactly match the values we are loading. Be very careful when loading data using this method, as any new attributes will be erased from the system. (They will default to NULL in the staging table and load as NULL into MDS.)

This import example shows the partial attribute update:

T-SQL	`INSERT INTO stg.Product_Leaf`
	`(ImportType, ImportStatus_ID, BatchTag, Code, Name, Fabric,`
	`Gender, Size) VALUES`
	`(1,0, N'New Member Load', N'1001', N'', 'Cotton', 'Female',`
	`'4')`

CSV File	ImportType, ImportStatus_ID, BatchTag, Code, Name, Fabric, Gender, Size 1,0,'New Member Load', 1001, '', 'Cotton', 'Female','4'

This example shows the exact member update:

T-SQL	`INSERT INTO stg.Raw_Materials_to_Product_Leaf`
	`(ImportType, ImportStatus_ID, BatchTag, Code, Name, Product,`
	`Raw Materials, Quantity) VALUES`
	`(2,0, N'Partial Member Load', N'1001', N'', 'Cotton',`
	`'Female', '4')`

CSV File	ImportType, ImportStatus_ID, BatchTag, Code, Name, Product, Raw Materials, Quantity 2,0,'Partial Member Load', 1001, '', 'Cotton', 'Female','4'

Delete a Member

There are two options to soft delete members from MDS using staging. An import type of 3 soft deletes a member from the system only if the member is not referenced by any other entity that has a relationship to the member. An import type of 5 removes these references, setting these related members' attribute values to NULL. All soft delete actions from staging only require the ImportType, ImportStatus_ID, BatchTag, and Code columns to have values. All other data provided in the row will be ignored.

This example shows how to soft delete data with no references:

T-SQL	```INSERT INTO STG.Color_Leaf ((ImportType, ImportStatus_ID, BatchTag, Code) VALUES (3,0, N'Soft Delete Member','Blue'))```
CSV File	ImportType, ImportStatus_ID, BatchTag, Code 3,0,'Soft Delete Member','Blue'

This example shows how to soft delete data and remove references:

T-SQL	```INSERT INTO STG.Color_Leaf ((ImportType, ImportStatus_ID, BatchTag, Code) VALUES (5,0, N'Soft Delete Member','Blue'))```
CSV File	ImportType, ImportStatus_ID, BatchTag, Code 5,0,'Soft Delete Member','Blue'

Purge a Member

In SQL Server 2012, you can now purge members from the system. While soft delete retains the member history and does not allow the code to be reused within the entity for the current version, purge completely removes the member and all history for the current version. There are two options to purge members from MDS using staging. An import type of 4 purges a member from the system only if the member is not referenced by any other entity that has a relationship to the member. An import type of 6 removes these references, setting these related members' attribute values to NULL. All purge actions from staging only require the ImportType, ImportStatus_ID, BatchTag, and Code columns to have values. All other data provided in the row will be ignored.

This example purges data with no references:

T-SQL	```INSERT INTO STG.Color_Leaf (ImportType, ImportStatus_ID, BatchTag, Code) VALUES (4,0, N'Purge Member','Blue')```
CSV File	ImportType, ImportStatus, BatchTag, Code 4,0,'Purge Member','Blue'

This example purges data and removes references:

T-SQL	```INSERT INTO STG.Color_Leaf (ImportType, ImportStatus_ID, BatchTag, Code) VALUES (6,0, N'Purge Member','Blue')```
CSV File	ImportType, ImportStatus, BatchTag, Code 6,0,'Purge Member', 'Blue'

Create a Consolidated Member

This example shows you how to create a consolidated member with the name Short Term Assets and the code STA for the Account entity.

T-SQL	```INSERT INTO STG.Account_Consolidated (ImportType, ImportStatus_ID, BatchTag, HierarchyName, Code, Name) VALUES (0,0,N'Consolidated Member Load', N'Chart of Accounts', N'STA', N'Short Term Assets')```
CSV File	ImportType, ImportStatus, BatchTag, HierarchyName, Code, Name 0,0, 'Consolidated Member Load', 'Chart of Accounts', 'STA', 'Short Term Assets'

Create a Collection

This example shows you how to create a collection with the name Boys Winter Set and the code BWS. Unfortunately, collections are not handled with the new entity-based staging. To manage collections using staging in SQL Server 2012, you need to use the old, deprecated tables from the prior release. This collection won't have any members in it. It is simply creating a collection with this name and code. To add members to collections, you can use the TblStgRelationship staging table.

Collections have a MemberType_ID of 3 to distinguish them from leaf members (1) and consolidated members (2).

T-SQL	```INSERT INTO mdm.tblStgMember (UserName, ModelName, EntityName, MemberType_ID, MemberName, MemberCode) VALUES (N'Domain\tyler', N'Product', N'Product', 3, N'Boys Winter Set', N'BWS')```
CSV File	UserName,ModelName,EntityName,MemberType_ID,MemberName,MemberCode Domain\tyler,Product,Product,3,Boys Winter Set,BWS

Update a Collection's Attribute

This example updates the Description attribute of the Boys Winter Set (BWS) collection to read "Boys 2011 Winter Set." If you have not defined additional attributes for your collections, the only attributes you can update are Owner_ID, Description, Name, and Code.

T-SQL	`INSERT INTO mdm.tblStgMemberAttribute (ModelName, EntityName, MemberType_ID, MemberCode, AttributeName, AttributeValue) VALUES (N'Product', N'Product', 3, N'BWS', N'Description', N'Boys 2011 Winter Set')`
CSV File	ModelName,EntityName,MemberType_ID,MemberCode,AttributeName,AttributeValue Product,Product,3,BWS,Description,Boys 2011 Winter Set

Add One Collection to Another

This example adds the Boys Winter Set (BWS) collection to the Fall and Winter Sets (FWS) collection.

T-SQL	`INSERT INTO mdm.tblStgRelationship (ModelName, EntityName, HierarchyName, MemberType_ID, MemberCode, TargetCode, TargetType_ID) VALUES (N'Product', N'Product', NULL, 5, N'BWS', N'FWS', 1)`
CSV File	ModelName,EntityName,HierarchyName,MemberType_ID,MemberCode,TargetCode,TargetType_ID Product,Product,NULL,5,BWS,FWS,1

Add a Leaf Member to a Collection

This example adds leaf member 1052 to the Boys Winter Set (BWS) collection.

T-SQL	`INSERT INTO mdm.tblStgRelationship (ModelName, EntityName, HierarchyName, MemberType_ID, MemberCode, TargetCode, TargetType_ID) VALUES (N'Product', N'Product', NULL, 5, N'1052', N'BWS', 1)`
CSV File	ModelName,EntityName,HierarchyName,MemberType_ID,MemberCode,TargetCode,TargetType_ID Product,Product,NULL,5,1052,BWS,1

Add a Consolidated Member to a Collection

This example adds the Boys (B) consolidated member to the Fall and Winter Sets (FWS) collection. The TargetType_ID of 5 tells the system that you are setting a collection member.

T-SQL	`INSERT INTO mdm.tblStgRelationship (ModelName, EntityName, HierarchyName, MemberType_ID, MemberCode, TargetCode, TargetType_ID) VALUES (N'Product', N'Product', NULL, 5, N'B', N'FWS', 1)`
CSV File	ModelName,EntityName,HierarchyName,MemberType_ID,MemberCode,TargetCode,TargetType_ID Product,Product,NULL,5,B,FWS,1

Using Staging to Deactivate Members

The soft delete process in the leaf and consolidated entity-based staging has replaced the deactivation process of the prior release of MDS. Unfortunately, there is no way to reactivate a member through the new staging process. When you deactivate a member, the member code no longer changes to a 32-character GUID, making that code unavailable for use. The purge import type will solve this issue. Entity-based staging does not support reactivating the member. This can be useful if you want to restore a member's attributes and its membership in hierarchies and collections. If you want to reactivate a member, you need to leverage the deprecated tblMemberAttribute table.

This procedure no longer requires that you look in database tables for information, as the code is not updated to a GUID. In Chapter 7 we will show you how to delete and reactivate members in the Master Data Manager web application. Using the web UI is simpler than using staging and leaves less room for error. The new purge functionality is only available in staging, and it should be noted that purging the member will cause you to lose attribute assignments and hierarchy relationships as well as any history stored within the selected purge version.

Example: Reactivate a Member

This example shows how to reactivate a member that was deactivated. Note that the member code is now the code and has not changed to a 32-character GUID.

T-SQL	`INSERT INTO mdm.tblStgMemberAttribute (ModelName, EntityName, MemberType_ID, MemberCode, AttributeName, AttributeValue) VALUES (N'Product', N'Product', 1, N'1101', N'MDMMemberStatus',N'Active')`
CSV File	ModelName,EntityName,MemberType_ID,MemberCode,AttributeName,AttributeValue Product,Product,1,1101,MDMMemberStatus,Active

Loading Relationships

The last staging table type within MDS entity-based staging is the relationship table. This table will be created only if the entity is hierarchy enabled. You use the stg.<*Staging Name*>_Relationship table to load explicit hierarchy relationships. Explicit hierarchy relationships can still be entered in two ways. You can load data as a parent relationship, or you can load data as sibling relationships.

In most cases, the easiest way to load data into MDS is to load it in parent-child format. Many systems care not about the order of members within the hierarchy but rather about the consolidations themselves; in these cases, parent-child format is the easiest way to load records through staging. When parent-child records are loaded through staging in this manner, the sort order is triggered in a standard way. Any new children of a consolidated member in the system are placed as the last siblings in the tree, similar to how birth order works in a family tree for humans.

If sort order matters and you cannot control the order of data within your staging load, you can load records into MDS using the sibling type. Using 2 as the relationship type, new relationships are created at the same level of the hierarchy as the next sibling to the target code specified. This allows you to directly set the order of records in an explicit hierarchy without reloading the entire hierarchy.

Creating a new record as the first sibling of any parent requires a two-step process. The first step is to load the new relationship as a sibling to the first child of the target parent. The second step is to set the first child as a sibling to the just loaded member. This reverses the order of these two child members.

Relationship Table Fields

Use stg.<*Staging Name*>_Relationship to move members in explicit hierarchies. You cannot use this table for updating derived hierarchies or for adding or removing members to or from collections. To update derived hierarchies, you must update the attribute values that determine the hierarchy. For more information about hierarchies and collections, refer to Chapter 6.

The following table describes the fields in tblStgRelationship.

Column Name	Required?	Description
RelationshipType	Yes	The type of relationship to be applied to the import record: 1 to make the target member the parent of the staged member or 2 to make the target member a sibling of the staged member.
ImportStatus_ID	Yes	The status of the import process. Enter 0 for records that are ready for staging. The system updates this value to 1 if the record is successfully loaded and to 2 if the record is not successfully loaded.

Column Name	Required?	Description
Batch_ID	No	Leave this field blank. When the batch is processed, an ID for the batch will populate this field. This value is also added to the ID field in the mdm.tblStgBatch table when the batch is processed.
BatchTag	Yes	This is the tag provided by the staging user or system to mark all records in the batch. Staging uses this tag to assign a common Batch_ID to all records at the start of the staging process. This is the tag you provide to the system when you trigger staging from the stored procedure or web UI. The BatchTag is added to tblStgBatch to help identify the batch in the future.
ErrorCode	Yes	This error code is a bit mask for all the errors that occurred on the member. This can be complicated to decipher. To review errors, open the stg.viw_ *<entity>*_ MemberErrorDetails view described later in this chapter.
HierarchyName	Yes	The explicit hierarchy name, if you are staging a relationship in an explicit hierarchy.
ParentCode	Yes	A unique code for the member that the ChildCode will be related to in the hierarchy. If the RelationshipType is 1, then the ParentCode must be a consolidated member. If you have a nonmandatory explicit hierarchy, use MDMUNUSED to add a leaf member to the Unused node. To add members to the root of any explicit hierarchy, use ROOT.
ChildCode	Yes	The member code to be moved or added to the hierarchy.
SortOrder	No	For explicit hierarchies, an integer that indicates the order of the member in relation to the other members under the parent. Each member should have a unique number. If this is not populated, then the order of records in the staging table is used as the order.

Relationship Staging Examples

The following examples show how to populate the Account Relationship staging table by using T-SQL statements or by using SSIS to import a CSV file. Again, many of the members referred to in these examples do not exist yet in the samples we've provided, and you will get errors if you try to update a member that doesn't exist. Use these examples to get ideas for how to stage your own data, or use the staging spreadsheets we've provided at www.mdsuser.com.

Set a Parent-Child Relationship in an Explicit Hierarchy

This example sets the Short Term Assets (STA) consolidated member as the parent of the Cash member in the Chart of Accounts explicit hierarchy.

TIP

If you want to specify the Unused node of an explicit hierarchy as the parent, use MDMUNUSED for the TargetCode. If you want to assign a hierarchy member to the root, use ROOT.

T-SQL	`INSERT INTO stg.Account_Relationship (RelationshipType, ImportStatus_ID, BatchTag, HierarchyName, ParentCode, ChildCode) VALUES (1,0, N'Relationship Batch', N'Chart of Accounts', N'STA', N'Cash')`
CSV File	RelationshipType,ImportStatus_ID,BatchTag,HierarchyName,ParentCode,ChildCode 1,0,Relationship Batch, Chart of Accounts, STA, Cash

Set a Sibling Relationship in an Explicit Hierarchy

This example sets Long Term Assets at the same level as Short Term Assets in the Chart of Accounts explicit hierarchy.

T-SQL	`INSERT INTO stg.Account_Relationship (RelationshipType,ImportStatus_ID, BatchTag, HierarchyName, ParentCode, ChildCode) VALUES (2,0,N'Relationship Batch', N'Chart of Accounts', N'STA', N'LTA')`
CSV File	RelationshipType,ImportStatus_ID,BatchTag,HierarchyName,,ParentCode,ChildCode 2,0,Relationship Batch, Chart of Accounts, STA, LTA

Add One Collection to Another

This example adds the Boys Winter Set (BWS) collection to the Fall and Winter Sets (FWS) collection. This is a deprecated table, but it is the only way to use staging to update a collection member in SQL Server 2012.

T-SQL	`INSERT INTO mdm.tblStgRelationship (ModelName, EntityName, HierarchyName, MemberType_ID, MemberCode, TargetCode, TargetType_ID) VALUES (N'Product', N'Product', NULL, 5, N'BWS', N'FWS', 1)`
CSV File	ModelName,EntityName,HierarchyName,MemberType_ID,MemberCode,TargetCode,TargetType_ID Product,Product,NULL,5,BWS,FWS,1

Add a Leaf Member to a Collection

This example adds leaf member 1052 to the Boys Winter Set (BWS) collection.

T-SQL	`INSERT INTO mdm.tblStgRelationship (ModelName, EntityName, HierarchyName, MemberType_ID, MemberCode, TargetCode, TargetType_ID) VALUES (N'Product', N'Product', NULL, 5, N'1052', N'BWS', 1)`
CSV File	ModelName,EntityName,HierarchyName,MemberType_ID,MemberCode,TargetCode,TargetType_ID Product,Product,NULL,5,1052,BWS,1

Add a Consolidated Member to a Collection

This example adds the Boys (B) consolidated member to the Fall and Winter Sets (FWS) collection.

T-SQL	`INSERT INTO mdm.tblStgRelationship (ModelName, EntityName, HierarchyName, MemberType_ID, MemberCode, TargetCode, TargetType_ID) VALUES (N'Product', N'Product', NULL, 5, N'B', N'FWS', 1)`
CSV File	ModelName,EntityName,HierarchyName,MemberType_ID,MemberCode,TargetCode,TargetType_ID Product,Product,NULL,5,B,FWS,1

Importing Data into the Staging Tables

You may already have decided how to get your data into the MDS database's staging tables. If you haven't, we'll show you how to do it by using SQL Server Integration Services. After you import your data into the tables, you can proceed with running the import, which puts the data from the staging tables into the appropriate MDS database tables. You can load files that are provided for later chapters by using the following process.

Procedure: How to Import Data into SQL Server by Using SSIS

In this procedure, we are going to use a flat CSV file with a header row that includes column names. To import a CSV file into the SQL Server MDS database staging tables by using SSIS, complete the following steps:

1. Open SQL Server Management Studio.
2. Right-click the MDS database.
3. On the submenu, select Tasks | Import Data.
4. On the Welcome page, click Next.

5. On the Choose a Data Source page, select Flat File Source as your data source.

6. Click the Browse button to browse to the file. (You must select CSV as the file type to view your files. TXT is selected by default.)

7. Select the "Column names in the first data row" check box.

8. Click Next.

9. On the next Choose a Data Source page, confirm that the preview of your data looks accurate and click Next.

10. On the Choose a Destination page, confirm that your MDS database is selected and click Next.

11. On the Select Source Tables and Views page, ensure that you select the appropriate staging table. You should load data only into tables in the stg schema. If you are not sure which table to load into, you can check in the Manage Entities screen in System Administration functional area. You can also click the Preview button at the bottom of this screen to preview your data.

CAUTION

The correct table is not selected by default. Be careful not to click Next without changing the destination table.

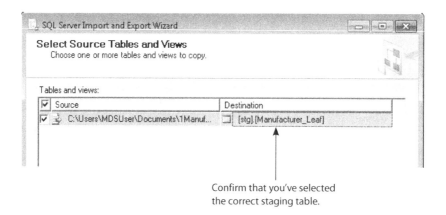

Confirm that you've selected
the correct staging table.

12. Click Next.
13. On the Review Data Type Mapping page, click Next.
14. On the Save and Run Package page, click Next.
15. On the Complete the Wizard page, click Finish.

When the process is complete, a message is displayed, stating that the execution was successful.

Initiating the Staging Process

After you have populated the staging tables with your data, you must run the batch process that loads the data from the staging tables into the MDS-specific tables. In SQL Server 2012 Master Data Services, Microsoft has created a specific staging stored procedure for each entity-based staging table.

To initiate the staging process, you can use

▶ The Master Data Manager web application
▶ A stored procedure in the MDS database

In an effort to align with other SQL Server features and to provide to users an efficient method to load data into MDS, the new web services for entity-based staging are not supported for customer use. Data stewards should plan to move all of their MDS staging processes to leverage the appropriate stored procedures.

Procedure: How to Use Master Data Manager to Initiate the Staging Process

To use the Master Data Manager web application to initiate the staging process after you've loaded data into the MDS staging tables, complete the following steps:

NOTE

In the latest release of MDS, staging batches are now processed by entity, and processing begins at an interval determined by a setting in Master Data Services Configuration Manager. As a data steward, you are responsible for initiating the processing of each table individually, so you should import only the records you intend to load in the proper order (for example, import colors before importing products set to that color).

1. On the Master Data Manager home page, click Integration Management. On the initial Import Data page, all batch tag grouped records that have not been cleared are displayed for the selected model. Even with identical batch tags, entity and type will be broken out in the table.

2. Select the model and then select a batch tag from the table to load into the system. The total number of records to be imported should be displayed in the Records column.

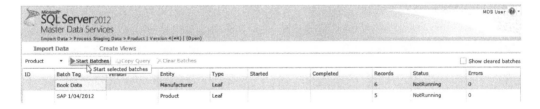

3. Above the batch list, click the Start Batches button.

4. In the Run Selected Batches dialog box, shown next, select the version to load selected batches into.

NOTE

Committed versions are available in the list even though you will not be able to load members into those versions. If the number of records to be imported does not seem correct or the batch tag is missing, ensure that your batch tag was properly entered, that the Batch_ID field for each record in the table is NULL, and that the ImportStatus_ID field for each record is 0.

Click OK. The batch is assigned an ID, and the Status column is updated to QueuedToRun.

The selected batch is assigned an ID of 43.   The selected batch is queued to run.

TIP

On the menu bar, click Import Data to refresh the page until the Status column is updated.

When the batch has finished processing, the Status column is updated to Not Running and errors are listed in the Errors column.

ID	Batch Tag	Version	Entity	Type	Started	Completed	Records	Status	Errors
	SAP 1/04/2012		Product	Leaf			5	NotRunning	0
	SAP 1/05/2012		Fabric	Leaf			1	NotRunning	0
	SAP 1/05/2012		Product	Leaf			8	NotRunning	0
	SAP 1/05/2012		Color	Leaf			2	NotRunning	0
	SAP 1/06/2012		Product	Leaf			5	NotRunning	0
	SAP 1/06/2012		Color	Leaf			1	NotRunning	0
	SAP 1/10/2012		Product	Leaf			6	NotRunning	0
	SAP 1/10/2012		Color	Leaf			2	NotRunning	0
43	Book Data	Version 4	Manufacturer	Leaf	5/1/2012 10:13:1!	5/1/2012 10:13:1!	6	Completed	0

You can go to Explorer functional area to view your staged members, or open the Staging Batch Errors view to view the details of your errors.

Procedure: How to Use Stored Procedures to Initiate the Staging Process

After you have loaded data into the staging tables by using either T-SQL or SSIS, using the web UI or web services to trigger a staging load process can be inconvenient. While we do not recommend coding against stored procedures as a general rule, the benefits outweigh the risks in this case.

You can trigger logging of transactions or validation by using staging stored procedures. The stored procedures, described in the following section, provide access to additional functionality that is not exposed in the UI. These stored procedures are also more accessible when loading data through SSIS.

NOTE

Microsoft does not guarantee that these interfaces will remain constant, nor does Microsoft provide any backward compatibility at the stored procedure level.

The End of Staging Sweep

The new batch tag approach has replaced the staging sweep process used in the prior release of MDS. While the deprecated three-table approach still requires staging sweep use, all new staging tables automatically receive a batch ID upon triggering the load process.

Using Web Services to Stage Data

There are a number of calls within the web service that leverage the staging tables and processes to load data into Master Data Services. Some of these calls provide support for bulk loading of data. These calls manage the entire process of populating the staging tables and triggering the staging process. The structure of these calls will be discussed in greater detail in Chapter 13.

In SQL Server 2012, all of the new staging calls have been tagged for "Internal Use Only." These calls were not created or tested for external consumption. The new staging tables provide a much more compelling integration with SSIS using the new stored procedures to trigger staging loads, and staging batches can be created when loading the staging tables.

Errors That Occur During Staging

Sometimes errors occur during the staging process. As each row in a staging table is processed, the Status_ID column is updated with a 1 if staging succeeded and a 2 if it failed. If staging failed, the ErrorCode column is updated with a new (to SQL Server 2012) complex error code that can help you troubleshoot the issue. This number is useful to humans only through the new staging error view created for each entity.

In SQL Server 2012, all errors are now determined for a record in the batch that is processed. In the new staging error view created for each entity, these errors are expanded into a new row for each error that is found on the record.

You can no longer see a translation of these error messages in the Master Data Manager web application; however, you can save a SQL script to the Clipboard to review in SQL Server Management Studio.

Procedure: How to View Staging Errors in Management Studio

To view details of your staging errors in SQL Server Management Studio, complete the following steps:

1. On the initial import data screen, click the row for the batch with errors you want to explore.

ID	Batch Tag				Started	Completed	Records	Status	Errors
	SAP 1/04/2012		Product	Leaf			5	NotRunning	0
	SAP 1/05/2012		Fabric	Leaf			1	NotRunning	0
	SAP 1/05/2012		Product	Leaf			8	NotRunning	0
	SAP 1/05/2012		Color	Leaf			2	NotRunning	0
	SAP 1/06/2012		Product	Leaf			5	NotRunning	0
	SAP 1/06/2012		Color	Leaf			1	NotRunning	0
	SAP 1/10/2012		Product	Leaf			6	NotRunning	0
	SAP 1/10/2012		Color	Leaf			2	NotRunning	0
44	Error Test Load	Version 4	Product	Leaf	5/1/2012 4:53:59	5/1/2012 4:53:59	4	Completed	4

Import Data   Create Views

Product ▾   ▶ Start Batches   Copy Query   ✗ Clear Batches   ☐ Show cle:

Copy a SQL query you can run to view error messages

2. Click the Copy Query button to load the SQL query onto the Clipboard. If this is your first time using this feature, Silverlight may ask permission to write to the Clipboard. If so, click Yes to continue.

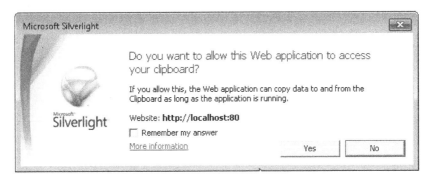

3. Open SQL Server Management Studio and connect to the database server running the MDS database.
4. Open a new query window and press CTRL-V.
5. Click the Execute button at the top of the screen. You will notice that many more errors than original member records can be present, as a row in the view has been created for each error found by the staging process.

Staging Errors View

To help you better manage errors in your staging batches, Microsoft includes in the latest release of MDS the errors view table, the columns for which are listed and described in the following table. A single view shows errors for all staging table types for an entity. Filtering this view by the appropriate batch ID is the best way to see your issues effectively. (This is what copy query provides.)

Column Name	Description
ID	The ID from the staging table. This allows data stewards to determine the exact member record the error refers to.
ImportType	Import Type for the record returning an error.
ImportStatus_ID	The status of the import record. This should initially be 2 for all error records.
Batch_ID	The ID assigned during import process; this is the best column for managing specific batch errors.
BatchTag	The Batch tag of the record returning an error.
Code	The Code value of the record returning the error shown.
Name	The Name value of the record returning the error shown.
NewCode	The New code value if it was provided in the original staging record.
MemberType	The member type of the member, used to determine the staging table of the record.
UniqueErrorCode	The specific error code broken out from the original error code bit mask.
ErrorDescription	The text description of the specific error in the view record.
AttributeName	The name of the attribute that created this error. This is completed only for attribute-specific errors.
AttributeValue	The value of the attribute that created this error.

Viewing the Staging Batch Table

The last table specifically related to staging is the batch table, mdm.tblStgBatch. This table stores information related to each load of data imported into the MDS system. Summary information related to the success and failure of each record is stored in the batch table indefinitely. As this table is not part of the stg schema, users should not modify this table directly.

Column Name	Required?	Description
OriginalBatch_ID	No	This is not currently implemented.
MUID	Yes	Unique identifier for the batch.
Entity_ID	Yes	Entity ID of the processed batch.
MemberType_ID	Yes	Member type of the data loaded into MDS.
BatchTag	Yes	The batch tag that was used to identify this group of staging records originally.
Version_ID	Yes	ID in the mdm.tblModelVersion table that identifies the model version that the data was or will be staged into.
ExternalSystem_ID	N/A	This column is not currently managed by the MDS system. The column was created to support the identification and tracking of staging records by external source systems in concert with the mdm.tblExternalSystem table. Neither this column nor the table is currently used in the staging process.
Name	N/A	The name for the batch. When using the UI or the staging sweep stored procedure, this is populated with the model name and "unbatched." This value will be blank for system staging loads. You can set this value to anything when using the staging batch creation stored procedure, udpStagingBatchSave.
Status_ID	N/A	1 = "Queued to run"—The batch will be processed the next time the Service Broker queue is activated.* 2 = "Not Running"—The batch staging process has completed. 3 = "Running"—The batch is currently processing. 4= "Queued to clear"—The request to clear staging table records for this batch has been set and the staging tables will be cleared the next time the Service Broker queue is activated. 5= Batch has been cleared—All corresponding records for the batch have been cleared from the staging tables.
TotalMemberCount	N/A	The total number of members in tblStgMember that were associated with this Batch_ID.
ErrorMemberCount	N/A	The total number of members with errors in tblStgMember that were associated with this Batch_ID.
TotalMemberAttributeCount	N/A	The total number of attributes in the tblStgMemberAttribute staging table that were associated with this Batch_ID. Not used in entity-based staging.
ErrorMemberAttributeCount	N/A	The total number of attributes with an error in tblStgMemberAttribute that were associated with this Batch_ID. Not used in entity-based staging.

Column Name	Required?	Description
TotalMemberRelationshipCount	N/A	The total number of relationships in the relationship staging table that were associated with this Batch_ID. Not used in entity-based staging.
ErrorMemberRelationshipCount	N/A	The total number of relationships with an error in tblStgRelationship that were associated with this Batch_ID. Not used in entity-based staging.
LastRunStartDTM	No	The time that the staging batch process was initiated.
LastRunStartUserID	No	The user who ran the process that invoked the staging process.
LastRunEndDTM	No	The time that the staging batch process completes.
LastRunEndUserID	No	The user who ran the process that invoked the staging process.
LastClearedDTM	No	The date and time that this batch was cleared from the staging tables. Even though all the imported records are cleared, the summary data stored in this batch table remains.
LastClearedUserID	No	The user who initiated the batch clearing process.
EnterDTM	No	The date and time that the batch was "queued for processing."
EnterUserID	No	The user who ran the process to create the batch.

*The Service Broker queue is used only as an asynchronous timer. Generic staging messages are placed on the queue and staging batches are triggered by the Queued to Run status only.

Procedure: How to Clear the Staging Queue

To clear a batch from the staging queue, complete the following steps:

1. On the Master Data Manager home page, click Integration Management.
2. In the pane, click the row for the batch you want to clear.
3. Click the Clear Batches button.

The value in the Status column changes to Queued to Clear. When it's done processing, the Status column changes to Not Running. This can be considered completed for any batch that is displayed.

Summary

In this chapter, we discussed techniques for using staging tables to load data into Master Data Services efficiently and effectively. We discussed the changes to the staging process in SQL Server 2012 and the benefits of entity based staging. We reviewed examples of using SQL Server Integration Services or standard SQL calls to populate records into the new staging tables. Within the discussion of staging tables, we also discussed types of errors that can occur during the data loading process from the staging into MDS and how to use the new error views provided in this release. We provided likely solutions to these errors. In the next chapter, we will discuss hierarchy types in greater detail.

Chapter 6

Working with Hierarchies and Collections

In This Chapter

- ▶ Ragged vs. Level-Based Hierarchies
- ▶ Creating Derived Hierarchies
- ▶ System Settings for Hierarchies
- ▶ Creating Explicit Hierarchies

- ▶ Recursive Hierarchies
- ▶ Derived Hierarchies with Explicit Caps
- ▶ Collections
- ▶ Creating Hierarchies by Using Web Services

usinesses are not built only on lists; they require more complex structures for data. Dollars, units, and hours must all be calculated to produce consolidated views of a business. For many years, companies have been using business intelligence (BI) applications to better understand their businesses and discover opportunities for both cost savings and revenue growth. At the heart of these applications are the hierarchies that make consolidations possible.

When managing consolidations within a business, it is imperative that all values are accounted for once and only once. To ensure this, hierarchies in Master Data Services enforce that all leaf members have one and only one parent. This limits your ability to manage many-to-many relationships within MDS and display these relationships hierarchically.

In this chapter, we review the two primary types of hierarchies supported in MDS. We then create these derived and explicit hierarchies within our models. Finally, we create a number of special hierarchies and discuss the various uses for these special hierarchies.

Before you start this chapter, go to www.mdsuser.com and download the ZIP file for Chapter 6, called chapter6.zip. This ZIP file contains the following files that you will use in this chapter:

File	When to Use	How to Use
Finance_data.pkg	Now	Open a command prompt as administrator and use ModelDeploy.exe to load into MDS (see Chapter 4). This executable is located in the MDS Program Files location.
Product_data.pkg	Now	Same as deploying the Finance package.
1Manufacturer.csv	Procedure: How to Create a Three-Level Derived Hierarchy	Import this CSV file into the stg.Manufacturer_Leaf staging table. Then use Integration Management to import these members.
2Line.csv	Procedure: How to Create a Three-Level Derived Hierarchy	Import this CSV file into the stg.Line_Leaf staging table. Then use Integration Management to import these members.
3Product.csv	Procedure: How to Create a Three-Level Derived Hierarchy	Import this CSV file into the stg.Product_Leaf staging table. Then use Integration Management to import these members.
4account_consolidated.csv	Procedure: How to Create an Explicit Hierarchy	Import this CSV file into the stg.Account_Consolidated staging table. Then use Integration Management to import these members.
5account_relationship.csv	Procedure: How to Create an Explicit Hierarchy	Import this CSV file into the stg.Account_Relationship staging table. Then use Integration Management to import these members.
6Employee.csv	Procedure: How to Create a Recursive Hierarchy	Import this CSV file into the stg.Employee_Leaf staging table. Then use Integration Management to import these members.

The Product model represents everything you created in Chapter 4, but it includes several hundred product members with their attributes already populated. This gives you a fair amount of data to work with and will help the samples in this chapter make more sense. The Finance model is similar insofar as it is fully populated with data and contains the structure you'll need to work with the hierarchies we create in this chapter.

Ragged vs. Level-Based Hierarchies

When you're working with hierarchies, it is important to understand some common terms used across applications. Any hierarchy can be either ragged or level based. *Ragged* describes hierarchies that support leaf members at multiple levels. A hierarchy is *level based* if leaf members always exist at the same level, regardless of the number of levels within the hierarchy.

Some business applications do not support ragged hierarchies, so it is important to know the limitations of downstream systems before you create hierarchies in MDS.

Derived Hierarchies

In MDS, derived hierarchies provide the ability to highlight preexisting data relationships within entities and display them hierarchically. Derived hierarchies are based on the preexisting data relationships within MDS. In SQL Server 2012, derived hierarchies have been expanded to allow more complex relationships to be managed effectively. It is clear that as the MDS product advances, derived hierarchies will continue to evolve to handle all data relationships, and explicit hierarchies will lose importance. Derived Hierarchies will continue to be expanded past the definition that every level within the hierarchy corresponds to a specific domain-based attribute within the entity–attribute chain (see Figure 6-1).

Explicit Hierarchies

Explicit hierarchies are multilevel hierarchies with very few restrictions. Explicit hierarchies are managed as name–value pairs, with consolidated members containing other consolidated or leaf members. Explicit hierarchies are created for one entity at a time. Derived hierarchies, in contrast, require multiple entities.

Consolidated members are almost always theoretical items, whereas leaf members represent physical items. Like leaf members, consolidated members can have attributes assigned to them. In the MDS database, a separate table exists to manage consolidated members and their associated attributes. Consolidated members are available only if an entity is enabled for explicit hierarchies. Each consolidated member can be associated with only a single hierarchy no matter how many explicit hierarchies have been created for the entity.

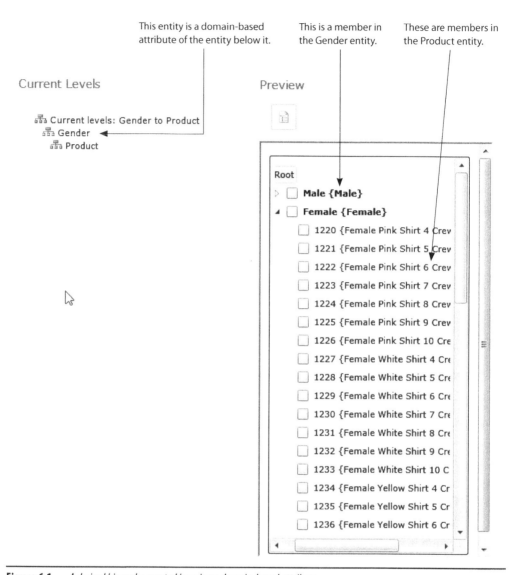

Figure 6-1 *A derived hierarchy, created by using a domain-based attribute*

Derived vs. Explicit: Which Hierarchy Is Best?

Derived hierarchies are determined by the structure of the model, and changes to the structure are rare. To illustrate the value of this rigor, consider the following scenario that organizations commonly encounter.

Our fictional company devises a regional hierarchy to manage sales. As with most of these hierarchies, this hierarchy begins as a level-based hierarchy, with each level within the hierarchy corresponding to a distinct type of attribute. To store the hierarchy, IT uses the parent-child format from its analysis system.

Over time, this hierarchy is modified by midlevel managers to help them manage their divisions better. Changes are not centrally managed, and new levels are added monthly. John is the manager of the Western region of the company. John has two managers who split duties managing the Southwest division for him: Bill and Margaret. Since Bill and Margaret are splitting the Southwest, John needs to split divisional data in the company's reports to measure this divisional structure. To do this, he creates two additional nodes within the hierarchy for the Southwest division, SWB (Southwest Bill) and SWM (Southwest Margaret).

Over time, Bill and Margaret move on to other jobs, either moving up in the company or on to other opportunities. Yet the Southwest division continues to be split into SWM and SWB. This is not an isolated occurrence, as many managers make isolated changes to the hierarchy structure. Some of these changes may not be warranted, and others may have a short shelf life. Soon the initial hierarchy is unrecognizable and difficult to manage. The ability to provide managers with rigid derived hierarchies, malleable explicit hierarchies, and focused collections allows BI professionals to provide the perfect tool for each scenario.

Hierarchy Type	Description
Derived	Uses multiple entities. Based on domain-based attribute relationships. Level based. Hierarchy structure is designed in System Administration. Hierarchy members are updated in Explorer.
Explicit	Uses one entity only. Consolidated members are used to group other consolidated and leaf members. Ragged. Entity must be enabled for explicit hierarchies in System Administration. Hierarchy structure is designed in Explorer. Hierarchy members are maintained and updated in Explorer.

Creating Derived Hierarchies

Derived hierarchies require that you have one or more entities, each of which has a domain-based attribute that you want to group members by. In MDS, you cannot group members by more than one domain-based attribute at a time. This doesn't mean that your derived hierarchy can't have multiple levels, just that each level must be based on a domain-based attribute relationship.

Procedure: How to Create a Derived Hierarchy

In this example, you'll create a derived hierarchy that has two levels. You will roll up products by gender. Product will be at the lowest level in the hierarchy, and Gender will be one level higher.

To create a two-level derived hierarchy, complete the following steps:

1. On the Master Data Manager home page, click System Administration.
2. On the menu bar, choose Manage | Derived Hierarchies.
3. From the Model list, select the model if it isn't selected already. In this case, select Product.
4. Click the "Add derived hierarchy" button.
5. In the "Derived hierarchy name" field, type a descriptive name for your hierarchy. In this case, we're going to name the hierarchy **Product by Gender**.
6. Click the "Save derived hierarchy" button. The page that is displayed has three panes.

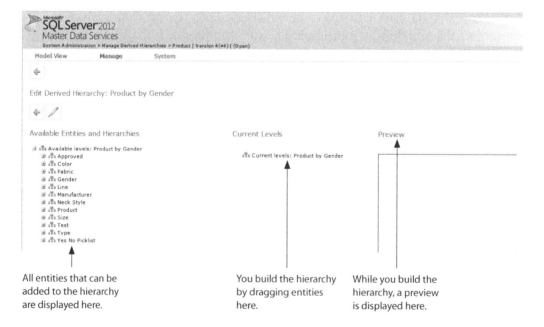

| All entities that can be added to the hierarchy are displayed here. | You build the hierarchy by dragging entities here. | While you build the hierarchy, a preview is displayed here. |

On the left are the entities that can be added to the current level in the hierarchy. In the center are all the entities in the derived hierarchy; right now there are none because you haven't added any yet. Each time you drag an entity from the left pane to the center pane, the left pane refreshes with the list of entities that remain available to add.

You should always drag the lowest-level entity first. In this case, we want a hierarchy with products at the lowest level.

7. In the left pane, click and drag Product to the "Current levels" label in the middle pane. Release the mouse button and the screen refreshes, with Product displayed in the Current Levels pane.

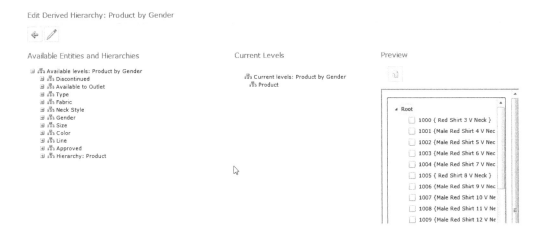

The Preview pane refreshes to show a list of products.

8. Now you can drag the entity you want to group by. In this case it's Gender, so click Gender in the left pane and drag it to the Current Levels pane.

The page refreshes and the Preview pane shows all products grouped by gender.

NOTE

The hierarchy is saved as you build it. No Save button is available on this page.

If you decide you do not want to group by gender, click Gender in the Current Levels pane and then click the Delete button that's displayed at the bottom of the pane. If you decide you want to rename your hierarchy, click the "Edit selected item" button on the top left of this page.

The real value of a derived hierarchy occurs when new products are created. You can configure a business rule so that each time a new product is added, if the Gender attribute is not populated, an e-mail notifies all interested parties. Business rules will be covered in more detail in Chapter 8.

Procedure: How to Create a Three-Level Derived Hierarchy

Now you are going to create a derived hierarchy with three levels. After completing this procedure, you should be able to build your own multilevel hierarchies.

In the Product model you have built so far, you don't have the ability to create a three-level derived hierarchy. This is because the Product entity is the only entity that has domain-based attributes. To create a hierarchy with multiple levels, each entity in the hierarchy must be used as a domain-based attribute of another entity.

For example, right now you can roll up products by Gender, Size, Type—any of Product's domain-based attributes. But you can't roll up products by size and *then* by gender. You have to choose one or the other.

In this example, you will create a derived hierarchy that rolls up products first by product line, then by manufacturer. This will require two relationships:

- ▶ The Product entity must have a Line domain-based attribute.

- ▶ The Line entity must have a Manufacturer domain-based attribute.

When you're done creating the structure, you will be able to roll up Product by Line by Manufacturer. The Product model doesn't have this structure right now, so let's create it.

Create a Manufacturer Entity

Create an entity called Manufacturer and populate it with six members. (Note: It does not need to have explicit hierarchies enabled.) You can get these members from chapter6.zip on www.mdsuser.com. Import 1Manufacturer.csv into stg.Manufacturer_Leaf and use Integration Management to start the staging process. Or, create these members manually in Explorer.

Name	Code
Pish Posh	Pish Posh
Hipsters	Hipsters
Rings with Rosie	Rings with Rosie
TumbleJacks	TumbleJacks
TumbleJills	TumbleJills
Candy Canes	Candy Canes

For the Product Entity, Create a Line Domain-Based Attribute

Now, for the Product entity, you're going to create a domain-based attribute that's based on the Line entity:

1. In Master Data Manager, click System Administration.
2. On the menu bar, choose Manage | Entities.
3. From the Model list, select Product.
4. Click the Product entity and then the "Edit selected entity" button.
5. In the Leaf attributes section, click the "Add leaf attribute" button.
6. Choose Domain-based, type **Line** for the name, and select Line for the source entity.
7. Click the Save attribute button.

For the Line Entity, Create a Manufacturer Domain-Based Attribute

Now in System Administration, perform the same steps as you just did, but edit the Line entity instead. Add a leaf attribute, domain based, called **Manufacturer**, based on the Manufacturer entity.

Create a Line Entity and Assign Manufacturer to Each Line

Create an entity called **Line** and populate it with 14 members. (Note: It does not need to have explicit hierarchies enabled.) You can get these members and their associated Manufacturer from chapter6.zip on www.mdsuser.com. Import 2Line.csv into stg.Line_Leaf and use the Integration Management functional area to start the staging process. Alternatively, create the members manually by referring to the following table. Remember, you create the entity in System Administration and add members in Explorer.

Line Name	Line Code
Boys Fall	Boys Fall
Boys Summer	Boys Summer
Boys Spring	Boys Spring
Boys Activewear	Boys Activewear
Girls Activewear	Girls Activewear
Springtime Collection	Springtime Collection
Summer Boys	Summer Boys
Summer Girls	Summer Girls
Fall Boys	Fall Boys
Fall Girls	Fall Girls
Spring Girls	Spring Girls
Boys Active	Boys Active
Summer Collection	Summer Collection
Accessories	Accessories

Assign a Line to Each Product, and a Manufacturer to Each Line

You can use 3Product.csv from www.mdsuser.com to assign a Line attribute to each product. Remember that attributes are now imported with the members in the stg.Product_Leaf staging table and you use Integration Management to start the staging import process. Or, you can assign attributes manually in Explorer.

If you decide to do this manually, here are a few things to consider:

▶ The Line attribute is not part of an attribute group yet, so it will not be displayed in Explorer. Add it to the Marketing attribute group if you want to edit it.

▶ You can edit members individually in the UI or use the MDS Add-in for Excel to perform bulk edits.

You are now ready to create your three-level derived hierarchy.

Create the Derived Hierarchy

Creating the hierarchy should be the easiest part of the process:

1. In System Administration, on the menu bar, choose Manage | Derived Hierarchies.
2. Ensure Product is selected in the Model list and click the "Add derived hierarchy" button.

3. For the name, type **Product by Line by Manufacturer**.

4. Click and drag Product to the Current Levels pane. A list of products is displayed in the Preview pane.

5. Click and drag Line to the Current Levels pane and drop it on Product.

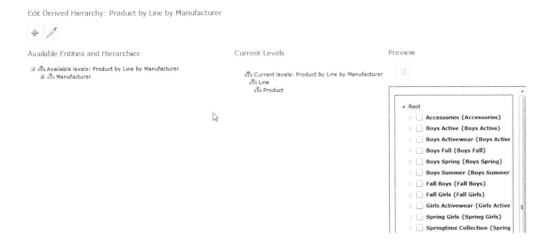

6. Manufacturer is the only entity available to add to the hierarchy. Click and drag it to Line in the Current Levels pane. When you release the mouse button, the full hierarchy is displayed in the Preview pane.

You can now expand and collapse nodes in the hierarchy to get an idea of the structure.

Hiding Levels

If you click any of the levels in the Current Levels pane, you can hide the level from users by selecting No from the Visible list. This can be useful when you have a multilevel hierarchy structure and users don't need to see many of the middle-tier levels when working with the hierarchy.

You can also change the name of a hierarchy level by updating the value in the Column name field.

System Settings for Hierarchies

There are two settings in Master Data Services Configuration Manager that apply to hierarchies and collections. Now that you know more about what hierarchies look like, you might want to change these.

▶ **Number of members in the hierarchy by default**   This setting determines how many members are displayed in a hierarchy node before a label named …more… is displayed. The default setting is to show 50 members.

▶ **Show names in hierarchy by default**   This setting determines whether the name and code of each member are displayed or only the code is displayed. The default setting is to show both name and code.

Creating Explicit Hierarchies

There are two types of explicit hierarchies in MDS: mandatory and non-mandatory. Before you create an explicit hierarchy, you should determine which type you'll need.

Non-mandatory Explicit Hierarchies

When you create a non-mandatory explicit hierarchy, all children are located in a node named Unused, as shown in Figure 6-2. Leaf members in the Unused node do not show up in subscription views based on the explicit hierarchy. This means that when you use subscription views as source data for subscribing systems, all the members in the Unused node are excluded. For more information on subscription views, see Chapter 12.

In non-mandatory explicit hierarchies, the consolidated members are at the root and the leaf members are in the Unused node by default.

Figure 6-2   *A non-mandatory explicit hierarchy, where all leaf members start in the Unused node*

Non-mandatory explicit hierarchies are easier to work with when you have large numbers of leaf members. To build an explicit hierarchy, you must create consolidated members, which are displayed at the root by default. You can then move leaf members from the Unused node to the consolidated members that live at the root.

Mandatory Explicit Hierarchies

When you create a mandatory explicit hierarchy, all leaf members are initially located at the root of the hierarchy. As you create consolidated members, they are also added to the root, but they are displayed at the end of the list. To find them, you must search or scroll to the end of the hierarchy. Figure 6-3 shows a mandatory explicit hierarchy where consolidated members exist but are not displayed because they follow hundreds of leaf members.

In mandatory explicit hierarchies, all members, including consolidated members, are initially at the root.

Figure 6-3 *A mandatory explicit hierarchy, where all leaf members start at the root*

Procedure: How to Create an Explicit Hierarchy

To create an explicit hierarchy, you are going to use the Finance model, which, if you deployed it from the web site, includes a full list of sample accounts. To create an explicit hierarchy, you complete the following tasks:

1. Enable the Account entity for hierarchies and collections.
2. Populate the consolidated members for the Account entity.
3. Create the explicit hierarchy.

Enable the Entity for Hierarchies and Collections

Before you can create explicit hierarchies, you must always enable the entity for explicit hierarchies by completing the following steps:

1. In Master Data Manager, click System Administration.
2. On the menu bar, choose Manage | Entities to open the Entity Maintenance page.
3. From the Model list, select Finance.
4. Click Account and then click the "Edit selected entity" button.
5. From the "Enable explicit hierarchies and collections" list, select Yes.
6. In the "Explicit hierarchy name" field, type **Chart of Accounts**.
7. You are going to create a non-mandatory explicit hierarchy where all leaf members start in an Unused node, so clear the "Mandatory hierarchy (all leaf members are included)" check box.

Edit Entity: Account

Entity Maintenance

Entity name:

Account

Name for staging tables (optional):

Account

If you do not complete this field, the entity name will be used.

☐ Create Code values automatically

Enable explicit hierarchies and collections:

Yes ▼

Explicit hierarchy name:

Chart of Accounts

☑ Mandatory hierarchy (all leaf members are included)

Leaf member attributes:

➕ ✏ ✕

Name
Code
Account Type

8. Click the Save entity button.

If you decide in the future that you want additional explicit hierarchies, edit the Account entity. You can now add explicit hierarchies, attributes for consolidated members, and attributes for collections from this page.

Edit Entity: Account

Entity Maintenance

Entity name:

Account

Name for staging tables (optional):

Account

If you do not complete this field, the entity name will be used.

☐ Create Code values automatically

Create explicit hierarchies.

Explicit hierarchies: ◄

Chart of Accounts

Leaf member attributes:

Name
Code
Account Type

Consolidated member attributes: ◄

Name
Code

Collection attributes:

Name
Code
Description
Owner_ID

Create attributes for collections.   Create attributes for consolidated members.

Populate the Consolidated Members for the Account Entity

You can use 4account.csv from www.mdsuser.com to populate the consolidated members (by using stg.Account_Consolidated), or you can complete the following steps in the Master Data Manager web UI:

1. On the MDS home page, select Finance and VERSION_1 from the Model and Version lists, respectively, and click Explorer.
2. On the menu bar, choose Hierarchies | Explicit: Chart of Accounts
3. Above the grid, select the Consolidated members option from the drop-down list, which is new in SQL Server 2012 MDS.

New selection drop-down list. You can select consolidated members for the currently selected parent or select all consolidated members in this hierarchy.

4. The drop-down list is blank. Click the Add button above the grid and add the following consolidated members (or create your own):

Name	Code
Cash	Cash
Cost of Goods Sold	Cost of Goods Sold
Fixed Expenses	Fixed Expenses
Long Term Assets	Long Term Assets
Long Term Liabilities	Long Term Liabilities

Name	Code
Marketing Expenses	Marketing Expenses
Revenue	Revenue
Salary Expense	Salary Expense
Shareholder's Equity	Shareholder's Equity
Short Term Assets	Short Term Assets
Short Term Liabilities	Short Term Liabilities
Variable Expenses	Variable Expenses
Revenue - Real	Revenue - Real
Revenue - Contra	Revenue - Contra
Revenue - INT	Revenue - INT
Expense	Expense
Assets	Assets
Liabilities	Liabilities
Profit and Loss Accounts	PL Accounts

Create the Explicit Hierarchy

The hierarchy structure was created when you enabled explicit hierarchies for the Account entity. Open Explorer to view it in more detail.

1. On the home page, select Finance and VERSION_1 from the lists and click Explorer.
2. On the menu bar, choose Hierarchies | Explicit:Chart of Accounts.

When you first open the hierarchy, only Root and Unused are displayed. If you expand Unused, all of the Account leaf members are displayed. If you click Unused, the grid on the right refreshes to display all of the Account leaf members.

You can now use 5account_relationship.csv with stg.Account_Relationship to move members in the hierarchy, or use the procedures in Chapter 7 that explain how to move hierarchy members. Figure 6-4 shows part of the hierarchy that will be created if you use the spreadsheet from www.mdsuser.com.

```
▲ Root
    ▲ ☐  Assets {Assets}
        ▲ ☐  Short Term Assets {Short Term Assets}
            ▲ ☐  Cash {Cash}
                    ☐  1200 {Bank Accounts}
                    ☐  1100 {Petty Cash}
                ☐  2000 {Accounts Receivable (Debtors)}
                ☐  2100 {Prepaid Expenses}
                ☐  3000 {Inventory (Stock on Hand)}
            ▲ ☐  Long Term Assets {Long Term Assets}
                ☐  4500 {Accumulated Depreciation and Other Assets}
                ☐  4100 {Buildings}
                ☐  4300 {Investments & Stocks}
                ☐  4000 {Land}
                ☐  4200 {Vehicles & Equipment}
    ▲ ☐  Liabilities {Liabilities}
        ▷ ☐  Long Term Liabilities {Long Term Liabilities}
        ▷ ☐  Short Term Liabilities {Short Term Liabilities}
    ▷ ☐  Shareholder's Equity {Shareholder's Equity}
```

Figure 6-4   *An explicit hierarchy that shows a chart of accounts*

Recursive Hierarchies

A recursive hierarchy is a special type of derived hierarchy. In a typical derived hierarchy, the members in an entity are grouped by a domain-based attribute. In a recursive hierarchy, the members are still grouped by a domain-based attribute, but this domain-based attribute is based on the entity itself. For example, each employee in an organization has a manager. And the manager can be any one of the employees. The following procedures show how to use this employee-manager relationship to create a recursive hierarchy that shows Main Street Clothing Company's organizational structure.

Procedure: How to Create a Recursive Hierarchy

To create a recursive hierarchy, you are going to use the Finance model, which, if you deployed it from the web site, includes a full list of sample employees. To create a recursive hierarchy, you are going to complete the following tasks:

1. Create a domain-based attribute for the Employee entity. This attribute will be named Manager and will be based on the Employee entity.

2. Assign a manager for each employee or load a list of Manager attributes.

3. Create the recursive hierarchy.

For the Employee Entity, Create a Manager Domain-Based Attribute

The Finance model has an entity called Employee. You need to create a domain-based attribute named Manager for the Employee entity:

1. In Master Data Manager, click System Administration.

2. On the menu bar, choose Manage | Entities.

3. From the Model list, select Finance.

4. Click the Employee entity and then the "Edit selected entity" button.

5. In the Leaf attributes section, click the "Add leaf attribute" button.

6. Choose Domain-based, type **Manager** for the name, and select Employee for the source entity.

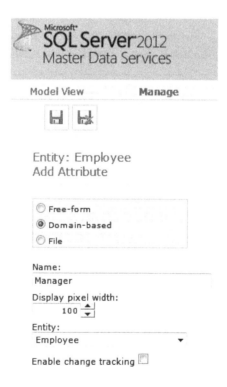

7. Click the Save attribute button.

Populate the Manager Attribute for Each Employee

You can use 6Employee.csv (from www.mdsuser.com) and stg.Employee_Leaf to populate each employee's Manager attribute.If you choose not to use the staging process, you can populate each employee's Manager attribute value manually by entering it in Explorer. Keep in mind that you should not populate a manager for the CEO. As long as you have one employee without a manager, you will have someone at the top of your organizational structure. If you used the Finance model provided, each employee's title is already populated in Explorer.

Create the Recursive Hierarchy

After every employee but the CEO has a manager (or even just a few employees have one, if you want to quickly see how this works), you can create the recursive hierarchy by completing the following steps:

1. In Master Data Manager, click System Administration.
2. On the menu bar, choose Manage | Derived Hierarchies.
3. From the Model list, select Finance.
4. Click the "Add derived hierarchy" button.
5. In the "Derived hierarchy name" field, type **Org Structure**.
6. Click the "Save derived hierarchy" button.
7. In the leftmost pane, click Employee and drag it to the Current Levels pane. When you release the mouse button, the Preview pane shows a list of employees.

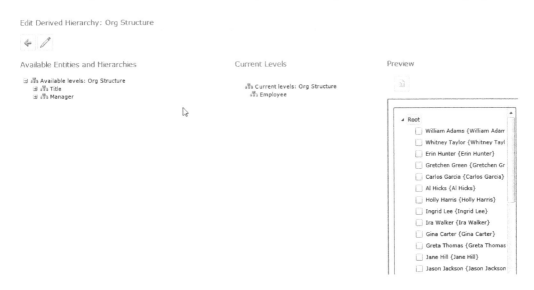

8. In the leftmost pane, click Manager and drag it to the Employee label in the Current Levels pane. When you release the mouse button, in the Preview pane, the CEO (or other employees without a manager assigned) is displayed at the highest level of the hierarchy, and the system recognizes that this hierarchy is recursive.

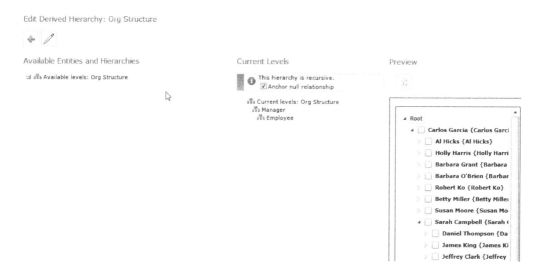

As you expand and collapse the hierarchy, you can see that each employee is listed only once. If you were to clear the "Anchor null relationship" check box, each employee would be listed individually, with any of his or her direct reports listed underneath. Anchor null relationship means that Carlos Garcia, who has a NULL value for his Manager attribute value, is considered the "anchor" for all other relationships. If there were multiple null relationships, these would all be displayed at the top of the hierarchy.

If you clear this check box, all employees are displayed with
the employees who report to them underneath.

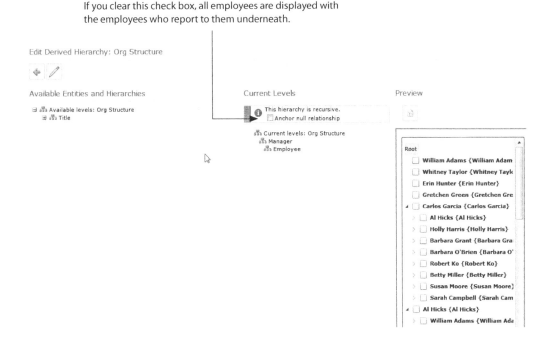

Derived Hierarchies with Explicit Caps

The last type of derived hierarchy within MDS is the derived hierarchy with explicit cap. This is a standard derived hierarchy that has an explicit hierarchy on top. The topmost entity of the derived hierarchy must be the bottom level of the explicit hierarchy.

Explicit cap hierarchies allow you to provide the best of both worlds. At the lower levels are derived levels that correspond to specific entities. At the top levels, you have the freedom to adapt the complex ragged structures allowed by explicit hierarchies. Explicit cap hierarchies allow you to define many lower bases to the same explicit hierarchy. These hierarchies are primarily used in finance domains such as Chart of Accounts and Organization Structure.

A global chart of accounts allows you to map disparate financial systems into your standard chart of accounts. This mapping allows corporate employees at large organizations to have common nomenclature when discussing financials with divisions across the globe. When working within multinational corporations, the complexities of accounting are further complicated by regional accounting laws that must be enforced. Corporate controllers cannot be expected to understand the intricacies of all these accounting practices worldwide, yet they must be able to hold individual business units accountable for their financial budgets and numbers. By creating a global chart of accounts and having each individual business unit map their country's unique chart of accounts into the global master account structure, individual countries can manage finances according to their regional requirements and corporate managers can still discuss their financials in a common manner.

As you can see in Figure 6-5, a company can use an explicit hierarchy for its global chart of accounts. This allows a ragged structure that's flexible and easy to update.

Each business unit can have its own standard chart of accounts that it maintains in a level-based derived hierarchy, as shown in Figure 6-6.

When you combine the derived hierarchy with the explicit hierarchy, the top levels are dictated by the explicit hierarchy and the bottom levels are populated by the derived hierarchy, as shown in Figure 6-7.

Figure 6-5   *An explicit hierarchy showing a multinational corporation's chart of accounts*

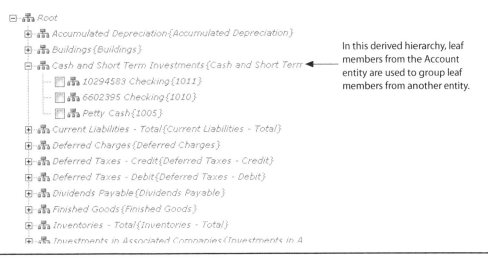

In this derived hierarchy, leaf members from the Account entity are used to group leaf members from another entity.

Figure 6-6   *A derived hierarchy for one division of the multinational corporation*

Figure 6-7   *A derived hierarchy with explicit cap*

Procedure: How to Create a Derived Hierarchy with Explicit Cap

To create a derived hierarchy with explicit cap, you must have your explicit hierarchy already created. You should also have an entity with domain-based attributes that you plan to use to create the derived hierarchy.

Then follow the directions for creating a derived hierarchy (in System Administration, choose Manage | Derived Hierarchies). Drag the entities for the derived hierarchy over to the Current Levels pane. When your derived hierarchy is complete and the top level of the hierarchy is the bottom level of the explicit hierarchy, drag the explicit hierarchy to the Current Levels pane and drop it above the other levels.

Current Levels

Current levels: Div1
Hierarchy: Chart of Accounts
Account
Div 1

The structure of the hierarchy looks similar to that of a derived hierarchy; the results, however, are ragged at the top and level-based at the bottom.

NOTE

You can use the same explicit hierarchy as a cap for multiple derived hierarchies.

Collections

While hierarchies provide structures to manage consolidations of entire entities, you or your users might need to group a small number of members for your personal use. Master Data Services provides the ability to manage these personal consolidations through collections. Collections are containers for members from a single entity. Collections can hold leaf members, consolidated members, or other collections within them. Collections do not follow the same rules as hierarchies. Collections can contain a member twice, as long as that member is contained in separate objects within the collection.

There are many different scenarios where collections can be a valuable tool. Collections can be used to manage personal charts of account consolidations or employee shifts. The Main Street Clothing Company uses collections a few times each year to manage sets of clothing (for example, a seasonal shirt, pants, belt, and hat). Collections allow Main Street to group members without using a hierarchy where all members need to be accounted for. It is simply a combination of random members that Main Street uses for analysis.

Weighting of Collection Members

In the SQL Server 2012 version of MDS, weighting has been surfaced to the UI. Weighting on collections enables users to apportion values across all members in a collection. This process can be invaluable in managing partnerships or managing sets where multiple quantity of the same member exists, such as a six-pack or a case. The default weighting for each member is 1.

NOTE

Once members are added to the collection, you can set the weight for each member in the collection. Make sure you save the weight for a member before setting the next weight. Every time you save a weight for a member, all other unsaved weight changes will be lost.

Procedure: How to Create a Collection

In this example, you'll create a collection that represents a set of clothes for boys. Main Street Clothing Company sells two sets every season: one set for boys and one set for girls.

Before you can create a collection, you must enable the entity to have collections. Some organizations never use collections, but Main Street uses a few. To create a collection, you complete the following tasks:

1. Enable the Product entity for hierarchies and collections.
2. Create a collection.
3. Add members to the collection.

Enable the Entity for Hierarchies and Collections

As with explicit hierarchies, you cannot create a collection for an entity until you enable the entity for hierarchies. To do so, complete the following steps:

1. On the Master Data Manager home page, click System Administration.
2. On the menu bar, choose Manage | Entities.

3. Select the Product model.

4. In the list, click Product and then the "Edit selected entity" button.

5. From the "Enable explicit hierarchies and collections" list, select Yes.

6. You are prompted to enter a name for an explicit hierarchy. Even though you don't need an explicit hierarchy, you must create one. Type **Product** for the name and leave the "Mandatory hierarchy (all leaf members are included)" check box selected.

7. Click the Save entity button.

Create a Collection

To create a collection, complete the following steps:

1. Go back to the Master Data Manager home page by clicking the SQL Server image in the top left.

2. Ensure the Product model and VERSION_1 are selected and click Explorer.

3. If you point to Hierarchies on the menu bar, you can see that a hierarchy is now displayed. This is the one you just created. Again, you don't need this hierarchy, but it is required to create collections.

   To create your collection, on the menu bar, choose Collections | Product. The Collections item on the menu bar shows the name of all entities that are enabled for explicit hierarchies and collections. None of the other entities in the model has enough members to merit collections, though, and right now you've enabled collections for Product only.

4. To create a collection, click the Add Collection button above the grid.

5. In the Details pane on the right side of the screen, enter the name and code, just as you would when you create a member. Enter **Boys Winter Set** for the name and **BWS** for the code.

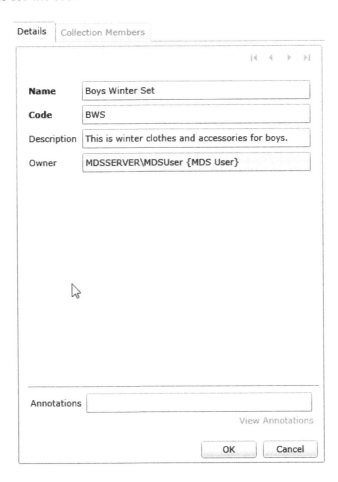

6. If you want to type a brief description for your collection, you can select the Description field in the Details pane and type a description. Click the OK button.
7. The collection is displayed in the grid. Every collection has a Name, Code, Description, and Owner attribute. By default, the user who created the collection is listed as the owner.
8. To save the changes to the collection, click the OK button at the bottom of the Details pane.

Add Members to the Collection

Now that the collection exists, you can add members to it:

1. In the list of collections, select the collection to modify, and in the right pane, click the Collection Members tab.

2. Click the Edit Members button.

The page that is displayed has two panes. In the left pane are the leaf members for the product entity. You can select to view other collections or any product hierarchy from the drop-down list at the top of this pane.

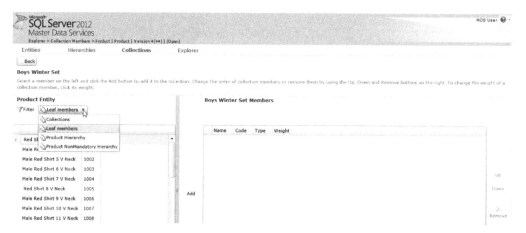

3. From the left pane, click the members you want to add and click the add button between the two panes. These represent a boy's shirt, pants, belt, and hat, which are sold together as a set.

If you have trouble finding any of these members, Microsoft has added full filter functionality to the collection member editor.

Members are added to the collection based on the structure of where they come from. If you add consolidated members from an explicit hierarchy, and that hierarchy already has a ragged structure, when you bring the members to the collection, that ragged structure is maintained. Any members in the collection can be reordered or removed using the buttons on the right side of the screen.

Creating Hierarchies by Using Web Services

While there are two types of hierarchies discussed within this chapter, we have only provided a derived hierarchy example here. Explicit hierarchies can be created as part of the MetadataCreate operation.

Creating a Derived Hierarchy with the MetadataCreate Operation

Derived hierarchies are created as a series of connected attribute levels. Each of these levels must be related properly within the system or the hierarchy will not be created. While creating derived hierarchies within the UI will limit the entities or hierarchies available at the current level, creating derived relationships within the web service does not provide this information until the error response is returned.

The following operation creates a three-level derived hierarchy that groups Product by Line by Manufacturer:

```
public OperationResult CreateDerivedHierarchy(string ModelName, string DHName)
        {
            // Create the request objects
            MetadataCreateRequest request = new MetadataCreateRequest();
            request.Metadata = new Metadata();
            request.Metadata.DerivedHierarchies =
            new Collection<DerivedHierarchy>();

            //Create the initial derived hierarchy container
            DerivedHierarchy dHier1 = new DerivedHierarchy();
            dHier1.Identifier = new ModelContextIdentifier
                    {
                        Name = DHName,
                        ModelId = new Identifier { Name = ModelName }
                    };
            dHier1.Levels = new Collection<DerivedHierarchyLevel>();

            //Level 1 - Product
            DerivedHierarchyLevel DHLevel1 = new DerivedHierarchyLevel();
            DHLevel1.LevelNumber = 1;

            //Levels will default to invisible without explicitly setting
            //visible to true
            DHLevel1.IsVisible = true;
            DHLevel1.Identifier = new DerivedHierarchyContextIdentifier
            { Name ="Product" };
            DHLevel1.DisplayName = "Product";
            DHLevel1.ForeignType = HierarchyItemType.Entity;
            DHLevel1.ForeignId = new Identifier { Name = "Product" };
            dHier1.Levels.Add(DHLevel1);

            //Level 2 - Line
            DerivedHierarchyLevel DHLevel2 = new DerivedHierarchyLevel();
            DHLevel2.LevelNumber = 2;
            DHLevel2.IsVisible = true;
            DHLevel2.Identifier = new DerivedHierarchyContextIdentifier
            {Name = "Line" };
            DHLevel2.DisplayName = "Line";
```

```
    //For standard MDS derived hierarchies all additional levels
    //will have the foreign type of DBA
    DHLevel2.ForeignType = HierarchyItemType.DBA;
    DHLevel2.ForeignId = new Identifier { Name = "Line" };

    //Provide the ForeignEntityID Connector for this DBA entity
    DHLevel2.ForeignEntityId = new Identifier { Name = "Product"};
    dHier1.Levels.Add(DHLevel2);

    //Level 3 - Manufacturer
    DerivedHierarchyLevel DHLevel3 = new DerivedHierarchyLevel();
    DHLevel3.LevelNumber = 3;
    DHLevel3.IsVisible = true;
    DHLevel3.Identifier = new DerivedHierarchyContextIdentifier
    { Name = "Manufacturer" };
    DHLevel3.DisplayName = "Manufacturer";
    DHLevel3.ForeignType = HierarchyItemType.DBA;
    DHLevel3.ForeignId = new Identifier { Name = "Manufacturer" };
    DHLevel3.ForeignEntityId = new Identifier { Name = "Line" };
    dHier1.Levels.Add(DHLevel3);
    request.Metadata.DerivedHierarchies.Add(dHier1);

    //Send the request object to the MetadataCreate Operation
    MetadataCreateResponse response =
    mds_Proxy.MetadataCreate(request);
    return response.OperationResult;
}
```

Summary

In this chapter we discussed a number of methods for managing relationships in Master Data Services. We showed derived hierarchies, which enforce a level-based structure based on domain-based attribute relationships. We showed explicit hierarchies, which allow ragged structures but still prevent duplicates or loss of data. We talked about the system settings that affect hierarchies and showed real-world examples meant to help you build your own hierarchies. Finally, we showed collections and special hierarchies that can be used to manage more complex relationships within MDS.

Chapter 7

Working with Master Data

In This Chapter

I n previous chapters we focused on creating the environment and architecture for managing master data in your organization. In this chapter, we begin to talk about how to work with your master data on a daily basis. We discuss the grid and filter that allow you to work with data within your master data entities.

The majority of MDS users will be entering the system to update data. Data stewardship activities in the Master Data Manager web application are managed within the Explorer functional area. A vast majority of users will only have access to the Explorer functional area. In this functional area, there are two major areas where users will work with data:

► In the Explorer grid, where they can update consolidated or leaf members within a grid control.

► On the hierarchy page, where they can navigate through a hierarchy to manage data changes in an integrated grid control.

Changes in SQL Server 2012

In the initial release of MDS, there were significant bugs that impaired users' ability to use MDS to manage their data. In SQL Server 2012, the MDS team addressed these issues by adding the SQL Server Master Data Services Add-in for Microsoft Excel (which we will discuss in detail in Chapter 10) and completely re-architecting the Explorer functional area. The new Explorer area streamlines the data editing process. All updates to an entity can be made on a single screen.

Viewing the Base Entity

The entity that is set as the first "base" entity you have security access to is displayed when you first open Explorer. Users will immediately be able to review and update data in the Explorer grid. MDS no longer shows the Explorer screen, which gave users an overview of all objects associated with the base entity, upon entering the Explorer functional area. For more information on base entities, see Chapter 4.

In this book, we show you how to take actions in Explorer by using the menu bar. The Explorer screen is still available from the menu bar if you want to use this screen to navigate the model's main entities.

Product Entity

Add Member   ✕ Delete Member   Apply Rules ▾   View Transactions   ▽ Filter   Settings

Logistics	Marketing	Pricing	Product Line	[All Attributes]			
	Name	Code	Safety Stock Level	Reorder Point	Discontinued	Available to Outlet	
▶ ?	Red Shirt 3 V Neck	1000	30	50	N {No}	N {No}	
?	Male Red Shirt 4 V Neck	1001	30	50	N {No}	N {No}	
?	Male Red Shirt 5 V Neck	1002	30	50	N {No}	N {No}	
?	Male Red Shirt 6 V Neck	1003	30	50	N {No}	N {No}	
?	Male Red Shirt 7 V Neck	1004	30	50	N {No}	N {No}	
?	Red Shirt 8 V Neck	1005	30	50	N {No}	N {No}	
?	Male Red Shirt 9 V Neck	1006	30	50	N {No}	N {No}	
?	Male Red Shirt 10 V Neck	1007	30	50	N {No}	N {No}	
?	Male Red Shirt 11 V Neck	1008	30	50	N {No}	N {No}	
?	Male Red Shirt 12 V Neck	1009	30	50	N {No}	N {No}	
?	Male Blue Shirt 3 V Neck	1010	30	50	N {No}	N {No}	
?	Male Blue Shirt 4 V Neck	1011	30	50	N {No}	N {No}	
?	Male Blue Shirt 5 V Neck	1012	30	50	N {No}	N {No}	
?	Male Blue Shirt 6 V Neck	1013	30	50	N {No}	N {No}	
?	Male Blue Shirt 7 V Neck	1014	30	50	N {No}	N {No}	
?	Male Blue Shirt 8 V Neck	1015	30	50	N {No}	N {No}	
?	Male Blue Shirt 9 V Neck	1016	30	50	N {No}	N {No}	

1-50 of 479 members |◀ ◀ Page 1   of 10 ▶ ▶|

Finding Data by Filtering

To begin working with data, you open an entity and, if necessary, filter the list of members to show those that you want to work with. Although the base entity is initially displayed, you can open a different entity by pointing to Entities on the menu bar and selecting the entity you wish to edit from the drop down list. All of the selected entity's members are displayed in a paged grid. The number of default members returned is 50, but because this release of MDS offers increased performance, you can increase this number significantly.

In SQL Server 2012, the filter is not always displayed. To display the filter grid, click the Filter button above the grid, as shown next. This button acts as a toggle to hide and display filter options. You can select any of the attributes of the entity from the Attribute drop-down list. Selecting the attribute limits the Operator list to those attributes available for that attribute type. The Criteria field will be an input box or a drop-down list based on prior column selections.

When you're ready to apply the filters to the members in the grid, click the Apply button.

NOTE

You can filter by multiple attributes by clicking the Add Criteria button and adding multiple rows of criteria before applying.

The filters that are currently applied will always be shown directly above the grid.

Product Entity

Add Member   Delete Member   Apply Rules ▼   View Transactions   Filter   Settings

Filter: [Cost] Is greater than 2.5

Logistics	Marketing	Pricing	Product Line	[All Attributes]			
Name		Code	Safety Stock Level	Reorder Point	Discontinued	Available to Outlet	
?	Female White Dress 4 Not Applicable	1275	20	30	N {No}	Y {Yes}	
?	Female White Dress 5 Not Applicable	1276	20	30	N {No}	Y {Yes}	
?	Female White Dress 6 Not Applicable	1277	20	30	N {No}	Y {Yes}	
?	Female White Dress 7 Not Applicable	1278	20	30	N {No}	Y {Yes}	
?	Female White Dress 8 Not Applicable	1279	20	30	N {No}	Y {Yes}	
?	Female White Dress 9 Not Applicable	1280	20	30	N {No}	Y {Yes}	

Filtering can either be accomplished through adding simple criteria where every record can be evaluated or through using matching algorithms. Standard filtering leverages a list of operators that encompass all of the available expressions that can be applied.

Operators

The operator determines how you're going to filter the list.

Operator	Use
Is equal to	Finds values that match your filter criteria exactly.
Is not equal to	Finds values other than those that match your filter criteria exactly.
Is like	Allows you to use the T-SQL LIKE expression.
Is not like	Allows you to use the T-SQL NOT LIKE expression
Is greater than	Finds values greater than your filter criteria. This works with both letters and numbers.
Is less than	Finds values less than your filter criteria. This works with both letters and numbers.
Is greater than or equal to	Finds values greater than or equal to your filter criteria. This works with both letters and numbers.
Is less than or equal to	Finds values less than or equal to your filter criteria. This works with both letters and numbers.
Matches	Finds values based on fuzzy match logic. In SQL Server 2012, all matching functionality has been exposed in the filter UI. For more information, see the "Using Matching" section that follows this table.

Operator	Use
Does not match	Finds values based on fuzzy match logic. In SQL Server 2012, all matching functionality has been exposed in the filter UI. For more information, see the "Using Matching" section that follows this table.
Contains pattern	Matches pattern expressed in Microsoft .NET Framework regular expressions format.
Does not contain pattern	Does not match pattern expressed in Microsoft .NET Framework regular expressions format.
Is NULL	Finds NULL values.
Is not NULL	Finds all values that are not NULL.

Using Matching

When you select the "Matches" or "Does not match" operator, a small icon for an extended drop down appears. This drop down lets you configure your matching parameters. The default values are Levenshtein for the algorithm and 0.30 for the minimum similarity, but you can change them by using the controls provided. The closer the number is to 1, the more specific the results. To return a wider variety of results, specify a number closer to 0 (for example, 0.20, 0.10, or 0).

The following table shows the four types of similarity matches you can do programmatically. In each of these cases, 1 indicates an exact match and 0 indicates no match.

ID	Match Type	Description
0	Levenshtein	The Levenshtein distance is based on the number of edits (for example, adds or deletions) that it takes for one string to match another. This is the default match for MDS.
1	Jaccard	The Jaccard index works best when trying to match multiple strings.
2	Jaro-Winkler	The Jaro-Winkler distance is best used for finding duplicate person names.
3	Longest Common Subsequence	A *subsequence* is when the letters in a pattern appear in order, although they can be separated. For example, MDS is a subsequence of MaDneSs. This works well where extra characters may have been inadvertently inserted into data.

The following example shows the Matches operator and the default matching settings.

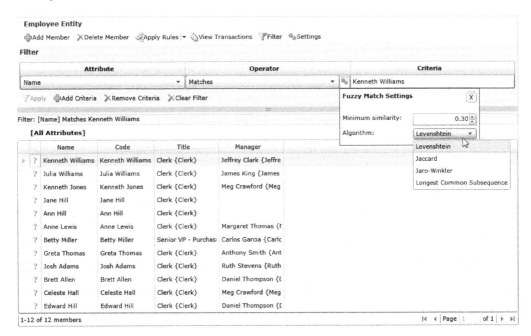

You can see by looking at the number of records displayed in the lower right that 12 results were found.

If you change the Algorithm setting to Jaccard with the default settings, you retrieve only four results, as shown next. Further research may be necessary to determine what algorithm works best for your dataset.

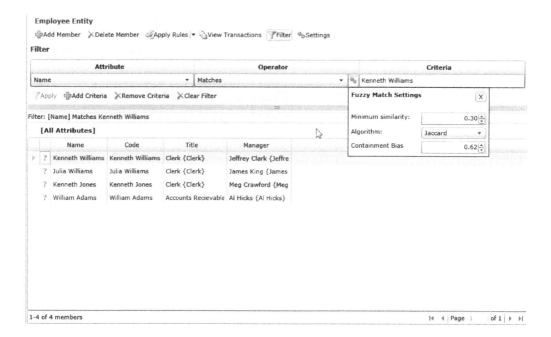

In general, 0.30 to 0.70 is a reasonable range to retrieve a list of results based on your dataset. If you want the default to be something other than 0.30, you can change it in the Master Data Services database, in the tblSystemSetting table. GridFilterDefaultFuzzySimilarityLevel determines the default Similarity Level.

NOTE

Some MDS system settings have not been exposed in Master Data Services Configuration Manager, and this is an example of one. All of the settings in Configuration Manager are in tblSystemSetting, and you can change the settings directly in the table or in Configuration Manager. Use care and ensure you're comfortable working in the database if you decide to make the change directly in the table.

Sorting and Pagination

When working in the grid, it is useful to understand sorting, pagination, and some other related settings.

Sorting

By default, the members in the grid are sorted in the order they were loaded in the entity. In the prior version, records were returned sorted by code, but this was modified in the SQL Server 2012 release to ensure initial results are returned as quickly as possible. You can click any column heading to sort the members by that column. Click once to sort in ascending order, and again to sort in descending order. You can sort by the values in only one column at a time. Each time you leave the page and return to the grid, the default sort is displayed. Clicking on a column to change the sort will reload sorted data from the server instead of sorting the records already displayed in the grid.

Pagination and Other Settings

In this release of MDS, a new Settings button has been added above the grid. To modify settings for the Explorer grid, click the Settings button in the menu bar to open the Settings dialog box, which has the following settings:

- ▶ **Records per page**   You can change the number of records to be displayed per page. The new Silverlight grid can handle any number of records per page. The number of records is then displayed, followed by arrows that you use to page through the members.

- ▶ **Display format**   This setting controls how all domain-based attributes are displayed within the Explorer grid and Details pane. Members in the grid can be sorted based on the order of the name and code values are displayed, whichever column you choose to display first will be used to sort the potential attribute values.

- ▶ **Freeze columns**   In the first release of MDS, the Name and Code columns were always pinned to the left side of the Explorer grid. In SQL Server 2012, each user can control how many columns are pinned to the left of the grid. The default value is no columns frozen to the left.

- ▶ **Show System Attributes**   In SQL Server 2012, MDS can now expose a number of system attributes in read-only format. Both the created and last updated timestamp will be displayed in the grid for all attribute groups. These columns can be used to sort or filter records in the grid. Since these system attributes are read-only for all users, they do not appear in the Details pane.

Type number of records per page.

Drop-down list to control how domain-based attributes are displayed.

New in 2012, users can now control how many columns are always displayed on left side of grid.

New in 2012, system attributes can now be added to the Explorer grid. These attributes are read-only.

New Explorer Format

In an effort to simplify the edit process of members in the web UI, users can now edit a selected member on a single screen. Any member selected automatically displays in the Details pane on the right side of the Explorer window.

Edit One Attribute for One Member

While you can no longer update values in the grid directly, any value for a member can be updated on the Explorer grid screen. Selecting any member in the grid displays that member in the new Details pane on the right side of the Explorer screen. Any value for the member can be updated in this pane. This Details pane displays all attributes available in the currently selected attribute group. To save your changes, click the OK button at the bottom of the pane. Edit controls are disabled for members or attributes a user does not have security permissions for. Security is discussed in more detail in Chapter 11.

Change the Number of Domain-Based Attributes Displayed in List

In MDS Configuration Manager, you can change whether a list of attribute values or a new filterable dialog box is displayed when you click the edit icon of a domain-based attribute value. The setting is called "Number of domain-based attributes in list," and you set the maximum number of members that will be displayed in the attribute selection drop downs. List maximums can be anything between 10 and 1000 members. Once the list exceeds this number a pencil will appear next to the attribute and a more complex selection dialog box is displayed instead of a list.

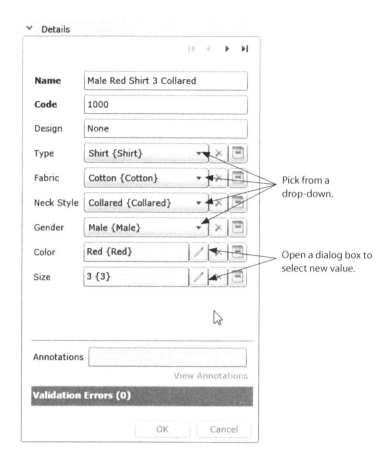

Edit One Attribute for Multiple Members

The ability to select multiple members and change the values in the grid has been removed in this release of MDS. The product team felt that this functionality was better handled in the freely available Add-in for Excel. The web UI has been designed to navigate easily between members in related entities. Batch data changes should now be completed in the MDS Add-in for Excel, as explained in Chapter 10.

Exporting Members

If you have used a previous release of Master Data Services, you may have used the Export to Excel function to send data to an Excel worksheet. This functionality has been replaced with the Add-in for Excel. For more information on editing members in Excel, please see Chapter 10.

Working with Data in Hierarchies

In the Explorer functional area of the user interface, you can view, edit, and move members in a hierarchy. As with most of the screens in the Explorer UI, the hierarchy screen has been redesigned in the latest release of MDS. The new hierarchy screen has been designed to allow users to navigate and manage data in a single screen. This screen is very similar to the original Explorer grid but with an additional hierarchy pane added to the left side of the Explorer window. Consolidated members can be managed only from the hierarchy screen.

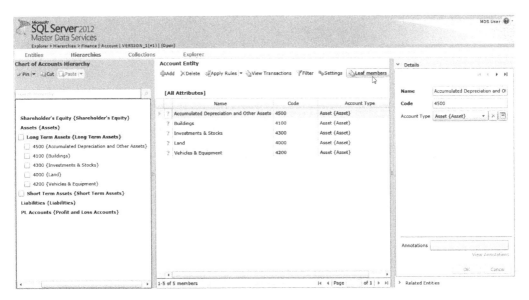

Hierarchy members can also be organized using the hierarchy Explorer screen. There are a few different methods for moving members; the one you choose will be based on how many members you want to move and the type of hierarchy you are working with. Moving members in a derived hierarchy is slightly different from moving members in an explicit hierarchy.

Moving Members by Dragging and Dropping

This procedure is basically the same for both hierarchy types. The only difference is the location you can drop members to. If you are working in an explicit hierarchy, you can

▶ Drop a leaf member beneath a consolidated member or at the root.

▶ Drop a consolidated member beneath a consolidated member or at the root.

If you are working in a derived hierarchy, you can

▶ Drop a leaf member anywhere beneath a domain-based attribute value that applies to the member. For example, you can drop products beneath colors, because Color is a domain-based attribute of Product.

To move a member in a hierarchy, click the label of the member you want to move. (The mouse pointer will become a pointer with a plus or not icon based on the suitability of the drop location.)

Holding the mouse button down, drag the member to the new location and, when the pointer cursor becomes a plus sign (+), release the button.

The member is moved to the new location.

Moving Members by Using the Clipboard

This procedure is also the same for both hierarchy types. To move members in any type of hierarchy by using the Clipboard, complete the following steps:

1. In the hierarchy tree, select the check box for each member you want to move (Stores 101 and 105 in this example).

2. Click the Cut button at the top of the hierarchy.

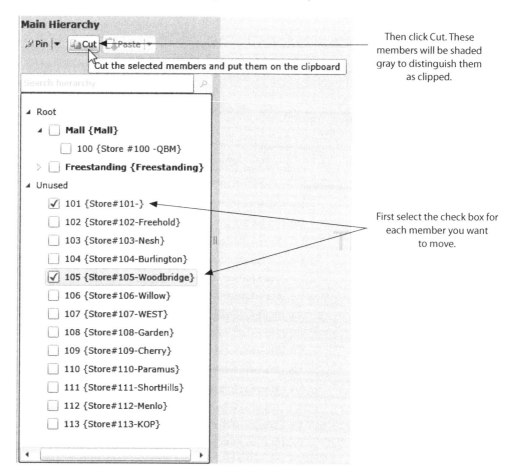

Then click Cut. These members will be shaded gray to distinguish them as clipped.

First select the check box for each member you want to move.

3. Click the label of the member you want to move the members to (Freestanding in this example).

4. You can click the Paste dropdown button or select Paste from the drop-down selections to add Stores 101 and 105 as children of Freestanding.

The members are displayed in the location you specified.

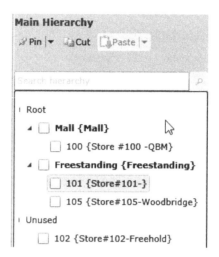

Moving Members in a Derived Hierarchy by Updating Attribute Values

In addition to using the Clipboard or dragging and dropping, you can move a member in a derived hierarchy by updating the member's attribute value that determines its location in the hierarchy.

When you first open a derived hierarchy, the top levels are displayed in the hierarchy structure on the left.

In the grid in the middle, the top-level members are displayed. To display the members contained in any level, click a node in the hierarchy tree. The grid in the middle refreshes. For example, when you click Female in the hierarchy tree on the left, all of the female products are listed in the grid in the middle.

Click the Female node. The grid displays all the members underneath this parent.

The top member is selected by default and is exposed for editing in the Details pane.

In the grid, find the attribute that determines where the member is displayed in the hierarchy. In this example, we'll click the Marketing tab and scroll to the right until the Gender column is visible. Find the member you want to move, select its row, and then, just as you would do to update any other attribute value, click the drop-down arrow in the Details pane, as shown next.

Now change the value. When you click the OK button at the bottom of the Details pane, the grid and hierarchy are updated, and the member is moved to the node based on your selection. In this case, the product moved from the Female to the Male hierarchy node.

Searching for Members in a Hierarchy

You can use the search field above the hierarchy to find members. Unfortunately, the search functionality has a number of limitations:

▶ The text you enter must be an exact match of either the full name or the code. To search for partial matches, use the % wildcard.

▶ The search does not find members in the Unused node of explicit hierarchies.

▶ If you have so many members in your hierarchy that the …more… label is displayed, members that aren't displayed are still included in the search results.

To use the search field, type your search text and click the magnifying glass icon. Your search is applied and the hierarchy is updated. To remove the search, click Close Search button at the top of the hierarchy control.

Setting the Number of Members That Are Displayed

In MDS Configuration Manager, you can change the number of members displayed in each hierarchy node before you have to click …more….

The setting is called "Number of members in the hierarchy by default," and you set the maximum number of members that will be displayed. If you have more than that number, the …more… label is displayed.

Managing Hierarchy Display Settings

The hierarchy grid uses the display format settings to control how members are displayed in the hierarchy. Members will be displayed either as Code, Code (Name), or Name (Code). You can change these settings using the settings button above the grid.

Transactions

Every change made to data in Master Data Services is logged as a transaction. All transactions log the type, prior value, new value, the user who made the change, and the time the change was made. In the Explorer functional area, all users have access to their own transactions and can reverse any transaction they have access to. In the Version Management functional area, administrators can review and reverse transactions for all users.

The following types of transactions are logged and displayed in the Master Data Manager web application:

Transaction Type	Description
Member created	A new leaf or consolidated member has been added to the entity.
Member status changed	The member has been deleted from the system. Because this is a soft delete, the member can be reactivated by reversing the transaction. The reversal will display as a status change as well.
Attribute value specified	An attribute value has changed.
Member moved to parent	A member was moved to a new location, based on its parent's location.
Member moved to sibling	A member was moved to a new location, based on its sibling's location.
Member annotated	An annotation was added to the member or an annotation was modified. You cannot reverse this type of transaction.

NOTE

By default, transactions are not logged for data that's staged into the system. Transaction logging for staging can be turned on in the MDS Configuration Manager system settings.

Reviewing Transactions

In SQL Server 2012, transactions can be reviewed only in the Version Management functional area. On the menu bar, choose Transactions. Transactions are displayed in a grid. You can filter the grid by using the Filter Criteria section. In this release of MDS, the transaction manager has not been upgraded to Silverlight.

Filter the list of transactions.

Reversing Transactions

To reverse a transaction, in the grid, click the row of the transaction you want to reverse, and then click the Revert Transaction button.

Transactions

↺   Revert Transaction

Entity	Reverse selected transaction	Explicit Hierarchy
Line	Accessories	
Line	Accessories	
Product	BWS	
Product	BWS	
Product	BWS	
Product	Consolidated Member	Product NonMandatory
Product	Consolidated Member	Product NonMandatory
Product	1010	
Product	1005	
Product	1000	

In the previous release of MDS, deactivated members were given a GUID identifier to allow those members' code to be reused. In this release, members that are deleted in the UI keep their code. This keeps the member's prior transactions tied to the member they were made on. If a member code that has been soft deleted in the system must be reinstated, you can reverse the transaction that shows the member changing from Active to De-Activated.

If you reverse this transaction, the member and its original code will be reactivated. The member will be part of all hierarchies and collections it was a member of before it was deleted; it will be as though the member was never deleted in the first place.

Annotations

You can annotate transactions to explain why you took an action. In the prior MDS release, these actions were hard to find after you entered them. In the current release, as you update individual member attributes in the Details pane, you can add an annotation to apply to the transaction. Transactions and their annotations for an individual member can be viewed in the same location.

Annotating Transactions on Update

To annotate updates to attributes, open Explorer to an entity. In the grid, select the member you want to update. Update the attributes you want to change. After you update the attributes, type the annotation in the Annotations box at the bottom of the Details pane.

After you have typed the annotation, click OK.

To review the transactions from that member, click the View Annotations link below the Annotations box and you will see all transactions for the member. The transactions you just made will show the annotation as well as a time and date stamp. Additional annotations can be added to any transaction from this screen as well.

All transactions for the specified member will display in this
sortable grid. The grid is sorted by the latest date first.

Additional annotations can be added
to any transaction for the member.

Annotations for the selected
transaction will display in this area.

Navigating Related Entities

One of the key value propositions of the MDS Explorer UI is the ability for users to navigate quickly through an entity and understand a total view of a member. In SQL Server 2012, a number of new features have been added to ensure that this full view can be easily navigated by data stewards.

Navigating Attributes

Many domain-based attribute values have their own information to provide to users. Consider the scenario of managing customers in MDS. One of the fields in the customer record is a domain-based attribute of ZIP code. This system uses a table for postal codes to store additional demographic information for each code. Within MDS, a data steward can drill down from a selected customer into the associated demographic information by clicking a single button in the Details pane.

Clicking this additional button attached to all domain-based attributes of a member opens a new tab in your browser with the new entity filtered by the selected value of the member you were reviewing.

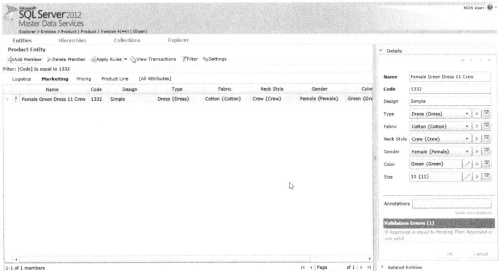

Navigating Many-to-Many Relationships

While many relationships within a model follow the one-to-one pattern or the one-to-many pattern, some data may require the support of many members from one entity relating to many different members in another entity. This relationship is termed many-to-many.

As an example, suppose Main Street Clothing Company has decided to start doing its own manufacturing of some simpler items for its stores. To manage this data in MDS, Main Street had to create two additional entities. The Raw Materials entity stores all of the items that Main Street combines to create its finished goods (the items it will sell to customers). The Raw Material to Product entity maps these combinations. As previously discussed, each manufactured product is made of multiple raw materials, and a raw material is reused in many different products.

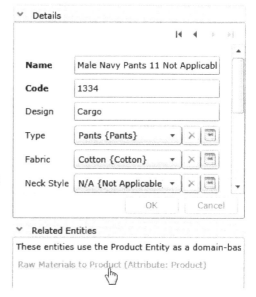

The bottom-right corner of the Explorer screen in MDS is the Related Entities section. If the current entity has any many-to-many relationships defined in the system, a link will be displayed.

Metadata

Prior users of MDS may notice that Metadata has been removed from the Explorer functional area. This feature has been marked for deprecation and can be accessed only from the metadata model or web services.

Using Web Services to Work with Members

The calls associated with getting and changing master data within Master Data Services are the most commonly used web service calls by organizations looking to customize their MDS implementation. These calls allow users to enter new member records, update existing member records, or bring back existing entity member record sets.

Retrieving Members

The EntityMembersGet operation will retrieve member records from any entity that exists within MDS. This operation supports paging to allow users to show a subset of the entity within a customized UI. This operation also supports subselecting a set of attributes to be retrieved. If you are going to use the paging criteria to retrieve a subset of records, be sure to lock down the sort criteria before you page; otherwise, inconsistent records will be returned.

There are three types of member return options. An EntityMembersGet operation can return either data, counts, or both data and counts. Some systems may require the total number of records to be returned before they return any member detail, and the "record counts only" return option provides this functionality. For organizations interested in using the paging mechanism to return records, the "data and counts" return option can provide a preview of the number of records in the full entity record set.

In the following code sample, we provide an example that returns a standard EntityMembersGet request with a standard page size of 50 members. This request has no complex filter.

```
public EntityMembers GetMembersFromEntity(string ModelName,
string VersionName, string EntityName, MemberType memType)
{
    //Create the Request and Criteria Objects
    EntityMembersGetRequest Request = new EntityMembersGetRequest();
    EntityMembersGetCriteria Criteria = new EntityMembersGetCriteria();
    //Build Context Criteria for Member Request
    Criteria.ModelId = new Identifier { Name = ModelName };
    Criteria.VersionId = new Identifier { Name = VersionName };
```

```
      Criteria.EntityId = new Identifier { Name = EntityName };
      Criteria.MemberType = memType;

      //Add Return Options to Criteria
      Criteria.MemberReturnOption = MemberReturnOption.DataAndCounts;
      Criteria.PageNumber = 1;
      Criteria.PageSize = 50;
      Criteria.SortColumnId = new Identifier { Name = "Name" };
      Criteria.SortDirection = SortDirection.Asc;

      //Assign Criteria to the Get Request
      Request.MembersGetCriteria = Criteria;
      EntityMembersGetResponse Response =
       mds_Proxy.EntityMembersGet(Request);
      return Response.EntityMembers;
}
```

When retrieving large amounts of data from the web service, it is quite likely that you will run into the following error:

System.ServiceModel.CommunicationException was unhandled
Message=The maximum message size quota for incoming messages (65536) has been exceeded. To increase the quota, use the MaxReceivedMessageSize property on the appropriate binding element.

This is to protect users from themselves. Each organization must determine how large the maximum message size can be, but this can be set in the client's app.config file by changing the following parameter:

```
maxReceivedMessageSize="2147483647"
```

Creating and Updating Members

Master Data Services provides the following three operations for managing entity members within the system. They support three different types of data loads.

▶ **EntityMembersCreate**   Only new member records with unique codes can be created with this operation. If a member code already exists, an error will be thrown in the returned error collection and the member will not be created or updated.

▶ **EntityMembersUpdate**   Only existing members can be updated using this operation. If a member code or ID is provided that does not exist within the system, an error will be returned in the error collection passed in the operation result and the member will not be created.

▶ **EntityMembersMerge**   Many users have been confused by this operation and believe it has something to do with record survivorship or match merge functionality. This operation does nothing to look for possible matches or provide any survivorship functionality; it only allows users to create and update records simultaneously within MDS.

The following example shows only the EntityMembersMerge operation because this operation provides the most flexibility for users programming against MDS. For simplicity in programming and to show all of the capabilities of setting attributes, we have hard-coded some defaults from the Main Street Clothing Company product example. If you are using this call within your organization, you need to replace the defaults with attribute parameters that are passed into the operation.

```
public OperationResult SimpleEntityMembersMerge(string ModelName,
string EntityName, string VersionName, MemberType memType,
string memCode, string memName)
{
    EntityMembersMergeRequest request = new EntityMembersMergeRequest();
    request.Members = new EntityMembers();

    //Set Context Identifiers for EntityMembers Object
    request.Members.ModelId = new Identifier { Name = ModelName };
    request.Members.EntityId = new Identifier { Name= EntityName };
    request.Members.VersionId = new Identifier { Name = VersionName };
    request.Members.MemberType = memType;

    //Create Members Collection object
    request.Members.Members = new Collection<Member>();

    //Add member to member collection
    Member newMem = new Member();
    newMem.MemberId = new MemberIdentifier { Code = memCode,
    Name = memName, MemberType = memType };
    newMem.Attributes = new Collection<MDS_WS.Attribute>();
```

```
        //Add default attribute values (In this example we are
        //adding attribute values for product)
        newMem.Attributes.Add(new MDS_WS.Attribute { Identifier =
         new Identifier { Name = "Safety Stock Level" },
         Type = AttributeValueType.Number, Value = 50 });
        newMem.Attributes.Add(new MDS_WS.Attribute { Identifier =
         new Identifier { Name = "Discontinued" },
         Type = AttributeValueType.Domain,
         Value = new MemberIdentifier { Code = "N" } });

        //Add the new member to the members collection
        request.Members.Members.Add(newMem);

        EntityMembersMergeResponse Response =
          mds_Proxy.EntityMembersMerge(request);
        return Response.OperationResult;
}
```

Summary

In this chapter we looked at how users will manage data within Master Data Services on a daily basis. We discussed using the new Explorer screen to update individual members. Every change made in MDS is logged as a separate transaction. All users can view all the transactions on a specific member. Transactions cannot be reversed in the explorer screen, this requires access to the Versioning functional area. Users can however provide additional annotations to any prior transaction on a member.

Chapter 8

Using Business Rules

In This Chapter

- ▶ Business Rules Overview
- ▶ Creating a Business Rule
- ▶ Editing a Business Rule and Configuring a Rule's Expression
- ▶ Publishing Business Rules
- ▶ Applying Business Rules

- ▶ Other Business Rule Tasks
- ▶ Configuring E-Mail Notifications
- ▶ Creating and Triggering Workflows
- ▶ Using Web Services to Manage Business Rules

anaging data is not just about storing the data in a customized entity; it is also about ensuring that the data is both accurate and complete. Master Data Services provides business rules to achieve this aim. In this chapter, we review business rules and discuss how to create both simple and complex rules. We discuss how to create simple workflows in MDS and how to integrate with external workflows such as those provided by SharePoint.

Business Rules Overview

In many organizations, no matter what the size, the business owners responsible for managing the master data don't have the technical knowledge needed to implement the related processes. If the business owners don't know how to use SQL Server or how to code business rule engines, they can be left at the mercy of their IT departments. At the same time, because the IT department has the technical know-how, the burden often falls on them to learn business domains they don't necessarily need to know. MDS strives to simplify the creation of business rules to empower business users to manage their own data quality.

In MDS, business rules are declarative expressions that govern the conduct of business processes. These expressions are compiled into stored procedures that perform the task of validating the data. The area of the Master Data Manager web application used for business rules was created to empower business users to write relatively complex business rules without knowledge of Transact-SQL.

Business Rule Structure

Business rules are IF…THEN statements. IF certain conditions evaluate to true, THEN perform specific actions. Conditions can be combined using either AND or OR logical operators. These operators can be used to create extremely complex business rules. You can use as many as seven levels for complex conditioning.

Although you have the ability to create complex rules, there are some real benefits in creating multiple, more granular rules. You should consider breaking any rule that uses the logical OR operator into multiple rules. This makes rules easier for other users to read and understand. Multiple rules also allow you to exclude specific rules and to provide more granular notifications. Rules built with the AND operator must be kept together to function as a unit.

Business rules are always applied to attribute values. For example, if an attribute value is blank, you might want to send an e-mail to notify someone or set the value to Pending.

Or you might want to update the value of one attribute based on the value of another attribute. Because business rules are applied to attribute values, you should determine which attributes you're going to work with before you start creating rules. Each time you create a rule, you must select the model, entity, and type of member that contains the attribute you're looking for.

Business Rule Workflow

Business rules must be created, configured, and published before you can validate data against them. The workflow includes the following steps:

1. Create a business rule, which adds it to the list of available rules.
2. Edit the rule and configure its expression.
3. Publish the rule so it's active and can be used to validate data.
4. Apply the rule to members.

When you apply the rule to members, the attribute values for each member are validated and they either pass or fail validation. If they pass, no action is required. If they fail, you must update the attribute values and re-validate your data successfully against the rules. If you don't take action, your hierarchies may not be complete or your data might otherwise be invalid.

Creating a Business Rule

The first step in the workflow is to create a business rule. Creating a rule means adding it to the list of existing rules. This procedure doesn't configure the rule to do anything, nor does it publish the rule. It's simply the first step necessary in using business rules to validate data.

1. On the Master Data Manager home page, click System Administration.
2. On the menu bar, choose Manage | Business Rules.
3. On the Business Rule Maintenance page, choose a model, entity, and member type to be validated. In this example, select Product, Product, and Leaf, respectively. For the attribute, leave it at the default, All. The Attribute list works as a filter for the list of business rules. In general, you should leave this as All to ensure that all rules are displayed.

4. Click the "Add business rule" button.

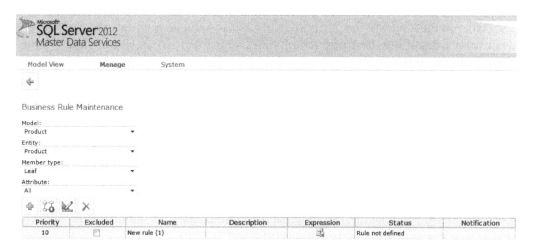

A new row with a light blue background is displayed in the table. The blue highlight indicates that the row is selected.

Priority	Excluded	Name	Description	Expression	Status	Notification
10	☐	New rule (1)			Rule not defined	

You are now ready to edit the business rule and configure its expression.

Editing a Business Rule and Configuring a Rule's Expression

A business rule frequently consists of a condition and an action. The condition is evaluated, and if it evaluates to true, one or more actions are initiated. If a rule contains no conditions, the rules engine will always initiate the actions.

Rules on the Edit Business Rule page are defined by using the following format:

IF *<condition>* THEN *<action>*

You can configure business rules to evaluate a wide variety of expressions. In this chapter we will strive to show you some common business rules and give you the knowledge needed to create some of your own.

Procedure: How to Require Attribute Values

In this first example, a business rule ensures that the Cost, Retail Price, and Gender attributes of all products are populated with values. The expression for this rule will be

IF *<nothing, because it applies to all cases>*

THEN require an attribute value for Cost, Retail Price, and Gender

To create the structure of a rule to perform this type of validation, complete the following steps:

1. Follow the procedure to create a new business rule. In this example, on the Business Rule Maintenance page, select the Product model, Product entity, Leaf member type, and All attributes and click the "Add business rule" button.
2. Click the row for the rule you want to edit and then click the "Edit selected business rule" button.

Business Rule Maintenance

Model:
Product

Entity:
Product

Member type:
Leaf

Attribute:
All

Priority	Excluded	Name
10	☐	New rule (1)

3. The Edit Business Rule page is displayed. In the Components pane on the top left, expand the Actions node.

4. Scroll down. Under the Validation node, click "is required" and drag it to the THEN pane in the middle right. Drop it on the Actions label.

Click "is required" and drag it to Actions.

5. The Edit pane in the lower right becomes the Edit Action pane. In the Attributes pane on the lower left, click Cost and drag it to the Edit Action pane. Drop it on the Select attribute label.

Edit Business Rule: New rule (1)

Click Cost and drag it to Select attribute.

6. At the bottom of the Edit Action pane, click the Save item button. This saves the action you just added.

7. Repeat steps 4, 5, and 6 for the Retail Price and Gender attributes. When you're done, you should have three actions displayed in the THEN pane.

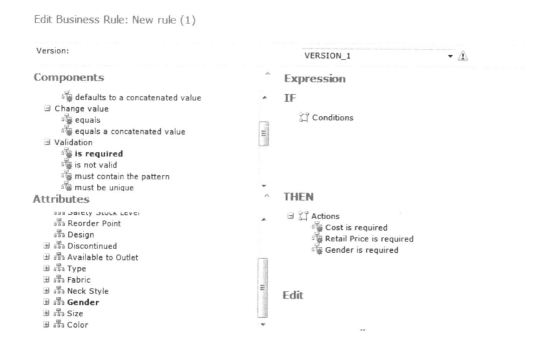

8. In the top-left corner, click the green arrow to return to the Business Rule Maintenance page. Because the rule was saved as you created it, there is no need to save again when you leave the page.

Now that the rule exists, you must publish it if you want to apply it to your data. The procedure for publishing the rule is covered in "Publishing Business Rules," later in the chapter. First, we'll look at more functionality on the Business Rule Edit screen.

Deleting a Condition or Action

While you're working on the Edit Business Rule page, you may realize you've selected the wrong action or condition. In either the IF pane or the THEN pane, you can right-click any condition or action and click Delete to remove it.

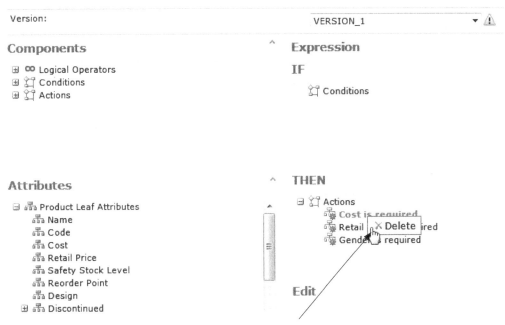

Right-click any action or condition to delete it.

More Expression Examples

Now we'll continue with other examples of business rules you might want to create. Later in this chapter, we'll explain how to validate your data against active business rules.

Procedure: How to Populate One Value Based on Another Value

You can populate an attribute value based on other attribute values. This is probably the most common use for business rules.

In this example, we want to indicate that discontinued products that have fewer than 50 items in stock are now available to outlet stores. The expression will be

IF Discontinued = Y AND Safety Stock Level < 50
THEN Available to Outlet = Y

To create this rule, complete the following steps:

1. Follow the procedure to create a new business rule. In this example, on the Business Rule Maintenance page, select the Product model, Product entity, Leaf member type, and All attributes and click the "Add business rule" button.

2. Click the row for the rule you want to edit and then click the "Edit selected business rule" button. The Edit Business Rule page is displayed.

3. In the Components pane, expand the Conditions node.

4. Under the Value comparison node, click "is equal to" and drag it to the IF pane on the top right. Drop it on the Conditions label.

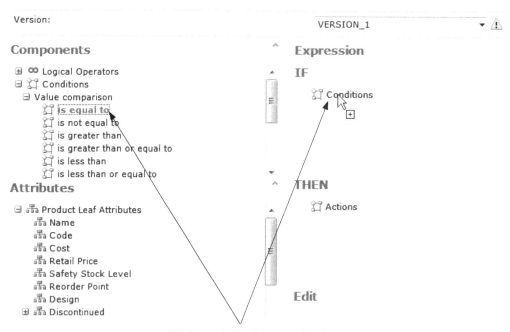

Click "is equal to" and drag it to Conditions.

5. The Edit pane in the lower right becomes the Edit Condition pane. In the Attributes pane, click Discontinued and drag it to the Edit Condition pane. Drop it on the Select attribute label.

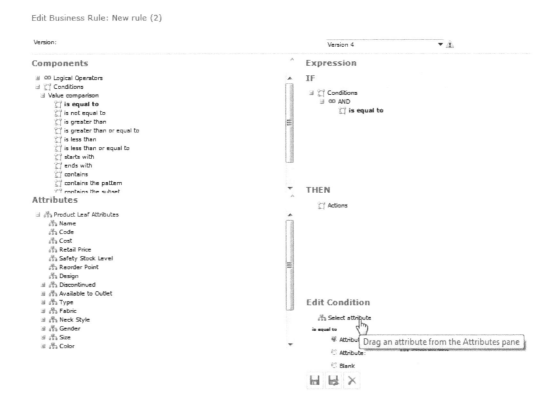

6. The Attribute value radio button is selected. Next to it, select Y from the list. This selector will vary depending on the type of attribute you select. Numeric attributes will allow a number to be entered in a numeric control, and free-form text fields would provide a text box.

7. At the bottom of the Edit Condition pane, click the Save item button. The IF pane is populated with the condition: Discontinued is equal to Y.

8. In the Components pane, click "is less than" and drag it to the IF pane. Drop it on the And label.

9. In the Attributes pane, click Safety Stock Level and drag it to the Edit Condition pane. Drop it on the Select attribute label.

10. The Attribute value radio button is selected. Next to it, type **50**.

11. At the bottom of the Edit Condition pane, click the Save item button. The IF pane is populated with the condition: Safety Stock Level is less than 50.

12. In the Components pane, expand the Actions node.

13. Scroll down. Under the Change value node, click "equals" and drag it to the THEN pane. Drop it on the Actions label.

14. In the Attributes pane, click Available to Outlet and drag it to the Edit Action pane. Drop it on the Select attribute label.

15. The Attribute value radio button is selected. Next to it, select Y from the list.

16. At the bottom of the Edit Action pane, click the Save item button.

The business rule is complete.

Procedure: How to Concatenate Values

In this example, a business rule creates a member name that is a concatenation of several attribute values. For example, one of our product names is

M Red Shirt 3 V Neck

This is a concatenation of these attribute values:

Gender Code + Color Name + Type Name + Size Name + Neck Style Name

Before we imported our products, we did this concatenation in Excel. Now we want to do this concatenation in MDS for all products, new and existing. We've also decided to use the full Gender name (Male) as part of the product name, rather than just the code (M). To create this rule, complete the following steps:

1. Follow the procedure to create a new business rule. In this example, on the Business Rule Maintenance page, select the Product model, Product entity, Leaf member type, and All attributes and click the "Add business rule" button.

2. Click the row for the rule you want to edit and then click the "Edit selected business rule" button. The Edit Business Rule page is displayed.

3. In the Components pane, expand the Actions node.

4. Under the Change value node, click "equals a concatenated value" and drag it to the THEN pane. Drop it on the Actions label.

5. In the Attributes pane, click Name and drag it to the Edit Action pane. Drop it on the Select attribute label. (You drag the attribute whose value you want to concatenate; in this case, you want to concatenate the Product's Name value.)

6. Also in the Attributes pane, expand the Gender node and click Name. Drag it to the Edit Action pane and drop it on the Value label.

7. Right-click DBA.Gender.Name and choose Add text.

8. Double-click the label that instructs you to do so (shown next). A text box is displayed. Type a single space to indicate the space between values. Then click away from the field to make the text box back into a label.

Edit Action

🔗 Name

equals a concatenated value
⊟ Value
    ⊞ 🔗 **DBA.Gender.Name**
    ⊞ ✎ Double-click to edit text

9. In the Attributes pane, expand the Color node and click Name. Drag it to the Edit Action pane and drop it on the Value label.

Edit Action

🔗 Name

equals a concatenated value
⊟ Value
    ⊞ 🔗 DBA.Gender.Name
    ⊞ ✎
    ⊞ 🔗 DBA.Color.Name

10. Right-click DBA.Color.Name and choose Add text.

11. Double-click the label that instructs you to do so. A text box is displayed. Type a single space to indicate the space between values.

12. Repeat steps 9–11 for Type Name, Size Name, and Neck Style Name.

13. At the bottom of the Edit Action pane, click the Save item button. The THEN pane is updated with all of the actions you specified.

THEN   ⌃
⊟ 🔧 Actions
  🔗 Name equals a concatenated value DBA.Gender.Name + + DBA.Color.Name + + DBA.Type.Name + + DBA.Size.Name + + DBA.Neck Style.Name +

The business rule is complete. Now, when you validate your data, all product names will be updated based on this rule.

TIP

You can use concatenation to create link attributes, like those used for Bing maps (for example, http://bing.com/maps/default.aspx?where1=15%20Cherry%20Street%20Springfield%20WA%2098000). In this case, you would concatenate the Name attribute values for the Location entity's Street Address, City, State, and Zip Code attributes to create a link.

Procedure: How to Populate an Attribute Value from a Different Entity

In Chapter 6, we created a three-level hierarchy:

Product > Line > Manufacturer

In this example, the Product entity had a Line attribute, and the Line entity had a Manufacturer attribute. But the Product entity did not have a Manufacturer attribute.

This structure is required in order to create the hierarchy. But you probably want to see the manufacturers at the same time as you look at the products; that is, you want the Product entity to have a Manufacturer attribute.

You can set up the structure required for the hierarchy but then use business rules to populate the Manufacturer value, in this case. The following procedure describes how to show the manufacturers along with the products without losing the hierarchy structure. This is going to require some work before we proceed to creating the business rule.

1. For the Product entity, create a free-form attribute called **Manufacturer**. See Chapter 4 for information on how to create free-form attributes.
2. For the Product entity, create an attribute group called **Product Line** and add the Manufacturer and Line attributes to it. You can also see Chapter 4 for how to create attribute groups.
3. Create a business rule to populate products with the appropriate manufacturer. This means that the rule will populate the Product entity's Manufacturer attribute with the Line entity's Manufacturer attribute values.
    a. Follow the procedure to create a new business rule. In this example, on the Business Rule Maintenance page, select the Product model, Product entity, Leaf member type, and All attributes and click the "Add business rule" button.
    b. Click the row for the rule you want to edit and then click the "Edit selected business rule" button. The Edit Business Rule page is displayed.

c.   In the Components pane, expand the Actions node.

d.   Under the Change value node, click "equals" and drag it to the THEN pane. Drop it on the Actions label.

e.   In the Attributes pane, click Manufacturer and drag it to the Edit Action pane. Drop it on the Select attribute label. (You drag the attribute whose value you want to populate; in this case, you want to populate the Manufacturer value.)

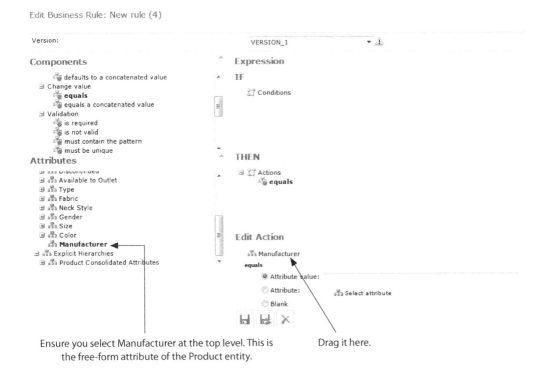

Ensure you select Manufacturer at the top level. This is the free-form attribute of the Product entity.

Drag it here.

f.   In the Attributes pane, expand the Line node and click Manufacturer. Drag it to the Edit Action pane and drop it on the Select attribute label.

Select the Manufacturer domain-
based attribute of the Line entity.

Drag it here.

    g. At the bottom of the Edit Action pane, click the Save item button.

The business rule is complete.

NOTE

In Chapter 11, we will discuss how to set security assignments, but it is usually best practice to limit access to columns populated by business rules.

Procedure: How to Use Incremental Values for Code Attribute in SQL Server 2012

You might want to populate an attribute value with an incremental number. For example, maybe you want each new product to have a unique number as its Code value and you want to increment each new product number by five. In the first release of MDS, you used business rules to do this. In SQL Server 2012, this special action of creating Code values was moved to the entity creation screen.

    In the current Finance model, the Code attribute values for the Location entity start with 100 and additional Code values are incremented by one. As new locations are added, the Code value should be one number higher than the highest number that's already used. The following example shows how to set up the entity to do this incremental numbering. This can be turned on and off for an entity at any time.

NOTE

Even though you're going to populate the Code attribute, you will notice in Explorer that the Code attribute is editable.

To update the entity to automated code creation, complete the following steps:

1. In this example, on the Entity Maintenance page, select the Finance model and the Location entity and click the "Edit selected entity" button.
2. On the Edit Entity page, select the "Create Code values automatically" check box.
3. Checking the box displays an integer input box labeled Start with. If you are not sure which number to start with, you can leave 1 for the Start with value. MDS will populate the Code value with the next possible value.

Edit Entity: Product

Entity Maintenance

Entity name:
Product

Name for staging tables (optional):
Product
If you do not complete this field, the entity name will be used.

☑ Create Code values automatically

Start with:
1

Create Code values automatically

Explicit hierarchies:

➕

Product

Leaf member attributes:

➕

Name
Code
Cost
Retail Price

Consolidated member attributes:

➕

Name
Code

Collection attributes:

➕

Name
Code
Description
Owner_ID

4. At the top of the Edit Entity page, click the Save entity button.

The automation is complete.

This new code-generation process was implemented to provide speed and functionality outside of the business rule process. In SQL Server 2012, members created through staging and the web service can now generate Code values. In order to maintain performance on large entities, the last integer used is stored in the tblCodeGenInfo table of the MDS database. This will track the largest Code value for each entity. If a user inadvertently updates a code member to a large integer, you may need to fix the problem in this table directly.

Creating Your Own Expressions

The following reference tables explain the possible conditions and actions you can use to create business rule expressions.

Conditions

If a condition evaluates to true, an action is taken. For example, if an attribute value is greater than another attribute value (the condition), then the attribute value is changed (the action).

Condition	Description	Column Types Supported
Is equal to	The value must match exactly.	Text, Number, DateTime, Link
Is not equal to	The value must not be equal.	Text, Number, DateTime, Link
Is greater than	The value must be greater.	Text, Number, DateTime
Is greater than or equal to	The value must be greater or equal to.	Text, Number, DateTime
Is less than	The value must be less than.	Text, Number, DateTime
Is less than or equal to	The value must be less than or equal to.	Text, Number, DateTime
Starts with	The value must start with the value.	Text, Link
Ends with	The value must end with the value.	Text, Link
Contains	The value must contain the value.	Text, Link
Contains pattern	The value must contain a .NET regular expressions pattern.	Text, Link
Contains subset	The value must contain a subset of a string value from either a provided value or another attribute. The match must occur at the provided starting position.	Text, Link
Has changed	The value has changed since the last time business rules were applied.	Change Tracking Group 1–31
Is between	The value is between two other attribute values.	Number, DateTime

Actions

There are four categories of actions you can take by using business rules.

Default Value Actions

Default value actions set a blank value to a value specified by the rule. If a value is already populated, default actions do not have an effect.

Action	Description	Supported Attribute Types
Defaults to	Change the value.	Text, Number, DateTime, Link
Defaults to generated value	Increment the value. You can specify a starting value and a number to increment by.	Number Note: This can no longer be applied to the Code column. See Chapter 4 to auto-increment the code of an entity.
Defaults to concatenated value	Concatenate the value. You can type text and use attributes to create the value.	Text, Number, DateTime, Link

Change Value Actions

Change value actions update values to new values each time business rules are applied.

Action	Description	Supported Attribute Types
Equals	Change the value.	Text, Number, DateTime, Link
Equals a concatenated value	Concatenate the value. You can type text and use attributes to create the value.	Text, Number, DateTime, Link

Validation Actions

Validation actions are used to send e-mail notifications when data fails business rule validation.

Action	Description	Supported Attribute Types
Is required	Require the value (it cannot be null or blank).	Text, Number, DateTime, Link
Is not valid	The value is not valid. Use this action in conjunction with conditions, otherwise all values will be considered not valid.	Text, Number, DateTime, Link
Must contain the pattern	Require the value to contain a .NET regular expressions pattern.	Text

Action	Description	Supported Attribute Types
Must be unique	Require each value for members in the entity to be distinct. You can also specify unique combinations. For example, you might want the Name and Color attributes to be unique when combined, but Color by itself does not need to be unique.	Text, Number, DateTime, Link
Must have one of the following values	Require the value to be one of those you specify.	Text, Number, DateTime, Link
Must be greater	Require the value to be greater than the specified value.	Number, DateTime
Must be equal to	Require the value to be equal to the specified value.	Number, DateTime
Must be greater than or equal to	Require the value to be greater than or equal to the specified value.	Number, DateTime
Must be between	Require the value to be between the specified values.	Number, DateTime
Must have a minimum length of	Require the value to be longer than the specified value.	Text, Link
Must have a maximum length of	Require the value to be shorter than the specified value.	Text, Link

External Actions

External actions start applications outside of Master Data Services.

Action	Description	Supported Attribute Types
Start Site Workflow	Initiates a SharePoint workflow or triggers an external process. For more information, see "Triggering an External Workflow" later in this chapter.	Not applicable. You can select any attribute; it's not used as part of the rule.

Publishing Business Rules

After you have created a business rule, you must publish it. Publishing a business rule means making it available to validate data against it. You can create as many rules as you want, but if you don't publish them, they aren't applied to your data when you start validation.

After you publish a business rule, you can always exclude it if you decide you don't want to apply it to data. Any time you edit a rule, you must republish it or it won't be applied to data as part of the validation process.

Procedure: How to Publish a Business Rule

To publish a business rule, click the "Publish business rules" button.

For all business rules that have expressions defined, the value in the Status column changes to Active. Data can now be validated against the rules. You can exclude rules you do not want to publish. For more information, see "Procedure: How to Exclude Business Rules," later in this chapter.

Business Rule Statuses

The following table describes all possible statuses for rules on the Business Rule Maintenance page.

Status	Description	Can Data Be Validated Against?
Rule not defined	A complete expression for the rule has not yet been defined.	No
Active	The rule expression is complete and the rule has been published to the validation process. Subsequent validations will include this rule.	Yes
Excluded	The rule is saved but has been excluded from the validation process.	No
Activation pending	The rule is complete, but until the rule is published, the rule will not be enforced when validation is triggered.	No
Changes pending	Changes have been made to the rule; the rule must still be published.	Previously published version of the business rule is still considered active.

Status	Description	Can Data Be Validated Against?
Exclusion pending	The business rule is still active and needs to be removed from the validation procedure by publishing business rules.	Yes
Deletion pending	The business rule is still active and needs to be removed from the validation procedure by publishing business rules.	Yes

Applying Business Rules

Business rules are not valuable until you validate data against them. Data can be validated against business rules in the following ways:

- ▶ You can validate the members for a single entity at a time in the Explorer functional area of the Master Data Manager web application. Business users with Explorer permissions can do this.

- ▶ You can validate the members for a single entity that you have loaded into an Excel worksheet using the Master Data Services Add-in for Excel. If the number of members loaded into the sheet exceeds the limit configured on the server, the whole entity will be validated asynchronously.

- ▶ You can validate all entities in a model in the Version Management functional area of the Master Data Manager user interface.

- ▶ You can use web services to validate all or some members as they are passed in.

- ▶ You can run a stored procedure to validate at different model object levels. While using the stored procedures directly is not encouraged, you may find it necessary to implement the data management process for your organization.

- ▶ Validations can be triggered through the staging stored procedures. For more information about this stored procedure, see Chapter 5.

Procedure: How to Apply Business Rules in Explorer

Users with permission can apply business rules in Explorer. To do so, complete the following steps:

1. On the Master Data Manager home page, select the Product model and VERSION 1 from the drop-down lists.
2. Click Explorer.

3. On the menu bar, choose Entities | Product (or whichever entity you want to validate against business rules).

4. Above the grid, click the Apply Rules button. In this release of MDS, the button can now be expanded to apply rules to the entire entity or to look at the current status of a validation request.

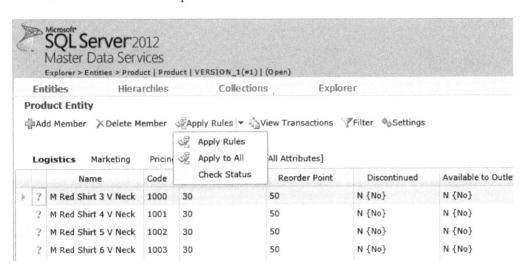

A green check mark indicates success. A red exclamation point indicates failure.

Product Entity

Add Member ✕Delete Member Apply Rules ▼ View Transactions ▼Filter Settings

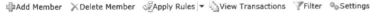

		Name	Code	Safety Stock Leve	Reorder Point	Discontinued	Available to Outle
▶	✓	Male Navy Pants 12 Not Applicable	1449	25	30	Y {Yes}	Y {Yes}
	✓	Male Navy Pants 13 Not Applicable	1450	25	30	Y {Yes}	Y {Yes}
	❗		1500				

Logistics   Marketing   Pricing   Product Line   [All Attributes]

NOTE

Only the members on the current page in the grid are validated. So if you are showing 50 members, only those 50 members are validated against business rules.

Resolving Validation Issues in Explorer

In Explorer, you can no longer view validation issues in a list format. The newly streamlined Explorer UI and the new Add-in for Excel should replace the need for the My Validation Issues page. In the Explorer UI and the Add-in for Excel, you can now filter on validation status, allowing you to display all members that failed validation, as shown here:

By selecting a specific member, you can see all validation issues related to the member at the bottom of the Details pane to the right. This provides a single screen to correct validation issues that have been found.

Procedure: How to Validate a Version

In the Version Management functional area of Master Data Manager, you can validate an entire model version at once. For more information and full instructions, see Chapter 9.

Other Business Rule Tasks

Now that you have created rules, you might want to update the name and description of each to ensure you can tell them apart. You can also change the order in which the rules run, or exclude rules from running.

Procedure: How to Change the Rule Name and Description

You should give each business rule a name and description so you can keep track of what the rule is used for. To change the name or description of a business rule, complete the following steps:

1. On the Business Rule Maintenance page, in the row for the rule you want to rename, double-click the Name column. The cell becomes editable.

Business Rule Maintenance

Model:
Product

Entity:
Product

Member type:
Leaf

Attribute:
All

Priority	Excluded	Name	Description	Expression	Status
10	☐	New rule (1)			Active
20	☐	New rule (2)			Active
30	☐	New rule (3)			Active
40	☐	New rule (4)			Rule not defined

2. Type the text you want and press ENTER. The Status column changes to Changes pending.
3. Click the "Publish business rules" button.
4. In the confirmation dialog box, click OK. The status changes to Active.

The text is updated. Follow this same procedure to update values in the Description column.

NOTE

The name cannot be more than 50 characters and the description cannot be more than 255 characters.

Procedure: How to Set the Rule's Priority Order

Business rules execute based on the priority order provided in the Priority column. If you change the priority, you're changing the order in which the rules are applied to data. It is possible to have two rules with the same priority. In this case, MDS will determine the order for these two rules, usually the order of creation.

To change a business rule's priority, complete the following steps:

1.   On the Business Rule Maintenance page, in the row for the rule with the priority you want to change, double-click the Priority column. The cell becomes editable.

Business Rule Maintenance

Model:
Product

Entity:
Product

Member type:
Leaf

Attribute:
All

Priority	Excluded	Name	Description	Expression	Status
10	☐	Require Cost, RP, Gender		🔲	Active
20	☐	Available to Outlet	Make products available	🔲	Active
30 ⇕	☐	Concatenate Product Nam		🔲	Active
40	☐	Populate Manufacturer	Use Line dba	🔲	Rule not defined

2.   Type the number you want and press ENTER. The status changes to Changes pending.
3.   Click the "Publish business rules" button.
4.   In the confirmation dialog box, click OK. The status changes to Active.

TIP

You can click the column heading to sort by the Priority column.

In Master Data Services Configuration Manager, you can change the number that the Priority column is increased by when you create a new rule. The default is 10 but you can change it by updating the "Number to increment new business rules by" setting.

Procedure: How to Exclude Business Rules

You can exclude rules if you're not ready to publish or if you're troubleshooting. If you wish to save the business logic but temporarily exclude the rule from validation processes, you can check the Excluded check box and republish the rules.

To exclude a business rule, complete the following steps:

1.   On the Business Rule Maintenance page, in the row for the rule you want to exclude, select the Excluded check box. The status changes to Exclusion pending.

Business Rule Maintenance

Model:
Product ▾

Entity:
Product ▾

Member type:
Leaf ▾

Attribute:
All ▾

➕ 🔧 ✎ ✕

Priority	Excluded	Name	Description	Expression	Status
10	☐	Require Cost, RP, Gender		🔳	Active
20	☑	Available to Outlet	Make products available	🔳	Exclusion pending
30	☐	Concatenate Product Nam		🔳	Active
40	☐	Populate Manufacturer	Use Line dba	🔳	Rule not defined

2. Click the "Publish business rules" button.

3. In the confirmation dialog box, click OK. The status changes to Excluded.

Configuring E-Mail Notifications

You can configure MDS to send e-mail notifications when an attribute value fails validation against certain types of business rules. First, you must configure e-mail settings to ensure e-mail can successfully be sent. Then, you must edit the business rule to indicate who to send e-mail notification to if validation fails. If you don't need e-mail notifications, you can skip this section.

A few notes before you get started:

▶ If you trigger e-mails to a group, only the users who have accessed the Master Data Manager web application will receive the mails.

▶ To confirm that the e-mail is sent to the user's correct address, on the Master Data Manager home page, click User and Group Permissions. To the left of the user, click the down arrow, then choose Edit | General. If the e-mail address listed is not correct, click the Edit button and update it.

Procedure: How to Configure E-Mail Notifications

Before you can configure e-mail notifications, you must know the IP address of the SMTP server that will send the mail. You should also have an e-mail address and display name for the account that will send the mail.

After you get this information, you can configure e-mail notifications by completing the following steps:

NOTE

This is a one-time process in Configuration Manager. If you need to update the Database Mail profile after you've set it up initially, you must do so in SQL Server Management Studio.

1. Open Master Data Services Configuration Manager.
2. In the left pane, click Database Configuration.
3. In the right pane, click the Select Database button.
4. In the Connect to Database dialog box, connect to a database and click OK. The System Settings section is populated with settings for the database.
5. In the System Settings area, scroll down to the end of the list.
6. Click the Create Profile button.
7. Populate the Create Database Mail Profile and Account dialog box as follows:

Setting	Description
Profile name	A unique name for the mail profile. It must be different from the name of any other mail profile in the database. An example might be MDS Email Profile.
Account name	A unique name for the account that's associated with the profile. Again, it must be different from the name of any other account in the database. This account name is used to create the account in SQL only; it is not a domain or local computer account. An example for this might be MDS Email Account.
E-mail address	The e-mail address that will be the From address on e-mails sent from MDS.
Display name	Optional. The display name for the e-mail address.
Reply e-mail address	Optional. If a user replies to an e-mail from MDS, this is the address replies are sent to.
SMTP server	The SMTP server used to send e-mail. You can use a server name or IP address.
Port number	The port number for the SMTP server, if needed.
This server requires a secure connection (SSL)	Select if you use SSL encryption.
SMTP Authentication	**Windows Authentication**—Database Mail uses the credentials of the service account used for SQL Server Database Engine. **Basic Authentication**—Specify a user account that can authenticate on the SMTP server. **Anonymous Authentication**—No credentials will be used when accessing the SMTP server.

8. Click OK to save and close. The Database Configuration page is updated with the name of your Database Mail profile.

Other E-Mail Settings in Configuration Manager

There are a few other settings you can use to customize e-mails for your implementation:

- ▶ **Master Data Manager URL for notifications** The URL that's used in the link in the e-mail notification. You should enter the name of your web site so users who get the e-mail can go directly to the validation issue by clicking the link.

- ▶ **Notification e-mail interval (in seconds)** How often e-mails are sent. The default is every two minutes.

- ▶ **Number of notifications in a single e-mail** How many validation issues are included in a single e-mail.

- ▶ **Default e-mail format** Format for e-mails.

- ▶ **Regular expression for e-mail address** Used to validate e-mail addresses in the User and Group Permissions functional area of Master Data Manager. It determines the format that is allowed when entering e-mail addresses. Unless you have reason to change it, leave the default setting.

- ▶ **Database Mail account** You cannot change this setting. It is intended to show you the name of the Database Mail account in SQL Server in case you need to update it.

Procedure: How to Configure a Business Rule to Send E-Mail

After you configure Database Mail in Configuration Manager, you must specify who will be notified when data fails validation against business rules.

NOTE

To send e-mail notifications, the rule must have a **validation** *action. (Validation actions are listed on the Edit Business Rule page, in the Components pane, under Actions | Validation.) Other types of actions do not send e-mail.*

To configure a business rule to send e-mail, complete the following steps:

1. On the Master Data Manager home page, click System Administration.
2. On the menu bar, choose Manage | Business Rules.
3. On the Business Rule Maintenance page, choose a model, entity, and member type for your rule to apply to. In this example, select Product, Product, and Leaf. For the attribute, leave All.

4. For the business rule for which you want to send e-mail, double-click the Notification column. Expand the Users node or Groups node to find the user or group you want to send mail to.

5. Click the name of the user or group. The Notification column is updated with the value you selected. The Status column is updated to Changes pending.

6. Click the "Publish business rules" button.
7. In the confirmation dialog box, click OK.

Creating and Triggering Workflows

By using business rules and customizing your data model, you can create relatively simple workflows for managing the flow of data through Master Data Services. If you want to manage a one- or two-step approval process or notify users when more data is required, you can simply use the MDS interfaces provided to create these workflows.

Some organizations will require more complex event processing. If your organization requires multitiered approvals or complex decision trees, then integration with a SharePoint workflow may better suit your needs. Integration with SharePoint workflow will require some coding expertise and basic understanding of Windows workflow foundation.

Creating a Workflow in MDS

A simple MDS workflow might include getting approval when an attribute changes. For example, if someone in Purchasing needs to change the cost of a product, the head of Purchasing might want to be notified so that he can approve or deny that change.

You can create workflows in MDS based on any condition, but we're going to show you an example where an attribute value changes. In this case, you don't know what the attribute has changed to; you just know that it has changed.

To address this scenario, MDS uses change tracking groups attached to attributes. Each entity within Master Data Services has up to 31 change tracking groups that can have any number of attributes allocated to them. An attribute can be managed by only one change tracking group at a time.

NOTE

Change tracking is still not triggered through the staging process in the SQL Server 2012 release of MDS. If you require automatic updates to trigger change tracking, you must use the web service to update data.

To create a workflow within MDS, complete the following steps:

1. Add attributes to a change tracking group (so you can be notified when their values change).
2. Add a domain-based attribute named Approved and populate it with Yes, No, and Pending members.
3. Create a business rule to send notification when the attribute values change.

These steps create a simple workflow. Any time the cost of a product changes, the Approved attribute changes to Pending and the purchasing manager is notified. It is the purchasing manager's job to open MDS, review the change, and approve or deny it.

Procedure: How to Add an Attribute to a Change Tracking Group

You must add an attribute to a change tracking group before you can use rules to determine if the attribute value has changed. To add an attribute to a tracking group, complete the following steps:

1. On the Master Data Manager home page, click System Administration.
2. On the menu bar, choose Manage | Entities.
3. Select a model from the Model list. In this case, select Product.
4. Click the row of the entity that contains the attribute and click the "Edit selected entity" button. In this example, edit Product.
5. In the Leaf attributes section (or whichever section contains your attribute), click the attribute and click the "Edit selected attribute" button. In this example, edit Cost.
6. At the bottom of the page, select the "Enable change tracking" check box.

7. The "Change tracking group" field is displayed. You can set this number to any number you want. It is just used as a grouping for multiple attributes. If you want to include more than one attribute in this group, use the same group number for each attribute.

Entity: Product
Edit Attribute: Cost

◉ Free-form
○ Domain-based
○ File

Name:
Cost
Display pixel width:
100
Data type:
Number
Decimals:
2
Input mask:
-####
Enable change tracking ☑
Change tracking group:
1

8. Click the Save attribute button.

Now if you want, you can edit other attributes and add them to the group with the same number. To do this, follow the same steps and make sure to use the same number for the group.

Viewing Change Tracking Group Reports

In the first release of Master Data Services, managing change tracking group attributes was a time-consuming task because there was no way of seeing all change tracking group associations in one place. While there is still no way in the UI to see a complete list of associations, two new views have been provided to give administrators insight into which attributes each change tracking group consists of and which business rule leverages that group:

▶ **viw_SUBSCRIPTION_CTG_ATTRIBUTES**   This view provides a list of all attributes associated with a change tracking group in any model in the database.

▶ **viw_SUBSCRIPTION_CTG_BUSINESS_RULES**   This view provides a list of all business rules that leverage a change tracking group as a condition. This view does not filter out rules that are excluded or not currently active.

Procedure: How to Create an Approved Attribute

Now you're going to create an attribute that will change whenever the Cost attribute changes. This attribute acts as a flag to make others aware that the cost has changed.

By now, you should be able to create an entity and attribute in System Administration and create members in Explorer. If you need a refresher, see the procedures in Chapter 4.

To continue with this example:

1. In System Administration, for the Product model, create an entity named **Approved**. This entity does not need to be enabled for hierarchies.
2. In System Administration, create a leaf-level domain-based attribute for the Product entity. This domain-based attribute should be based on the Approved entity and be named **Approved**.
3. Add the Approved attribute to the Pricing attribute group so you can view the attribute in Explorer.
4. In Explorer, open the Approved entity and create three members: **Yes**, **No**, and **Pending**. If you have created multiple versions of the Product model, make sure you do this in the latest version.

Procedure: How to Create a Business Rule That's Triggered by Change Tracking

Now you're going to create the business rule to update the Approved attribute when the Cost attribute changes. You can create your own rules for any attributes that change by using similar steps.

1. On the home page, click System Administration.
2. On the menu bar, click Manage | Business Rules.
3. Select a model, entity, member type, and attribute. In this case, choose Product, Product, Leaf, and All.

4. Click the "Add business rule" button.

5. The row is highlighted. Select the "Edit selected business rule" button. The Edit Business Rule page is displayed.

6. In the Components pane, expand the Conditions node.

7. Under the Value comparison node, click "has changed" and drag it to the IF pane. Drop it on the Conditions label.

8. In the Attributes pane, click Cost and drag it to the Edit Condition pane. Drop it on the Select attribute label. (Important: The attribute you drag here does not have any effect on MDS. It's required to create the rule, but the change tracking group and the attributes assigned to it, not the attribute, is what the rule is based on.)

Edit Business Rule: Change Tracking

9. Click Save item.

10. In the Components pane, expand the Actions node. In the Change value node, click "equals" and drag it to the THEN pane. Drop it on the Actions label.

11. In the Attributes pane, click Approved and drag it to the Edit Action pane. Drop it on the Select attribute label.

12. Select Pending from the list.

13. Click Save item.
14. Click the Back button in the top-left corner.
15. Click the "Publish business rules" button.

Now any time a cost changes and business rules are applied, the Approved column changes to Pending.

To have e-mail sent to the manager, create another business rule that sends e-mail when the Approved column is Pending. To do this, use the "is equal to" condition and the "is not valid" action.

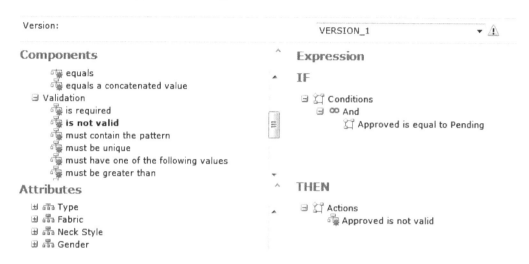

On the Business Rule Maintenance page, in the Notification column, choose the user or group you want to notify. This user or group is responsible for changing the Approved attribute from Pending to Yes or No.

Business Rule Maintenance

Model:
Product

Entity:
Product

Member type:
Leaf

Attribute:
All

Priority	Excluded	Name	Description	Expression	Status	Notification	Modified Date
10	☐	Require Cost, RP, Gender			Active	MDSSERVER\MDSUser	1/18/2012 4:14:54 PM
20	☐	Available to Outlet	Make products available		Active		1/18/2012 4:08:21 PM
30	☐	Concatenate Product Nam			Active		1/18/2012 4:00:29 PM
40	☐	Populate Manufacturer	Use Line dba		Rule not defined		1/18/2012 4:02:44 PM
50	☐	Change Tracking			Active		1/18/2012 4:34:01 PM
60	☐	Approved Pending Sends I			Active	MDSSERVER\MDSUser	1/18/2012 4:38:17 PM

NOTE

You might want to create an additional business rule that notifies a different user or group if the Approved attribute value changes to No.

Triggering an External Workflow

Workflows external to MDS are triggered by using the external action business rule. When business rules are applied, all entity members that evaluate to true by the conditions provided are sent to the external action Service Broker queue.

To enable external actions, the workflow integration service must be installed separately. Otherwise, the data gathered by external action business rules just sits in the external action Service Broker queue without triggering any effect. Because this workflow listener pulls requests from a Service Broker queue, only a single workflow listener should be connected to an MDS database at a time and no other custom components should be pointed at the external action Service Broker queue.

A diagram of the process is shown in Figure 8-1. The workflow integration service queries the database periodically, and if the external action business rule has put data in the Service Broker queue, the data is passed by the service to either a SharePoint workflow or some other, custom workflow.

NOTE

If the SharePoint or other workflow is not configured properly, the service still clears the data from the queue and attempts to pass it to the workflow. At this point, even if you re-validate against business rules, the change tracking has already occurred and the data won't be re-added to the queue.

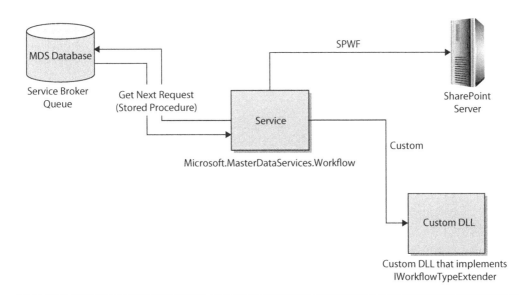

Figure 8-1   *The workflow integration service interacting with workflows external to MDS*

The following procedures should help you get started with installing the workflow integration service and configuring MDS to trigger external workflows. We've also written a white paper specific to triggering SharePoint workflows, which you can view here: http://msdn.microsoft.com/en-us/library/ff459274(SQL.100).aspx.

Installing the Workflow Integration Service

The first step in triggering an external workflow is to install the workflow integration service. It is called Microsoft.MasterDataServices.Workflow.exe and it can be found in Program Files\Microsoft SQL Server\110\Master Data Services\WebApplication\bin. You can use InstallUtil.exe to install the service. When you are ready to begin pulling data from the Service Broker queue, you will start this service.

As administrator, open a command prompt and enter the following command:

```
C:\Windows\Microsoft.NET\Framework64\v4.0.30319\InstallUtil.exe
"C:\Program Files\ Microsoft SQL Server\110\Master Data Services\
WebApplication\bin\ Microsoft.MasterDataServices.Workflow.exe"
```

Updating the Web Configuration File

Depending on the type of external action you want to trigger, different settings must be made in the Workflow configuration file. This file is called Microsoft .MasterDataServices.Workflow.exe.config and can also be found in Program Files\ Microsoft SQL Server\110\Master Data Services\WebApplication\bin.

If the only external actions that will be triggered are SharePoint workflows, then only the link to the MDS database is necessary. An example of the database connection string needed for a SharePoint workflow is shown here:

```xml
<?xml version="1.0" encoding="utf-8" ?>
<configuration>
    <configSections>
        <sectionGroup name="applicationSettings" type="System.Configuration.ApplicationSettingsGroup, System,
Version=2.0.0.0, Culture=neutral, PublicKeyToken=b77a5c561934e089" >
            <section name="Microsoft.MasterDataServices.Workflow.Properties.Settings"
type="System.Configuration.ClientSettingsSection, System, Version=2.0.0.0, Culture=neutral,
PublicKeyToken=b77a5c561934e089" requirePermission="false" />
        </sectionGroup>
    </configSections>
    <applicationSettings>
        <Microsoft.MasterDataServices.Workflow.Properties.Settings>
            <setting name="ConnectionString" serializeAs="String">
                <value>Server=MDSServer;Database=MDS;Integrated Security=SSPI</value>
            </setting>
        </Microsoft.MasterDataServices.Workflow.Properties.Settings>
    </applicationSettings>
</configuration>
```

Update this value with your server and database names.

In this example, MDSServer is the name of the server and MDS is the name of the database.

For each external DLL that you want to install into MDS, you must add a reference in the configuration file. Multiple external references must be added to the same XML node and separated by a semicolon. An example of two external actions is shown here:

```
<?xml version="1.0" encoding="utf-8" ?>
<configuration>
    <configSections>
        <sectionGroup name="applicationSettings" type="System.Configuration.ApplicationSettingsGroup, System,
Version=2.0.0.0, Culture=neutral, PublicKeyToken=b77a5c561934e089" >
            <section name="Microsoft.MasterDataServices.Workflow.Properties.Settings"
type="System.Configuration.ClientSettingsSection, System, Version=2.0.0.0, Culture=neutral,
PublicKeyToken=b77a5c561934e089" requirePermission="false" />
        </sectionGroup>
    </configSections>
    <applicationSettings>
        <Microsoft.MasterDataServices.Workflow.Properties.Settings>
            <setting name="ConnectionString" serializeAs="String">
                <value>Server=MDSServer;Database=MDS;Integrated Security=SSPI</value>
            </setting>
        </Microsoft.MasterDataServices.Workflow.Properties.Settings>
        <setting name="WorkflowTypeExtenders" serializeAs="String">
        <value>TAS=IntegrationWorkflow.AddressStandardizationIntegrationWorkflow, IntegrationWorkflow,
            Version=1.0.0.0, Culture=neutral, PublicKeyToken=null;
          TEST=Microsoft.MasterDataServices.Workflow.WorkflowTypeTest,Microsoft.MasterDataServices.Workflow,
            Version=10.0.0.0, Culture=neutral, PublicKeyToken=89845DCD8080CC91
        </value>
        </setting>
    </applicationSettings>
</configuration>
```

Multiple workflows are both between the <value> tag and are separated by a semicolon.

Creating a SharePoint Workflow in Visual Studio

If you decide you want to use SharePoint for your workflow, use these steps to get started designing a workflow in Visual Studio:

NOTE

You must use Microsoft Visual Studio 2010 and Microsoft SharePoint Foundation 2010 or Microsoft SharePoint Server 2010 to create your SharePoint workflow.

1. Open Visual Studio 2010.
2. Using the SharePoint 2010 templates, create a Sequential workflow project.
3. Drag the OnWorkflowActivated control from the toolbox to the designer area.
4. Right-click the control and choose Generate Handlers.

The data passed from the business rule process into the Service Broker queue will be contained in the string MDSData = workflowProperties.InitiationData. You must now parse the MDS data string into separate data fields and use the MDS web service to interact with Master Data Services.

Creating a Business Rule That Starts a Workflow

To trigger an external workflow from within MDS, you must create a business rule that starts the workflow. To do so, create a business rule as you normally would.

NOTE

Workflow business rules should always contain a condition. Otherwise, the workflow would be continually triggered.

The action needed to start the workflow is the last item in the node of the Components pane. Under the External action node, click "start workflow" and drag it to the THEN pane and drop it on the Actions label.

Edit Business Rule: New rule (1)

Version: VERSION_1 ▼ ⚠

Components   **Expression**

    must be equal to   IF
    must be greater than or equal to
    must be less than   Conditions
    must be less than or equal to   ∞ AND
    must be between   **has changed**
    must have a minimum length of
    must have a maximum length of
  External action
    start workflow

Attributes   **THEN**

  Type   Actions
  Fabric   **start workflow**
  Neck Style
  Gender
  Size
  Color
  Manufacturer
  Line   **Edit Action**
  Approved
  Explicit Hierarchies   Select attribute
    Product Consolidated Attributes   **start workflow**
                                                           Workflow type:
                                                           SPWF
                                                           ☐ Include member data in the message
                                                           Workflow site:

Then populate the Edit Action pane as follows:

Field	Description
Select attribute	Choose any attribute; this field is not used by MDS in this case.
Workflow type	SPWF for SharePoint; name of DLL file if other custom workflow.
Include member data in the message	Select this check box to include attribute names and values in the information passed to the workflow.
Workflow site	SharePoint only—the name of the site, e.g., http://site.
Workflow name	The name of the workflow. In Visual Studio Solution Explorer, this value is in the Display Name field.

Then save the item and publish the business rule as you normally would. When the business rule is applied, it populates the queue. When you start the service, the queue is cleared and an attempt is made to pass the data to the workflow.

In SQL Server 2012, Master Data Services has broken out the SharePoint Workflow DLL. You can get this open source DLL in the MDS workflow sample at http://sqlserversamples.codeplex.com. Search for Master Data Services to find the samples page.

Using Web Services to Manage Business Rules

Business rule management is the most complicated process exposed by the Master Data Services web service. Although we provide a couple of simple examples in this section, writing more complex business rules is significantly more intricate and would require a significant amount of this book to explain. Automation of MDS business rules should only be attempted by experienced developers working on a specific project that requires business rule automation.

Getting a List of Rules

There may be instances where you want to programmatically consume Master Data Services' business rules in external systems. While we have seen significant interest in this, we believe the internal ruleset limits the capability for MDS to be used as a rule warehouse. Users interested in this type of solution should look at using standard MDS entities to store this data. For users interested in getting rules out of MDS, the following procedure shows a common request to get a list of business rules:

```
public BusinessRules GetBusinessRules(string ModelName,
string EntityName, BREntityMemberType memType)
{
    //Instantiate the request and criteria
```

```
        BusinessRulesGetRequest Request = new
        BusinessRulesGetRequest();
        Request.GetCriteria = new BRGetCriteria();

        //Set Model, Entity, and MemberType
        //to filter the business rule request
        Request.GetCriteria.ModelId = new Identifier { Name =
ModelName };
        Request.GetCriteria.EntityId = new Identifier { Name =
EntityName };
        Request.GetCriteria.MemberType = memType;
        Request.ResultOptions = new BRResultOptions();
        Request.ResultOptions.BusinessRules = ResultType.Identifiers;
        BusinessRulesGetResponse Response =
          mds_Proxy.BusinessRulesGet(Request);
        //This operation will primarily return a BusinessRuleSet
        return Response.BusinessRuleSet;
    }
```

Creating a Business Rule Using Web Services

The most complex operations in MDS are the creation and update of business rules in MDS. If you are interested in automating the business rule process, we suggest that you keep the processes simple, by not adding complex conditions or actions in the beginning. At the conclusion of this procedure, a new business rule will be created but will not be published. You will need to publish the rule in another operation or through the UI.

```
        public OperationResult MandatoryAttributeBusinessRuleCreate
(string BRName, string ModelName, string EntityName, string
AttributeName,
 MemberType memType, int Priority)
        {
            BusinessRulesCreateResponse Response = new
              BusinessRulesCreateResponse();
            BusinessRulesCreateRequest Request = new
              BusinessRulesCreateRequest();
            Request.ReturnCreatedIdentifiers = true;
            Request.BusinessRuleSet = new BusinessRules();
```

```
Request.BusinessRuleSet.BusinessRulesMember =
  new Collection<BusinessRule>();

//Create New Business Rule Object and assign the properties
BusinessRule newBR = new BusinessRule();
newBR.Identifier = new  MemberTypeContextIdentifier
{ Name = BRName };
newBR.Identifier.ModelId = new Identifier
{ Name = ModelName };
newBR.Identifier.EntityId = new Identifier
{ Name = EntityName };

//Each Business Rule must be given a priority order to run
newBR.Priority = 1;
newBR.Identifier.MemberType = memType;

//Add Action to Action Collection
newBR.BRActions = new Collection<BRAction>();
BRAction BRActionItem = new BRAction();

//Add Attribute and Action type to the collection
BRActionItem.PrefixArgument = new BRAttributeArgument();
BRActionItem.PrefixArgument.PropertyName = BRPropertyName
.Anchor;
BRActionItem.PrefixArgument.AttributeId = new Identifier();
BRActionItem.PrefixArgument.AttributeId.Name = AttributeName;
BRActionItem.Operator = BRItemType.Mandatory;

//All Action and Condition Items must have a sequence
//greater than zero
BRActionItem.Sequence = 1;
newBR.BRActions.Add(BRActionItem);

//Add the New Business Rule to the Business RuleSet
Request.BusinessRuleSet.BusinessRulesMember.Add(newBR);
Response = mds_Proxy.BusinessRulesCreate(Request);

return Response.OperationResult;
}
```

Summary

In this chapter we discussed the ability to manage master data by using business rules. These business rules were created to allow business users to quickly and efficiently create logical constructs to manage the data within their entities. Business rules are entity and type centric. Using notifications and business rules, simple workflow processes can be managed using only Master Data Services functionality. If more complex workflows need to be managed, you can trigger SharePoint workflows using the external action business rule. The functionality of business rules did not significantly change in this latest release with the limited exception of new views for change tracking groups and a new process for auto-generating Code values. In the next chapter we will discuss using validation as part of a version management process.

Chapter 9

Creating Versions of Data

In This Chapter

After you understand the workflow for adding and modifying the data stored in MDS, you must learn how to manage that data over time. For each model within MDS, a historical record of the data can be stored. These data snapshots are called *versions*.

Each time you create a version of a model, the data for all the entities within the individual model are versioned at the same time. Only the data is stored; any changes to the structure of the model affect all versions and can create unintended consequences.

Version flags are another important component of versioning in MDS. By assigning flags to versions, integration with other systems can be better managed.

There were no significant changes to versioning in the SQL Server 2012 release. Administrators should continue to use versions to manage snapshots of their models over time.

Versions Overview

In order to manage data within your organization effectively, you may be required to create versions of the data stored within a model. In MDS, the data in all entities within each model is versioned simultaneously. A benefit of this design is that you can manage relationships between entities without worrying about time and version. A side effect of this design is that entities in different models cannot interact with one another.

There is often a natural cadence to many data domains. This cadence can help define which entities should be managed in the same model. For example, in many organizations, the accounting department manages structural changes on a monthly basis. As each month ends, everyone in the accounting department goes through standard routines to ensure that the month's books can be closed properly. Any entities related to this process—accounts, divisions, departments, or other internal business entities that are central to this process—should be managed together, versioned in concert with the month-end process.

In another example, an organization may release products on a quarterly basis. All entities central to the product development process would follow this quarterly versioning scheme. Other entities may not require a versioning scheme at all.

Versions provide a number of benefits to the data management process:

▶ **Complete model history for a specific point in time**   MDS model versions can be committed to ensure that an exact record of a model's data can be stored for later review. These committed versions can provide a portion of the required audit trail for new, more rigorous compliance requirements.

▶ **Limited access during sensitive processes**   When performing certain processes, like validating the entire model or loading large numbers of records, it may be prudent to restrict access to the model by locking it.

▶ **Additional version copies for analysis**   Additional versions can be created outside of the standard cadence for a variety of purposes. These versions can be used to examine new hierarchy configurations or potential acquisitions without affecting the current regular processes.

Changing the Structure of Your Model

MDS does not version metadata changes. Any changes to the model structure affect all open and committed versions. If an attribute or entity is deleted, for example, all history for that attribute or entity is lost from all versions *forever*. When you need to maintain historic data, we suggest that you use security permissions to hide attributes or entities instead of deleting them. You can also hide attributes by setting the display width to zero or by not adding them to attribute groups.

When you add an attribute or entity, the model structure is updated in all versions as well. You can add the corresponding data to any version of the model; if you add data to a later version, the structure exists in the earlier versions but the data does not.

Committing Versions

Sometimes users and downstream systems need to be certain that all data has been validated and reviewed. Because MDS allows incomplete members to be added to the system and encourages users to manage the data creation and correction workflow from within MDS entities, it may not be reliable for external production systems to use open or locked versions. Only committed versions ensure that all members in every entity within the model have passed all business rules successfully. Once a version is committed, no additional changes can be made to the data, and the status of the version cannot be changed.

Figure 9-1 shows the most common version control workflow.

A few notes about Figure 9-1:

▶ Each time the status changes, if notifications are configured, an e-mail is sent to model administrators. For more information about notifications, see Chapter 8.

▶ You can change a setting in MDS Configuration Manager so that you can copy versions with a status other than Committed, but Figure 9-1 shows the default behavior.

▶ You can validate a version at any time. Locking the version ensures that users don't make changes after you've validated, but it's only necessary if you plan to commit the version or otherwise prevent users from making changes.

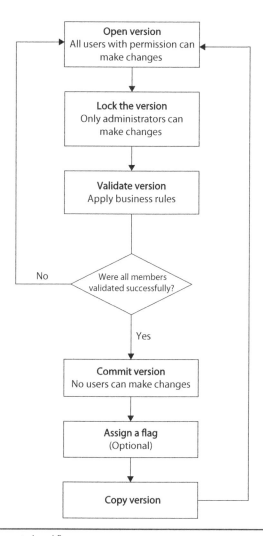

Figure 9-1 *Default version control workflow*

Versioning for Main Street Clothing Company

Main Street Clothing Company has separated its entities into two separate domains: Account and Product. A major reason for this split was the version cadence of each domain.

As a clothing company, Main Street finds that its product lines change significantly based on the season. This creates a natural cadence for managing major changes to its product list on a quarterly basis. The account model is managed on a monthly basis as part of the accounting team's regular month-end close process.

Updating Your Version Name and Description

Before you lock, validate, commit, or copy a version of your model, you might want to customize the version name and description. You can do this at any time. The new version name is displayed in many places in the Master Data Manager web UI, but you will probably notice it most on the home page, when you select the model name and version from the drop-down lists.

Procedure: How to Change the Version Name and Description

To change the version name and description, complete the following steps:

1. On the Master Data Manager home page, click Version Management.
2. From the Model list, select the model with the version name or description you want to change.
3. Double-click the cell that contains the version name or description that you want to change. The cell becomes editable.

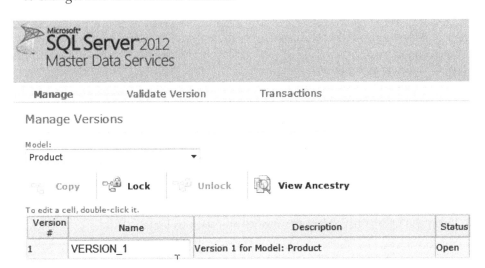

4. Change the text.
5. Press ENTER.
6. Double-click the cell with the version description.
7. Change the description to the text you want.
8. Press ENTER.

The name and description are updated.

NOTE

The date/time shown in the Last Changed Date column is based on the last change to any of the version information on this page, including the status.

Version Statuses

As you work with versions of your model and its data, you change the status of the version and then make copies of it. The version status indicates whether or not the model structure and its data can be updated. The following table lists the possible statuses for a version.

Status	Meaning
Open	Users can change the data; model administrators can change the data and the model structure. (See Chapter 11 for more information about model administrators.)
Locked	Users cannot change the data; model administrators can change the data and the model structure.
Committed	Neither users nor administrators can change the data or the structure. At this point, you can copy the model. *Note: MDS Configuration Manager has a setting you can use to change which statuses you can copy. By default, you can copy Committed only.*

Procedure: How to Lock a Version

When you're ready to save a version of the model, you first lock it. Then you can validate the model data and work on resolving issues that occur when data fails validation against business rules. To lock a version, complete the following steps:

1. On the Master Data Manager home page, click Version Management.
2. From the Model list, select the model you want to lock.
3. Select the row for the version you want to lock. The background is shaded when the row is selected.
4. Click the Lock button.

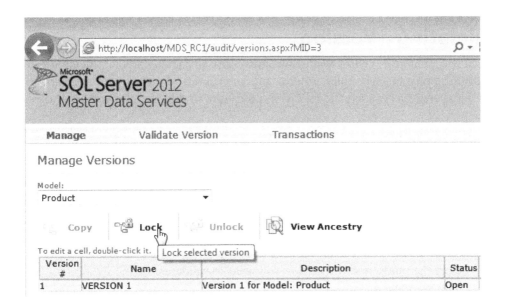

5. In the confirmation dialog box, click OK.

The Status column changes to Locked.

The status changes to Locked.

Now you can proceed with validating the version against business rules so that you can commit the version and create a copy of it.

Validating a Version

When you validate a version against business rules, all the members in the model are validated against business rules. You can validate subsets of members in the Explorer functional area, but you use the following procedure to validate all members at the same time.

Procedure: How to Validate a Version

To validate the members from a version against business rules, complete the following steps:

1. On the Master Data Manager home page, click Version Management.
2. On the menu bar, click Validate Version.
3. Select the model and the version you want to validate.
4. Click the Validate button.

5. In the confirmation dialog box, click OK.

(You may have to do steps 4 and 5 twice. You will know that the process is complete when the Commit button is enabled. Depending on the number of rules and members needing validation, this may take a long time to complete.)

Validation Statuses

The statuses that are displayed on this page help you determine which members have passed business rule validation and which members have failed. The following table lists the possible validation statuses.

Status	Meaning
Awaiting validation	These new members have never been validated.
Awaiting revalidation	These existing members are waiting to be validated.
Validation succeeded	These members passed business rule validation and there are no issues to fix.
Validation failed	These members failed validation and you must resolve the issues before you can commit.
Awaiting dependent member validation	These consolidated members are validated after leaf members are validated.

Procedure: How to Resolve Validation Issues

Before you can commit the version, you must resolve all business rule validation issues by completing the following steps:

NOTE

In Explorer, users can no longer view their own individual business rule issues, if they are recipients of notifications that are sent when validation fails users will need to use the links in the e-mail they receive or use the Excel Add-in described in Chapter 10. As an administrator, you can view all issues for all users by following this procedure.

1. On the Master Data Manager home page, click Version Management.
2. On the menu bar, choose Validate Version.
3. Select the model and the version.

A list of all validation issues is displayed at the bottom of the screen. Unlike the old Explorer functional area, this page shows validation issues for all users.

4. If you need to unlock the version at this point so that users can update data, return to the Manage Versions page, select the model, and click the Unlock button.

NOTE

To fix the validation issues, you can now filter based on the validation status in Explorer as well as the new Add-in for Excel, which is discussed in more detail in Chapter 10.

Reviewing and Reversing Transactions

To help resolve business rule validation issues, you can review transactions for all users in the Version Management functional area. To do so, choose Transactions. For the steps required to reverse a transaction or annotate it, see Chapter 7.

Committing and Copying a Version

You should not commit a version until you are sure it's complete and accurate. Once you commit a version, you cannot undo it without opening the database. You also have the ability to delete a version, but you must also go into the database to do so. In either case, you should only do these procedures if you're not concerned with compliance issues and if you're comfortable working in the database.

In general, you should commit the version and then copy it, giving users the ability to continue updating the data.

Procedure: How to Commit a Version

When all members pass validation against business rules and the version is locked, you can commit the version by completing the steps that follow.

CAUTION

After you commit a version, you cannot reopen it from the UI. Before committing, you should be sure that you no longer want to modify the data.

1. On the Master Data Manager home page, click Version Management.
2. On the menu bar, click Validate Version.

If all rows in the table show 0 except the Validation succeeded row, then the version can successfully be committed. Click Commit.

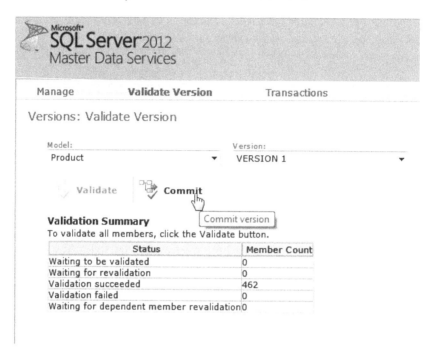

3. In the confirmation dialog box, click OK.

When the version is successfully committed, a success message is displayed. Back on the Manage Versions page, the Status column is updated to Committed.

Now you can copy the version.

Procedure: How to Reopen a Committed Version

You can change a committed version back to an open version by completing the steps that follow.

CAUTION

This action should be performed by a DBA only in those rare situations in which the version was committed by mistake. If production systems have pulled this data and used the results for reporting that is subject to compliance, the more appropriate action is to copy the version and commit a new, revised version for compliance purposes.

1. Open SQL Server Management Studio and connect to the MDS database.
2. In the table mdm.tblModel, in the ID column, note the ID of the model.
3. In the table mdm.tblModelVersion, in the Model_ID column, find the ID from step 2.
4. In the row for the version of the model you want to open, change the value in the Status column from 3 (Committed) to 1 (Open) or 2 (Locked).

The version is now displayed as open or locked in the web UI.

Procedure: How to Copy a Version

When you copy a version, a new version with the next version number is created. Newly created versions have the status of Open and are available for editing by users and administrators. To copy a version, complete the following steps:

NOTE

By default, you can copy Committed versions only.

1. On the Master Data Manager home page, click Version Management.
2. On the menu bar, choose Manage | Versions.
3. From the Model list, select a model.
4. Click the row for the version you want to copy.
5. Click the Copy button.
6. In the confirmation dialog box, click OK.

A new row is displayed in the grid. You can update the name and description to indicate which version you want this to be.

Copy Versions Other Than Committed

In MDS Configuration Manager, you can change whether you can copy models with any status or just those with a status of Committed. The setting is called "Copy only committed versions" and the default is Yes. Set it to No if you want to copy versions of any status.

If your organization acquires another organization, or you want to work with a hypothetical version of the data, it can be useful to copy other versions of the data. If you have more than one open version, however, remember that users can modify it. You can set security to prevent access, but it is not a straightforward process. See "Hierarchy Member Permissions" in Chapter 11 for more information.

Version Flags

While versions can provide a myriad of benefits, managing the integration with other systems can be a nightmare as the current version changes over time. MDS addresses this issue with the implementation of version flags. Each version in MDS can be flagged with a custom flag specific to the selected model. These flags allow data stewards to tag a version as current, prior, draft, or some unique identifier for downstream systems. Each version can have only one version flag associated with it at a time.

Because downstream systems rely on the validity of data being presented in a version, MDS can require versions to be committed before the flag can be applied. For most production systems, it is important to ensure that committed versions require flags. This check will be the only way to ensure that a specific version has passed validation before being used by downstream systems.

Procedure: How to Create a Version Flag and Assign It to a Version

To create a version flag and assign it to a version of a model, complete the following steps:

1. On the Master Data Manager home page, click Version Management.
2. On the menu bar, choose Manage | Flags.
3. From the Model list, select a model.
4. Click the Add button.

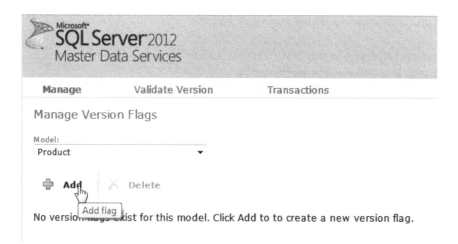

5. A grid is displayed. Type a name and description and select whether the flag is available to apply to Committed versions only (True) or to versions of any status (False).

6. Click the Save button.
7. On the menu bar, choose Manage | Versions.
8. In the row of the version you want to assign the flag to, double-click the Flag column. A list is displayed.
9. Select the flag from the list.

10. Press TAB or ENTER.

The Flag column is updated.

NOTE

You can assign a flag to one version at a time only.

Viewing a Version's Ancestry

You can copy any previous versions to create new versions; for example, you can copy versions in this order:

▶   Version 1 to Version 2

▶   Version 2 to Version 3

▶   Version 1 to Version 4

If you create several versions of a model and you are trying to determine where each version came from, you can view the Copied From column on the Manage Versions page.

This column shows where the version came from.

Version #	Name	Description	Status	Flag	Validation	Copied From
1	Version 1	Fall 2011 Products	Committed		Validated	
2	Version 2	Copy of Version 1	Committed		Validated	Version 1(#1)
3	Version 3	Copy of Version 2	Open		Validated	Version 2(#2)
4	Version 4	Copy of Version 1	Open		Validated	Version 1(#1)

This column shows only the most recent version in the version's history. You can view a more in-depth historical record by viewing the version ancestry. On the Manage Versions page, click the row you want to see a history for and click the View Ancestry button. In this example, we'll view Version 3, which was a copy of Version 2.

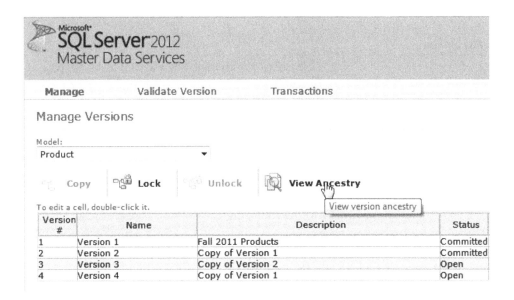

The Version Ancestry dialog box that is displayed shows the history. You read this dialog box from bottom to top; 0 is the first time the version was generated, 1 is the second time, 2 is the third, and so on. In this case, the first version of this model was Version 1, then it was copied to Version 2, and then to Version 3.

Procedure: How to Delete a Version

Normally, you should not need to delete a version of your model. This procedure is intended to help you with testing or if some circumstance forces you to take this action. Use with caution.

CAUTION

If you delete the only version for the model, the model becomes unusable.

To delete a model version, complete the following steps:

1. Open SQL Server Management Studio and connect to the MDS database.
2. In the view mdm.viw_SYSTEM_SCHEMA_VERSION, determine which version of the model you want to delete, and copy the value in the ID field.
3. Create a new query similar to the following:

```
EXEC [mdm].[udpVersionDelete] @Version_ID='value from step 2'
```

Replace *value from step 2* with the ID from step 2.

When you run the query, the version is deleted. The Master Data Manager web application reflects this change shortly after. To confirm the change, click the "Refresh cached information" link on the MDS home page. This link is located in the upper-right corner of the page.

Using Web Services to Work with Versions

Web services can be used to update information related to versions within a model. In this example, we use the MetadataUpdate method for the first time. Unlike the MetadataCreate operation, identifiers cannot be created using the Name field only to allow people to update the name.

Returning a List of Versions

When managing versions through the MDS web services, the GetVersion helper class will be very useful because version updates cannot be managed based on the name directly, as we have discussed. In this helper class, we will return the version based on the model and version name. Similar helper classes would be required to update any metadata objects.

```
public Collection<MDS_WS.Version>
GetVersion(string modelName, string verName)
    {
        MetadataGetRequest Request = new MetadataGetRequest();
```

```
//Create all required Search Criteria Objects
Request.SearchCriteria = new MetadataSearchCriteria();
Request.SearchCriteria.Models = new Collection<Identifier>();
Request.SearchCriteria.Versions = new Collection<Identifier>();
Request.SearchCriteria.SearchOption =
   SearchOption.UserDefinedObjectsOnly;

//Create model and version Search Identifiers
Identifier modelIdentifier = new Identifier { Name = modelName };
Identifier versionIdentifier = new Identifier { Name = verName };

//Add these identifiers to search criteria
Request.SearchCriteria.Models.Add(modelIdentifier);
Request.SearchCriteria.Versions.Add(versionIdentifier);

//Add Result Options to request
Request.ResultOptions = new MetadataResultOptions();
Request.ResultOptions.Versions = ResultType.Details;

MetadataGetResponse Response = mds_Proxy.MetadataGet(Request);

return Response.Metadata.Versions;
}
```

Changing the Version Status

Version information is updated using the MetadataUpdate operation. The following code leverages the helper class outlined in the prior section to retrieve the identifier for the version you want to update. In this code, we lock the version. A similar method could be used to commit the version, but committing a version requires that the version has been successfully validated first.

```
public OperationResult UpdateVersion(string modelName,
string verName, string verDesc, bool locked)
    {
        MetadataUpdateRequest Request = new MetadataUpdateRequest();

        Request.Metadata = new Metadata();
        Request.Metadata.Versions = new
          Collection<MDS_Wrapper.MDS_WS.Version>();
```

```
//Run the helper class to get reference to version
MDS_WS.Version targetversion = GetVersion(modelName, verName)[0];

//Create local instance of version and apply retrieved identifier
MDS_WS.Version ver1 = new MDS_Wrapper.MDS_WS.Version();
ver1.Identifier = targetversion.Identifier;

//Description or Name properties can be updated
ver1.Description = verDesc;

//VersionStatus can be freely changed between locked and open
//but committed requires a successfully validated model
if (locked == true)
{
    ver1.VersionStatus = VersionStatus.Locked;
}
else
{
    ver1.VersionStatus = VersionStatus.NotSpecified;
};

//Add the version to the versions collection
Request.Metadata.Versions.Add(ver1);

//Make the MDS Web Service request
MetadataUpdateResponse Response =
  mds_Proxy.MetadataUpdate(Request);

return Response.OperationResult;
}
```

Summary

Versioning provides you with the flexibility to manage models over time. Versions can be in one of three states: open, locked, or committed. Committed versions can provide users and downstream systems with the assurance that all members have been validated and the committed version will not be changed in the future. Integration with downstream systems can be facilitated by using version flags. Version flags can be used on draft versions, or you can require that versions be committed before they can be flagged. In the next chapter, we will discuss the new Excel Add-in for MDS.

Chapter 10

SQL Server 2012 MDS Add-in for Excel

In This Chapter

- ▶ Installing the Add-in
- ▶ Working with MDS Data in Excel
- ▶ Creating and Modifying Entities Rapidly
- ▶ Configuring Add-in for Excel Settings
- ▶ Leveraging Data Quality Matching in Excel

More master data is stored in Excel than in any other application on the planet. Some smaller companies use this solution because it is cost effective and easy to use. Others use it to store their "homeless" data in worksheets because it is the tool they are most comfortable with. Even the largest organizations with the greatest, most well-designed MDM systems that money can buy struggle with propagation of master data in Excel.

In SQL Server 2012, the Master Data Services team has attempted to harness the power of Excel to give users all the security, audit, and management features of MDS in a package that information workers are most comfortable with. In this chapter we will explore the current features available in Excel and how you can leverage those features for all types of data management.

Using the combination of Excel and MDS as a data management tool can provide organizations with significant advantages. Excel is a natural platform for managing data from a variety of sources. Its built-in data functionality can be used to parse and cleanse data before loading the data into MDS. The developer interfaces, whether code, macros, or formulas, can provide additional custom automation in a rapid fashion, without voiding any support in the MDS solution.

Many of Excel's limitations are also addressed by using it in conjunction with Master Data Services. Data sharing, security, and transaction logging have always posed problems that spreadsheet designers have struggled to solve. One of the biggest concerns with storing data in Excel is the lack of security and central management. Using the MDS Add-in for Excel can alleviate many of these concerns.

Installing the Add-in

The MDS Add-in for Excel is a separate, free installation available on the Microsoft website. The easiest way to download the latest edition of the Add-in is to use the link on the web UI's home navigation page. This link will be updated to the latest Excel Add-in download as new versions become available. It is important to understand that the Excel Add-in is not tied to the SQL Server update schedule. New versions of the Excel Add-in can and will include additional functionality that can be used with a SQL Server 2012 Master Data Services implementation.

Procedure: How to Install the Add-in for Excel

To install the Master Data Services Add-in for Microsoft Excel, complete the following steps:

1. Click the Install Master Data Services Add-in for Microsoft Excel link on the navigation page, shown next, and download the proper edition for your computer.

The edition required is based on whether you have the 32-bit or 64-bit version of Microsoft Office installed on your computer.

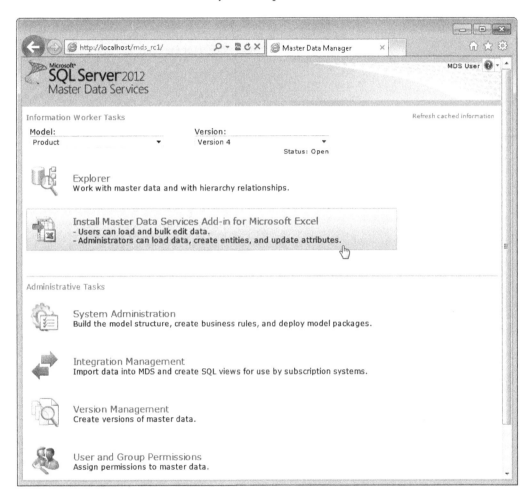

2. Run the setup until you see the following initial installation screen. Click Next.

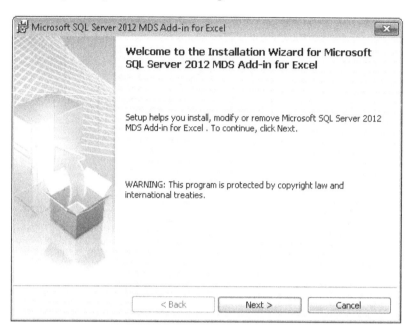

3. On the License Agreement page, you must accept the license agreement to enable the Next button and continue the installation. Once you accept the terms, click Next.

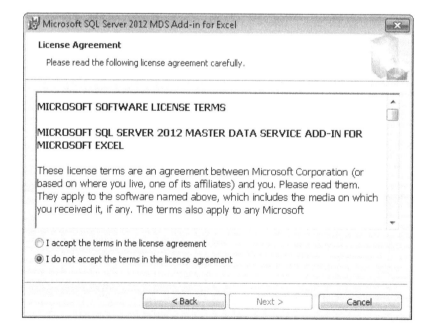

4. Click Install to begin the installation.

   The MDS Add-in for Excel installation may require Visual Studio 2010 Tools for Office Runtime to be installed. This is available for free on MSDN.

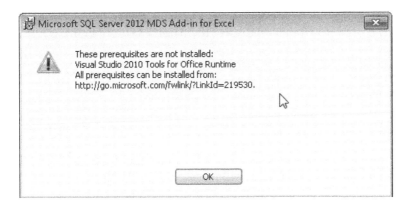

5. Once the installation has completed successfully, open Excel. If you already have Excel open, you will need to open a new instance for the Add-in to be available. A new Master Data ribbon should be available.

Working with MDS Data in Excel

The Master Data Service Add-in for Excel will allow you to load entity data into a worksheet as an Excel formatted table. An Excel table is really a perfect environment to review and manage reasonable amounts of data from Master Data Services. Filtering, sorting, and formula functions can be used to review the data in a friendly format without destroying the ability to write back to the server. Data can also be taken "offline" and modified without connectivity and then published back to MDS when connectivity has been restored.

Procedure: How to Connect to the MDS Server and Load an Entity

To load an entity from Master Data Services into Excel, complete the following steps:

1. Click the Master Data tab to display the Master Data ribbon.

2. Click the Connect button to create a new connection. After you have set up the connection, clicking this button will connect automatically to the stored connection.

3. The connection manager will display. In the possible event you are managing multiple Master Data Services implementations, you can manage them here. Click the New button at the bottom of the screen to add the connection to your server.

4. In the Add New Connection dialog box, provide a description and server address for the connection. You can use any name that is identifiable for the connection. Don't worry about this now, as you can always change the name as new servers are added. The MDS server address is just the base URL that you use to connect to the MDS server. Ensure this address does not contain a page such as default.aspx at the end. Click OK when you are finished.

5. Click the Connect button to connect to the server.

6. After making a new connection, the Master Data Explorer task pane displays on the right side of the screen. Select the Product model from the Model drop-down list. The most recent open version (Version 4) will be selected by default, but you can change to any available version in the Version drop-down list.

7. Double-click the Product entity from the list shown next. Data will immediately begin to load into the active sheet. If data already exists in the sheet, a warning message about data loss is displayed. If you select Yes, all data will be lost from the sheet. (Please be careful not to lose important data in this procedure.) Data on the MDS server is not affected.

A new Excel table with all the Product entity attributes as columns is created on the active sheet and all members of the Product entity are added as rows in the worksheet.

Publishing Changes

Unlike the web UI, the Add-in for Excel does not update members as changes are made to each cell. Instead, every change to a cell is monitored and the cell is colored to denote an unpublished change. Cells can be changed by direct edit or by leveraging any of the more efficient methods of updating a range of cells, such as copy and paste or autofill.

This coloring feature has the unwanted effect of removing the ability to undo changes in Excel. While we think that the benefit of having colored cells is worth this loss of functionality, you can turn off this feature in the settings.

Initially, when you click the Publish button, the following transaction annotation form appears. You can add a comment about the change to all changes or provide a comment for each change individually. If you want to suppress this form for future

Publish actions, select the "Do not show this dialog box again" check box at the bottom of the form.

Publishing changes will also trigger validation on those updated members. Any validation errors will be returned to the page, and two new columns will appear. You can toggle between showing and hiding these columns by clicking the Show Status button on the ribbon.

Refreshing Data from the Server

Once you have created an MDS managed sheet, controls in the Master Data Explorer pane become disabled. You cannot change the entity managed by the sheet, but all filter functionality is still available. You can save the parent workbook for this sheet and open it at a later time. All of the functionality should still be loaded. Instead of creating a new worksheet, you have two options to refresh data. Based on your needs, you can either refresh the entire managed sheet or refresh a selected range of cells. If you are ready to publish a worksheet that depends on certain attribute values that may have changed on the server recently, refreshing a selected range allows you to reload those attribute values before you publish your worksheet. You can also leverage this feature as a pseudo-undo.

While not recommended, a saved sheet can be sent to another MDS user. Sending data within an Excel workbook circumvents security on the server. We will discuss sharing this query with others later in this chapter.

Reviewing Transactions

You can review the transaction history of any member in a MDS managed sheet by using a new MDS menu item at the bottom of the Excel menu displayed when you right-click a row in a managed sheet. Annotations for any transaction will be displayed in the right-hand column, and you can add additional annotations at the bottom of the screen.

Making Deletions in Managed Sheets

Deleting members in an MDS managed sheet can be confusing. If you delete members using standard methods such as the right-click menu option, the member is removed only from the worksheet. It changes nothing on the MDS server. If you want to remove one or more members from the MDS system, you must use the Delete button on the Master Data ribbon. This method soft deletes all selected rows from the system. There is currently no way to purge members using the Add-in for Excel.

Combining Data

You can map data from a range into an MDS managed sheet by using the Combine Data button on the ribbon. This button is enabled only when the active sheet is an MDS managed sheet. You can select a range and then map to each of the attribute columns present in the managed sheet. It is not required to map all of the attributes to combine data.

Applying Rules

If you want to trigger validation on members awaiting validation without changing any data, you can apply validation to the managed sheet with the Apply Rules button on the ribbon. Only those members not currently validated will be processed. Any errors will display on the sheet and the validation status column will be shown.

Filtering Entity Results Members

While all of the datasets in our modest examples are small, many organizations may have entities that contain thousands or millions of members. The Add-in for Excel has been designed to hold up to a million MDS member records in a single managed sheet. There may be some instances when analyzing or managing a large number of records is warranted based on a business need, but most people should use the filtering function to limit results. The filtering function in Excel can limit both the number of columns and the number of rows returned from the MDS server.

Procedure: How to Load a Filtered Entity

To load an entity with filtered members and attributes, complete the following steps:

1. Open a blank worksheet or a new workbook.
2. Click the Master Data tab to display the Master Data ribbon in Excel.
3. Click the Show Explorer button to display the Master Data Explorer pane.
4. Select the Product model from the Model drop-down list at the top of the Master Data Explorer pane.
5. Select the Product entity in the list. Selecting an entity enables the Filter button in the Master Data ribbon, as shown here:

6. Click the Filter button to display the Filter dialog box.

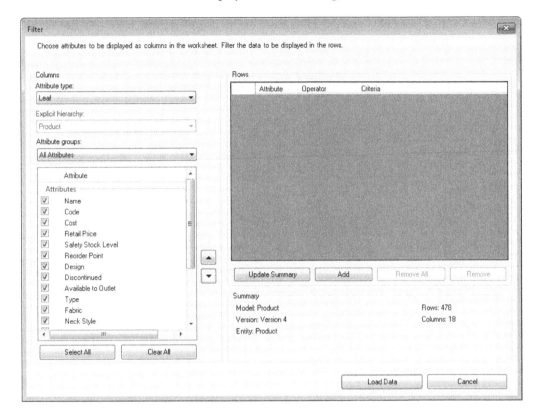

7. You can filter rows returned to the Excel worksheet by adding filter criteria in the Rows section. Select Validation Status from the Attribute drop-down list. You can now filter member records based on attribute values or the record's current validation status in SQL Server 2012.

8. Select the "is equal to" operator from the Operator drop-down list.

9. Select Validation failed from the Criteria drop-down list. Updates to row filter criteria do not automatically update the summary in the lower-right pane. To update this summary, you can click the Update Summary button at any time.

10. To limit the attributes returned, select Pricing from the Attribute groups drop-down list in the Columns section on the left. The Summary pane will immediately update to 5 rows and 5 columns returned.

11. Click the Select All button beneath the Attribute list box.

12. Uncheck the Design attribute in the Attribute list box. The summary will update to 8 columns returned.

13. Click the Load Data button to load the data into the active worksheet.

	MDS Connection: MDS(http://localhost/mds_rc1) Model: Product Version: Version						
$ValidationStatus$	$InputStatus$	Name	Code	Cost	Retail Price	Approved
Validation failed	Unchanged	*Cost is required*	1010	1.50	7.99	Pending {Pending}
Validation failed	Un	*Retail Price is required*	331			
Validation failed	Un		332	2.00	12.00	Pending {Pending}
Validation failed	Unchanged	Male Navy Pants 10 Not Applicable	1333	3.00	10.00	Pending {Pending}
Validation failed	Unchanged	Male Navy Pants 11 Not Applicable	1334	3.00	10.00	Pending {Pending}

Saving and Sharing Queries

Now that we have created a complex request to pull selected attributes and records from an entity, we need to save this request for later use. For years, MDS users have asked the Microsoft development team to provide a process to persist filter criteria for future use. The Add-in for Excel now provides this functionality while also allowing users to share those queries with other users through Outlook with the click of a button.

Procedure: How to Save a Filter Query and Share It Through Outlook

To save a previously created filter as a query, complete the following steps:

1. Activate the managed worksheet from the previous procedure.
2. Click the Master Data tab to display the Master Data ribbon in Excel.
3. Expand the Save Query button drop-down list and select Save as Query. This saves the filter setting for the active managed sheet as an XML query. This query is stored on your machine and can be reloaded into a new worksheet from the server at any time.

You can manage stored shortcut queries from the Manage Queries form, which you also access from the Save Query button drop-down list. Previously saved queries can be loaded, renamed, or deleted from this screen.

4. Click the Send Query button on the ribbon to share this MDS query with others. The benefit of sending the query rather than the worksheet itself is that the security configuration will trim results for each individual user. Only the members and attributes that each person has rights to will be returned when the Excel query is initiated.

5. An e-mail is generated with the query attached as an XML file with a new .mdsqx extension. This file opens automatically on any computer with the MDS Add-in for Excel installed on it.

6. Each user sees this warning message the first time that a file is opened, asking if the server connection should be allowed. You can add this server to a list of trustworthy servers and never see this message again by selecting the "Always allow connections to this address" check box and clicking the Yes button.

Creating and Modifying Entities Rapidly

Early in my career, after spending many days loading files into Excel and databases, I had grown tired of needing to solve all of my column choices before I could see the results. I didn't always know what I wanted. The wizards walked me through seemingly endless steps to determine an output that never matched all of my expectations, and once I clicked Finish, the process did not allow for revisions. If I wanted a different result, I had to start the wizard over again. When I was designing the wizard for Excel, the users I took into account first were the consultants and data stewards. They needed a tool that could be used to quickly model and load data into MDS, so that was the tool I hoped to design. My requirements were as follows:

▶ **Almost no information to do something** While it is nice to write a book on Master Data Services, I don't want reading this book to be a necessity for every user to get started. Master Data Services supports only a small subset of data types, so the Add-in should support determining the correct data type for the column and successfully loading all members.

▶ **Every action can be triggered automically** If I want to change a column to a domain-based attribute or change the decimal scale of a number attribute, I don't want to re-create the entire entity. I just want to replace the column in question. If I need to add a new column, I want to click on the column of unmanaged data and select the name of the attribute in MDS.

▶ **An entity is created for my DBA attribute automatically** If I select a column and determine that current values are the only values that I require, I want the supporting entity to be created. This entity should be populated with all of the unique values within the selected column.

The end result of successfully incorporating the preceding requirements into the tool's design is a very powerful feature that allows data stewards and consultants alike to quickly build and modify entities. The Add-in for Excel not only encapsulates MDS features in the Excel interface, but extends them into a much more powerful tool. The following examples and procedures will show you how these features work.

Using the Excel Add-In at the Main Street Clothing Company

At Main Street Clothing Company, each individual store manages a list of clerks and their schedules in Excel spreadsheets on the manager's laptop. Unfortunately, these spreadsheets are not currently backed up, nor are they integrated with headquarters' systems in any way. Store managers are concerned that any changes to their current process would add to their responsibilities, create inefficiencies in the process, and mandate unnecessary reliance on central IT.

IT proposes the creation of a new model for store managers. Within this model, all managers and the designees will be model administrators. IT will spend an afternoon with each manager to help them create a new entity for each store's clerks. The process is detailed in the following procedure, the worksheet for which you can download from www.mdsuser.com.

Procedure: How to Create an MDS Entity from Excel Data

To create an MDS entity from Excel data, complete the following steps:

1. Click the Master Data tab to display the Master Data ribbon.
2. Select all of the data to populate the new entity. The data area needs to be contiguous to be loaded correctly. To quickly select a large, contiguous range, select the uppermost cell of the range, hold down CTRL-SHIFT, press RIGHT ARROW, and then press DOWN ARROW.
3. Click the Create Entity button on the ribbon to open the Create Entity form.

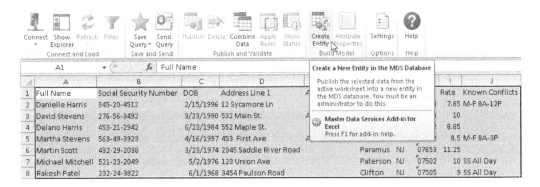

4. Note that the range for the Excel table appears in the Range field. If you had forgotten to select the range or if you wanted to change the range selected, you could click the range selection button to the right of the Range field and select the range.

NOTE

While there is a "My data has headers" check box for loading an entity without headers, I strongly discourage you from selecting this check box. Each column will be named Column A, Column B, etc. This is unlikely to be helpful to anyone and will probably just lead to more work later on.

5. Select the model in which to store the new entity. In Chapter 14 we will discuss some different options on modeling. For now, just store the new entity in the Finance model.

6. Select the version for the initial entity data to be loaded into. The entity will exist in all versions of the model, but members will only exist in the selected version.

7. Input the name for the new entity in the "New entity name" textbox. The name must be unique in the model for the operation to succeed.

8. Select "Generate code automatically" in the Code drop-down list. This sets up the entity with an automated code generated for each member. We could have selected a unique column, such as SSN, but that could lead to problems later on. While filling this column with unique values is not required for the entity to be created, only unique members and the first of the duplicate members would be created.

9. You can optionally select a name column for the entity. For this example, leave the Name drop-down list box blank.

10. Click the OK button to create the new entity.

11. A new sheet will be created similar to a loaded MDS managed entity. Any duplicate records will be colored to highlight them as errors.

MDS Connection: MDS(http://localhost/mds_rc1)		**Model:** Finance	**Version:** VERSION_1	**Entity:** Clerks_Loc_1	**Retrieved:** 5/20/2012 12:05:31 AM						
Name	Code	Full Name	Social Security Number	DOB	Address Line 1	Address Line 2	City	State	Zip	Rate	Known Conflicts
	1	Danielle Harri	345-20-4512	2/15/1996	12 Sycamore Ln		Paramus	NJ	07653	7.85	M-F 8A-12P
	2	David Steven	276-56-3492	3/23/1990	532 Main St.	Apt 204	Paramus	NJ	07653	10	
	3	Delano Harris	453-21-2942	6/23/1984	552 Maple St.		Paramus	NJ	07652	8.85	
	4	Martha Steve	563-49-3923	4/16/1997	453 First Ave	Apt 503	Paramus	NJ	07652	8.5	M-F 8A-3P
	5	Martin Scott	432-29-2038	3/23/1974	2345 Saddle River Road		Paramus	NJ	07653	11.25	
	6	Michael Mitch	521-23-2049	5/2/1976	123 Union Ave		Paterson	NJ	07502	10	SS All Day
	7	Rakesh Patel	232-24-3822	6/1/1968	3454 Paulson Road		Clifton	NJ	07505	9	SS All Day

When an entity is created, each column's contents are analyzed and a corresponding attribute is created in MDS of the appropriate type, string, number, or date. Sizes and scale will be determined by the initial members being loaded. This might be valuable in creating a model, but the ability to quickly modify an attribute is the new feature that will completely change project schedules.

Making Changes to an Existing Entity

Now that we have created a new entity, we want to modify this entity's attributes to take full advantage of MDS features and add value over Excel tables alone. In the initial version of MDS, there was no way to transform an attribute from one type to another while keeping the values stored in the column intact.

Procedure: How to Modify an Existing Entity's Structure

To load and modify an existing entity from Master Data Services in Excel, complete the following steps:

1. Click the Master Data tab to display the Master Data ribbon.
2. Click Show Explorer to display the Master Data Explorer pane.
3. Load the Clerks Loc 1 entity created in the previous procedure.
4. Select the State column header in the entity. This enables the Attribute Properties button on the Master Data ribbon.
5. Click the Attribute Properties button. This triggers the Attribute Properties form to display, as shown in the illustration. You can update the name or type of an attribute in MDS on this form.

6. Select "Constrained list (Domain-based)" from the Attribute type drop-down list. Selecting this option alters the form to provide a new drop-down list that enables you to select where to populate the values of the attribute from.

7. Initially this new drop-down list box is set to the selected column. This would create a new entity to store all unique values in this column. You will notice another input box, "New entity name," that allows you to name this new list of states. Select the State entity from the drop-down list. Changing this selection hides the "New entity name" input box.
8. Click the OK button.

NOTE

The attribute update process does not actually update the column. Instead, it creates a new column and then loads the values from the prior column into the new column. As long as the transition is completed successfully, the old column (and all its transaction history) will be deleted. If any errors occur, the column will remain with an _old suffix appended to the original column.

Configuring Add-in for Excel Settings

There are a number of settings for the Add-in for Excel that enable users to customize their installation to some extent. Unlike server settings, these options are stored on the client machine and are not sourced from the server in any way. Data stewards and IT administrators are encouraged to create internal policies on changing the data settings and provide guidance to your end users.

Settings provide value in two ways. One group of settings gives customers an opportunity to tweak data performance and usage from the MDS server. The other group of settings allows you to adjust how the Add-in works within Excel. These settings are not grouped together but rather span across both the Settings and Data tabs within the Settings dialog box.

Configuring Data Settings

As the value of MDS and the new Add-in for Excel are recognized across your organization, you may discover a significant number of Excel queries hitting the Master Data Services server. Depending on your hardware deployment and the size of your entities in MDS, it may become valuable to provide policies on data consumption through Excel. While you cannot stop authorized users from making large requests to the server, you can modify warnings and the size of batches retrieved.

▶ **Filter Warnings**   Unlike the web UI, which defaults to load only 50 members at a time, Excel users can potentially load up to 1 million members to their Excel worksheets for analysis. The most effective setting to combat large data requests initiates warnings to users before they retrieve large datasets. These warnings are initially set to trigger for datasets over 10,000 rows and 100 columns. You can modify these values or turn off filter warnings completely.

▶ **Batches size (in thousands)**   These two settings do not change the total amount of data retrieved, just the size of the data returned in each request. Obviously, smaller requests create more traffic to and from the server, but this can help on client computers with memory constraints. These options are initially set to 50,000 cells per batch. I would leave these settings alone unless you experience significant delays during loading or publishing.

Configuring Behavior Settings

These settings affect the behavior of the MDS selection and publish processes in Excel. These settings will allow users to customize their Master Data Services Excel experience.

▶ **Publishing**   When you initially publish changes, you can set whether or not a dialog box prompts you to provide transaction annotations to provide greater detail about the transaction. You can suppress or re-enable this dialog box, respectively, by clearing or selecting the "Show Publish and Annotate dialog box when publishing" check box.

▶ **Versions**   In the Master Data Explorer, selection of a model triggers a default version to be selected. The initial setting is for the newest version to be selected, but you can either suppress the default selection or choose to have the oldest version become the default by using the Version selection drop-down list box. In the initial release of the Add-in for Excel, the Oldest selection does not appear to select properly.

▶ **Logging**   Selecting the "Turn on detailed logging" check box will create a detailed log of web service calls and actions in the Add-in for Excel. This detailed log will be required by support staff to debug any issues with the MDS plug-in. These logs can get quite large, so clear this check box during normal operations.

▶ **Servers Added to Safe List**   In order to protect Excel users, the first time that you load a shortcut file sent through Excel, you will be asked if you trust the server. If you accidentally indicate that you trust a server, you can clear this list by clicking the Clear All button. Note that this will clear all servers, so you will need to reapprove all MDS server locations when the next file is opened.

Leveraging Data Quality Matching in Excel

In SQL Server 2012, Microsoft shipped a new feature, Data Quality Services (DQS), that provides project-level cleansing and matching tools for loaded datasets. Very little integration exists between MDS and DQS in this initial release. We expect this to change in future releases, but within 2012, the only integration between the two features is the ability to leverage DQS matching policies through the Add-in for Excel. This allows users to determine potential duplicates before loading new record batches into MDS. For more information on setting up Data Quality Services and creating matching policies, go to www.mdsuser.com.

Summary

The MDS Add-in for Excel really changes the game in master data management, providing a well-known and efficient interface for all members of the enterprise to load and manage their data. The intuitive interface can create new entities, thereby eliminating or reducing costly modeling phases of MDM projects. In Chapter 14, the new modeling process will be discussed in greater detail.

Chapter 11

Implementing Security

In This Chapter

- ▶ Security Overview
- ▶ Security Changes in SQL Server 2012
- ▶ Users and Groups
- ▶ Administrators
- ▶ Testing Permissions
- ▶ Functional Area Permissions
- ▶ Model Object Permissions
- ▶ Deleting Permissions
- ▶ Hierarchy Member Permissions
- ▶ Determining Which Permissions Apply
- ▶ Setting Security by Using Web Services

B y the time you are ready to implement security, most of the functionality in MDS has been enabled. Models have been built and refined, rules have been written, and the application has been integrated into your organization.

In order to deploy MDS, everyone needs access to the application. While transaction management can provide some accountability, limiting access based on needs and roles ensures that users are unable to change data without authorization. Limiting the number of models and functions available to users can also help them focus more quickly on the data they need. The ability to provide specific data access within the MDS system is the single most important feature of the application. The focused security access provided by MDS empowers business users and frees the IT organization to manage the overall process, not maintain the individual data points.

In this chapter we provide an overview of the security framework in Master Data Services. We discuss the process of managing user and group permissions and explain the highly customized access that can be granted. The rest of the chapter drills into each level of security by showing how permissions can be applied to your data.

Security Overview

MDS security is broken into three distinct areas:

- ▶ **Functional security**   Corresponds to each of the five functional areas displayed on the home page of the Master Data Manager web application. Most users need access only to the Explorer functional area of the web UI. All other functional areas are available only to administrators. Users must have permissions to the Explorer functional area to use the MDS Add-in for Microsoft Excel.

- ▶ **Model object security**   Provides access control to attributes, based on the model objects within the MDS architecture. For example, you can set permissions on an entity, which determines permissions for all attributes for the entity. Or you can set permissions on a single attribute, which affects that attribute only. Model object security is required; without it, a user cannot perform any tasks in MDS.

- ▶ **Hierarchy member security**   Provides the most granular level of security, and is optional. It is used to grant access to specific members, based on their location in a hierarchy.

Model object permissions (which apply to attributes) and hierarchy member permissions (which apply to members) are combined to determine the exact level of security for every attribute value. Figure 11-1 shows how attribute and member permissions intersect so that security can be determined for an individual attribute value.

Figure 11-1 *Model object and hierarchy member permissions are combined to determine permissions for every attribute value.*

Security Changes in SQL Server 2012

Security in the prior release of MDS was a double-edged sword. The ability to set security on multiple hierarchies simultaneously provided significant flexibility and complexity, but with so many pieces working together, it was easy for administrators to lose sight of what the effective permissions were for each user. A key effort for the second release of Master Data Services was to simplify the security model. In SQL Server 2012, attribute groups are no longer securable; you must set attribute security explicitly on each attribute. Direct hierarchy security has been removed from the security model.

Users and Groups

MDS relies on Active Directory for user and group authentication. While all security permissions are stored in the MDS database, no passwords or group memberships are managed in MDS.

To keep security as simple as possible, you should do the following:

▶   Create either Active Directory or local groups and add either Active Directory or local users to those groups.

▶   Assign security in MDS to these groups, rather than to individual users.

▶   If you decide to assign security to a user, don't also assign security to groups that the user is a member of. While MDS has rules for determining which permissions take effect, security becomes more complicated when you do this.

Before you begin working with security, you should take some time to determine which groups your users might be part of, and which attributes or members those groups might need access to. The following list should give you a general idea of the groups that Main Street Clothing Company might use. Some of the examples in this chapter show how you would assign permissions like these.

► **Product Administrators**   This group will have permission to all functional areas and to take any action available for the Product model. This includes changing the model structure and modifying all members, among many other things.

► **Finance Administrators**   This group will have the same type of permission as the Product Administrators, but for the Finance model.

► **Purchasing**   This group will be able to update the Cost attribute for all products.

► **Warehouse**   This group will be able to update the attributes on the Logistics tab only.

► **Logistics**   This group will be able to update the Safety Stock Level, Reorder Point, and Discontinued attributes. All other attributes will be read-only.

All of these groups will be able to access MDS after being assigned functional area and model object permissions. Main Street might also assign hierarchy member permissions to a few select members of the Purchasing group. These users should be able to view products for only the manufacturers they are responsible for.

Even though we recommend that you assign permissions to groups, for the rest of this chapter we'll refer to permissions that users receive, because at the end of the day, groups wouldn't mean anything if users weren't in them. Users are ultimately the ones who will access the data.

Procedure: How to Add a Group

After you've created your groups either locally or on the domain, you can add the group to the web UI by completing the following steps:

NOTE

Adding a group to the web UI does not give the users in the group permission to access models or data. It simply adds the group to a list, so that you can start to assign permissions.

1. On the Master Data Manager home page, click User and Group Permissions. The administrator account you specified in Configuration Manager when you set up MDS is shown in the Users list; for more information about administrators, see the following section.

2. On the menu bar, click Manage Groups.

3. Click the Add groups button.

4. In the Groups field, type the name of the group in the format Domain\ GroupName or Computer\GroupName.

5. Click OK.

Now that the group is displayed in the list, you can continue with assigning functional and model object permissions, which are described in upcoming sections. If you need to add a user instead of a group, click Manage Users on the menu bar and then click Add users.

NOTE

When you use groups, the users in the group aren't displayed in the list of users until after they have logged in.

Administrators

In MDS there are two types of administrators:

▶ The system administrator you specified in the Administrator Account field when creating the MDS database. This user has full control over all models and data. When new models are created, this user automatically has access. This user also has permission to access all functional areas of the web UI. To change this user, you must run a stored procedure in the database. See "Procedure: How to Change the Administrator Account" for more information.

▶ A model administrator who is manually assigned Update permission to a model, and no other model object or hierarchy member permissions. This user has full control over the model he or she has Update permission to. Model administrators do not necessarily have permission to access all functional areas of the application. For example, a model administrator might be responsible for integration only. However, they can perform all tasks in whichever functional area they have permission to access.

All model administrators with access to the User and Group Permissions functional area can assign permissions for other users. Keep this in mind when you're assigning someone permission to update a model.

In the following sections we explain how to manually assign the permissions that turn any MDS user into an administrator.

Procedure: How to Change the Administrator Account

When you created your database, you specified an administrator account. This user has access to everything, including any sensitive data you may be storing. If you want to change this user, complete the following steps:

CAUTION

This procedure deletes the former administrator's account from MDS.

1. On the Master Data Manager home page, click User and Group Permissions.
2. Add the new administrator to the list of users by clicking the Add user button.
3. Open SQL Server Management Studio and connect to your MDS database.
4. In the table mdm.tblUser, find the user you just added and copy the value listed in the SID column.
5. Create the following query:

```
EXEC [MDS_database].[mdm].[udpSecuritySetAdministrator]
@UserName='DOMAIN\user',
    @SID = 'SID', @PromoteNonAdmin = 1
```

6. Replace *MDS_database* with the MDS database name, *DOMAIN\user* with the new administrator's username, and *SID* with the value you copied.
7. Run the query.

This user now has permission to take all actions on all models and members. The former administrator is deleted from the list of MDS users. Note that if the former administrator was a member of a group that has security permissions, the user retains the permissions assigned to the group. You must remove the administrator from the local or domain group to fully remove his or her privileges.

Testing Permissions

As you begin assigning permissions to groups, you'll quickly realize that it would be great to log in as the user and confirm that they have the access you intended them to have. You can do this by creating a test user or group and assigning permissions to it. Then you can access the Master Data Manager web application by using the credentials of the test user and view the data that the user views.

To have Internet Explorer prompt you for credentials when you open an intranet site like Master Data Manager, you can change IE's security settings. Open IE and choose Tools | Internet options. On the Security tab, ensure that Local intranet is selected and click the Custom level button. Scroll to the bottom of the Security Settings dialog box, and in the User Authentication section, click the "Prompt for user name and password" option.

Now when you open a new browser, you are prompted for credentials.

After you enter the credentials of your test user, you can confirm that they have the access you expect them to have. Each time you make changes to the test user's security, you should close and reopen the browser to ensure you're viewing the latest changes.

> **NOTE**
>
> *You will learn later in this chapter that hierarchy member permissions are not applied immediately. Keep this in mind when testing security.*

If you are using IE 8 or IE 9, another setting to change before you start working with permissions is Compatibility View, which you should turn off. To do so, click Tools | Compatibility View. This makes the User and Group Permissions functional area work better. However, when you open the browser by using the test user's credentials and want to view data in the Explorer functional area, you should turn Compatibility View back on.

Functional Area Permissions

Functional area security determines which of the five functional areas on the Master Data Manager home page a user or group can access. Security at this level is either permitted or denied. If permission to access a specific functional area is denied, the area is not displayed in the web UI and related web service operations are denied.

The Explorer functional area is where users manage data. When you assign access to Explorer, you must assign access to specific model objects, so the user gets access to a specific set of data. When you assign access to any of the other functional areas, the user must have access to the entire model (on the Models tab) in order to use those areas. Without this access, the user can open the functional areas, but no models are displayed. This is how MDS handles permission for administrators.

Procedure: How to Assign Functional Area Permissions

To assign functional area permissions, complete the following steps:

1. On the Master Data Manager home page, click User and Group Permissions.
2. On the menu bar, click Manage Groups.
3. To the left of the group you want to edit, click the down arrow.
4. On the submenu, click Edit | Functions.

5. At the top of the page, click the Edit button.
6. In the Available functions list, select the functional areas you want the user to have access to.
7. Click the right-pointing arrows to add the functional areas to the Assigned functions list.
8. Click the "Save and continue" button to go to the Models tab, where you will set model object permissions.

At this point, the users in the group cannot do anything in MDS. If they open the web UI, they will see the functional areas but will not see models displayed either on the home page or in any of the functional areas.

Model Object Permissions

Model object permissions, assigned on the Models tab, are required. Users cannot view any models or data if they do not have model object permissions.

When you give users permission to model objects, you are giving them the ability to edit attributes for members, based on the object you select. For example, if you set Update permission on the Product entity, all attributes for all Product members (leaf and consolidated) can be updated. If you set Update on the Color attribute of the Product entity, only the Color attribute can be updated.

In addition to giving a user the ability to update attribute values, if you assign Update model object permissions to a model, entity, or to the word "Leaf" or "Consolidated," the user can also create and delete members. If permissions are assigned at a lower level, the user cannot create and delete members.

> **NOTE**
>
> *Permissions automatically cascade to all child objects within the current model unless permissions are assigned at a lower level. You do not need to explicitly set permission on every object.*

If you assign Update model object permissions to the model only, the user is an administrator, which means he or she can access the model in functional areas other than just Explorer if given access to that functional area.

Quick Facts About Model Object Permissions

Things to remember about model object permissions include the following:

▶   They are required.

▶   They determine which attributes a user can view or update (as opposed to which members).

▶   They apply to all lower-level objects unless another permission is explicitly assigned.

▶   Update permission to Leaf or Consolidated model objects and above gives users the ability to create and delete members.

▶   Update permission at just the model level makes the user an administrator.

Best Practice for Model Object Permissions

There are many different model objects you can assign permission to. Giving access to specific models, entities, or attributes should fulfill most of your security needs. In SQL Server 2012, most complicated security configurations have been simplified with the removal of attribute group and hierarchy object security.

Procedure: How to Assign Model Object Permissions

To assign model object permissions, complete the following steps:

1. On the Master Data Manager home page, click User and Group Permissions.
2. On the menu bar, click Manage Groups. In this example, we're going to update the Finance Administrators group.
3. To the left of the group you want to edit, click the down arrow.
4. On the submenu, click Edit | Models.
5. At the top of the page, click the Edit button.

6. If the correct model isn't visible, select the model you want to view from the Model drop-down list. In this case we'll select Finance.
7. Expand and collapse nodes in the tree until you see the object you want to give permission to.

8. Right-click the object you want to give permission to, and from the menu that's displayed, click Update, Read-only, or Deny. In this example, we're going to right-click the Finance model and choose Update.

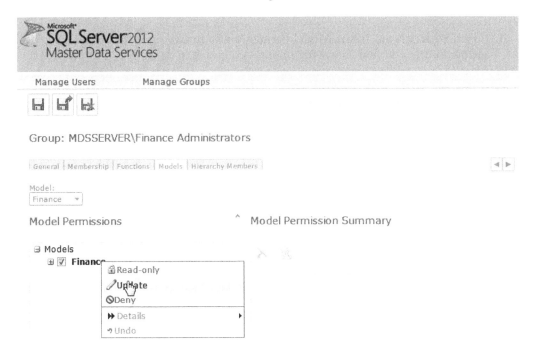

9. Click Save. If you intend to assign hierarchy member permissions, you can click the "Save and continue" button.

The Model Permission Summary grid is populated with the permissions you've assigned.

NOTE

You do not have to explicitly deny access to model objects you don't want users to see. Permissions cascade, so the user is implicitly denied access to any object that doesn't inherit permissions.

This was the simplest example, where you assign Update to the model and no other permissions. In this case, all of the users in the group can access all Finance members, as well as access the Finance model in any functional areas they have permission to access.

Procedure: How to Delete Model Object Permissions

Before you can test other permissions, you may want to delete those you already assigned. To do so, complete the following steps:

1. On the Models tab, in the Model Permission Summary grid, click the down arrow for the row that shows permissions you want to delete.

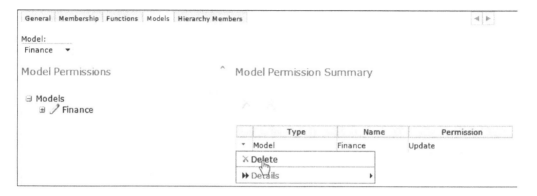

2. From the submenu that's displayed, click Delete.
3. In the confirmation dialog box, click OK.

The page refreshes and the permissions are deleted.

Now let's go through all of the possible model object permissions you can assign.

Access to Entities

When you assign Update permission to an entity, the user can create and delete members as well as update all attributes for the entity (assuming no other permissions are assigned). When you assign Read permission, the user can view all attributes for the entity.

Here is what Update permission to a single entity (in this case, the Line entity) looks like after you save:

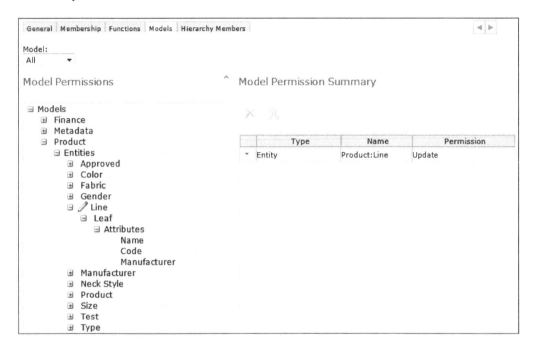

And the following illustration shows what Update access to the Line entity looks like in Explorer.

Line Entity

🔷 Add Member   ✖ Delete Member   ⚡ Apply Rules | ▼   📄 View Transactions

[All Attributes]

		Name	Code	Manufacturer
▶	✓	Accessories	Accessories	Candy Canes {Cand
	✓	Boys Active	Boys Active	Pish Posh {Pish Posl
	✓	Boys Activewear	Boys Activewear	Hipsters {Hipsters}
	✓	Boys Fall	Boys Fall	Pish Posh {Pish Posl
	✓	Boys Spring	Boys Spring	Pish Posh {Pish Posl
	✓	Boys Summer	Boys Summer	Pish Posh {Pish Posl
	✓	Fall Boys	Fall Boys	TumbleJacks {Tumb
	✓	Fall Girls	Fall Girls	TumbleJills {Tumble
	✓	Girls Activewear	Girls Activewear	Hipsters {Hipsters}
	✓	Spring Girls	Spring Girls	TumbleJills {Tumble
	✓	Springtime Collection	Springtime Collection	Rings with Rosie {Ri
	✓	Summer Boys	Summer Boys	TumbleJills {Tumble
	✓	Summer Collection	Summer Collection	TumbleJacks {Tumb
	✓	Summer Girls	Summer Girls	Rings with Rosie {Ri

1-14 of 14 members

As you can see, the user can update all attributes for all members in the Line entity. The user can also create and delete members when you assign permissions at this level. If the Line entity had hierarchies or collections, they would also be editable. When you have permission to read or update an entity, you can read or update any explicit hierarchies and collections for the entity.

In an effort to simplify security in this release, MDS gives access to change domain-based attributes in entities you have access to, but you no longer have Read access to those entities in the Explorer functional area. If you wish to provide Read access to the Manufacturer entity, for example, you must provide this security assignment explicitly.

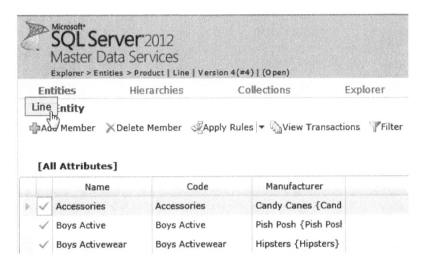

Access to Leaf Member Attributes

In the tree, you can assign permission to the word "Leaf" that's displayed beneath an entity. This is a shortcut for giving permission to all attributes for all leaf-level members. If you assign Update permission, the user can create and delete members, just as if you assigned permissions to the entity itself.

NOTE

If an entity does not have explicit hierarchies enabled, there is no difference between assigning permission to an entity and assigning permission to Leaf.

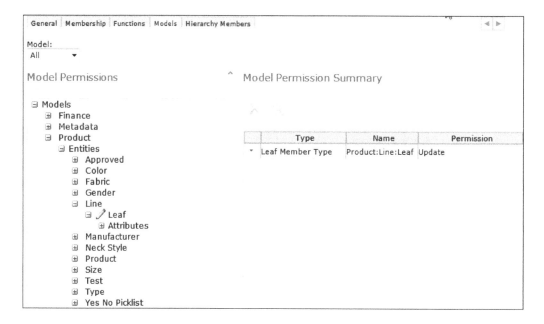

If the entity is enabled for explicit hierarchies, use this permission level to give a user access to update attributes for all leaf members or for all consolidated members. Otherwise, this permission does not need to be used, because you can assign permission directly to the entity.

Access to Individual Attributes

When you assign Update or Read permission to a specific attribute, the user can update or read that attribute. It doesn't matter if the attribute is domain-based; the user is able to update the attribute value for the entity that the attribute applies to only.

In this example, the user has Update permission to the Product entity's Cost attribute:

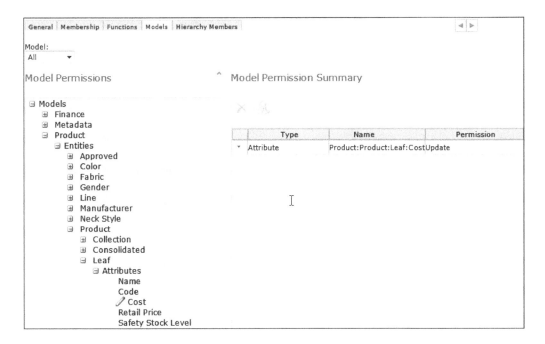

When the user accesses the Product entity in Explorer, the Name and Code attributes are read-only but the Cost attribute can be updated. While this is no longer displayed in the grid, the Name and Code columns are disabled in the Details pane.

Note that when you assign permission to an attribute, the user can't create or delete members. Also note that if the attribute is domain-based, the user can't make changes to the entity the attribute is based on. For example, if a user has permission to update the Color attribute for the Product entity, the user can change a product's color, but the user cannot open the Color entity itself and change the color name from Blue to Light Blue.

If you wanted the user to be able to do either of these things, you would choose these permissions:

In Explorer, you can view the results. The user can update the Color attribute for all products. In the latest release, the grid does not provide graphical security feedback, but the Edit button is enabled for changing the Color attribute. The input boxes for name and code are grayed out.

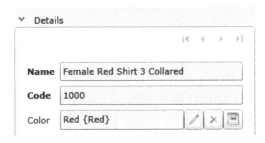

The user can also create, delete, and update members of the Color entity. Here is the other entity:

Access to an Explicit Hierarchy

In an effort to simplify security, you can no longer assign permissions to an explicit hierarchy. You can no longer separate the ability to move members in an explicit hierarchy but not create and delete members.

If you assign Update permission to the root entity, the user can move members in the hierarchy. If you assign Read-only permission, the user can view the hierarchy but not make any changes.

In this example, the user is assigned Update permission to the Account entity. This gives the user Update access to the Chart of Accounts explicit hierarchy; these permissions would be the same for any explicit hierarchies created on the Account entity.

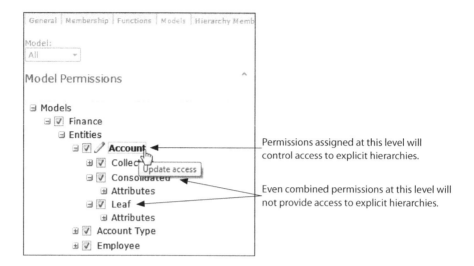

When you open Explorer to view the results of these permissions, you can open the hierarchy and move members in it. You can also view the members in the entity the hierarchy is for (in this case, the Account entity), and now you will be able to update attributes for these members as well as create new ones.

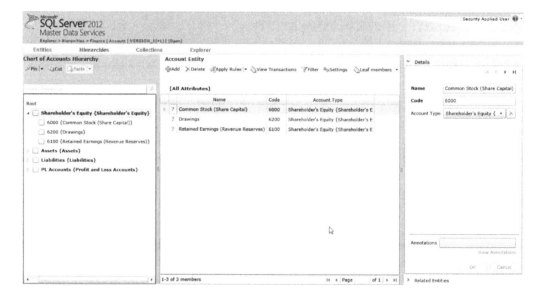

If the user has Update permission to an entity, the user can also view and update all explicit hierarchies for the entity. If the user has Read-only permissions to the entity, the user can only view all hierarchies within the system.

Access to Collections

When you assign Update or Read permission to the Collection object, you are assigning access to all collections. You can't give permission to an individual collection—it is an "all or nothing" scenario.

If a user has Update permission, he or she can create, delete, and update collections. In this example, the user has permission to update collections for the Product entity:

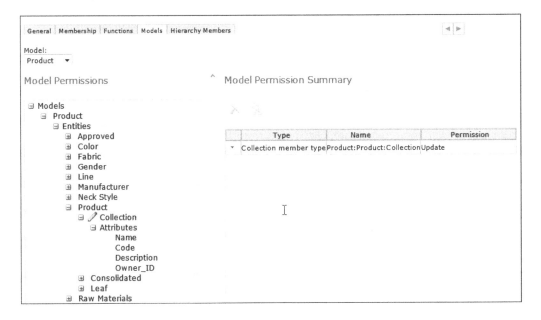

In Explorer, all collections for the Product entity are displayed, and the user can create and delete collections, as well as update collection attributes like Name, Code, Description, or Owner.

At this point, the user can delete members from the collection but can't add any members because the user doesn't have permission to other model objects. If the user had a minimum of Read-only permission to the Product entity, he or she could add members to the collection.

In User and Group Permissions, on the Models tab, you can give permission to attributes of collections, so you can lock down the description or names of all of your collections, for example. In SQL Server 2012, you can no longer set permissions on attribute groups, just as you cannot set them with attribute groups that apply to entities.

Access to Other Model Objects

Setting security directly on a derived hierarchy was removed in this release of Master Data Services. Derived hierarchy security is now based on access to all of the corresponding components of the derived hierarchy.

In addition, attribute groups should no longer be viewed as a way to secure attributes. All users have access to an All Attributes tab.

Access to a Derived Hierarchy

For any derived hierarchies to appear, the user must have or inherit Read or Update permissions on the model. This will obviously give the user Read or Update access to all of the entities in the model. Derived hierarchy access is now controlled by access to each of the components that make up the hierarchy. Every derived hierarchy where the user has access to all entities that make up the levels of the derived hierarchy will be displayed in the drop-down list in the Explorer UI. If any object is denied, the hierarchy will not be available, but the user may be able to affect the hierarchy by changing attributes within other represented entities they have access to.

In this example, the user is assigned Read permission to the Product model. To give the user Update access to the Product by Gender hierarchy, the user has Update permissions to the Product and Gender entities. Conversely, because the user is denied access to the Line entity that groups products by Line and then groups lines by Manufacturer, this hierarchy does not display in the hierarchy menu dropdown at the top of the explorer screen.

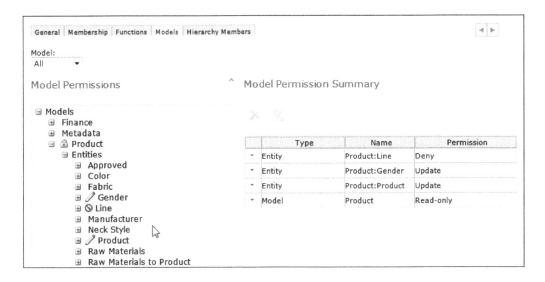

When you open Explorer with this user's credentials, you can see only the Product by Gender derived hierarchy. Due to the deny permissions on the Line entity, the only derived hierarchy that can be accessed is the Product by Gender hierarchy. Access to Product by Line by Manufacturer is not presented because the user does not have access to the Line entity.

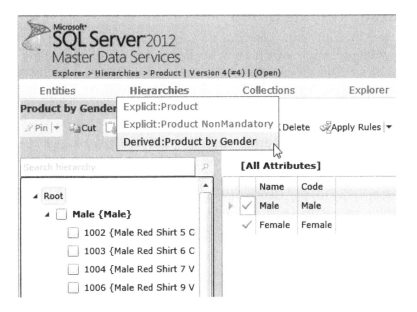

By updating the value of the Gender attribute, you change the location of a member in the hierarchy. For example, if you change the Gender attribute value for member 1000 to Female, the member would be displayed under the new line in the hierarchy. You don't need to view the hierarchy to know that this change has taken place.

However, assigning permissions to a derived hierarchy does allow the user to view the hierarchy structure and move members in the tree, rather than just update attribute values.

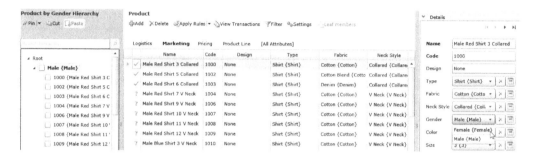

Although you can assign permissions to individual attributes, the user cannot work with the hierarchy structure unless you give him or her permission to the entity, model, or derived hierarchy model object.

Access to an Attribute Group

In SQL Server 2012, attribute groups are no longer a part of the security model in MDS. All attribute-level security must be applied at the individual attribute level. Permissions on attribute groups will now be evaluated as Hide(Deny)/Unhide(Update). The addition of the All Attributes tab has also rendered attribute group security obsolete.

Attribute Groups in System Administration   You may have noticed when you were creating attribute groups that users and groups were displayed on the Attribute Group Maintenance page. The Users and Groups nodes on this page are for viewing users and groups who have Update permission to the attribute group (users with Read-only permission are not displayed and no longer have meaning). This is the only way to manage which attribute groups are displayed for each user. *This is not for purposes of security!*

CAUTION

Do not attempt to edit users and groups on this page.

You should *not* use this page to try to administer security for attribute groups. This is for display management purposes only.

Deny Permissions

You'll notice that when you right-click a model object, Deny is listed on the submenu. In most cases you won't need to explicitly deny access to an object. Permissions cascade so that all lower-level objects inherit the assigned permissions. Objects that are at the same level or higher, and that don't have permissions explicitly assigned, are inherently denied.

For example, if you set Update permissions on the Product model but not on the Finance model, the user is denied permission to access the Finance model. You don't have to explicitly deny access. Or, for example, if you set Update permissions on the Color entity but not on any other entities, permission to access all other entities is denied.

These same rules apply to hierarchies on the Hierarchy Members tab. Hierarchy nodes at the same level and higher are inherently denied as soon as any Read-only or Update permissions are set. All other permissions cascade down the hierarchy.

Due to the changes in SQL Server 2012, giving permissions to derived hierarchies may lead to a number of entities requiring Deny access privileges. Once you have added Update or Read-only access to the model level, any entity you wish to restrict access to will require explicit Deny permissions to be set.

Navigational Access

Every user needs a certain degree of access to the system in order to open the members and attributes he or she has permission to. For example, if a user has permission to access three specific attributes, but not the model itself, the user can still view the list of models in the drop-down list on the home page. Users also have to be able to see the Name and Code attributes for the members so that they know what they are updating. This bare minimum required access is sometimes referred to as *navigational access*. We're not going to delve into the specifics of each model object, but you should know that when you give permissions to a user, you are also giving the user the navigational access required to work with the data they need.

Deleting Permissions

Earlier in this chapter, we showed you how to delete model object permissions. The procedure is the same for hierarchy member permissions. In the grid, click the down arrow next to the row with permissions you want to delete, and click Delete.

Model Permission Summary

Type	Name	Permission
Entity	Product:Line	Deny
✕ Delete	ender	Update
▶▶ Details	▶ roduct	Update
Model	Product	Read-only

If you want to remove a user so that he or she no longer has MDS access, you need to complete two procedures. First, confirm the user's group memberships. Then, remove the user from the list.

To confirm the user's group memberships, complete the following steps:

1. On the Manage Users page, to the left of the user, click the down arrow.
2. On the submenu, click Edit | Membership. Note any groups the user is a member of.

3. If the user is a member of multiple groups, go to the local or Active Directory group and remove the user from the group.

Now remove the user from the list:

1. On the Manage Users page, click the row of the user you want to delete.
2. Click the "Delete selected user" button.

Both of these procedures are required to keep your list of users accurate. Otherwise you might end up with users in the list who don't truly have access or retain access due to additional group permission.

Hierarchy Member Permissions

In an effort to provide the functional equivalent of row-level member security without providing all of the maintenance nightmares associated with it, MDS provides hierarchy member security. This type of security allows you to assign security to all the members in a node of a hierarchy. The same cascading feature that is found in model object security applies to hierarchy member security.

With MDS, you have the ability to set security on levels of either explicit or derived hierarchies. This powerful feature allows you to limit access to data within MDS on a number of axes simultaneously (one axis from model object permissions, and a second axis from hierarchy member permissions, as was shown in Figure 11-1 at the beginning of this chapter).

Because you may have thousands or millions of members, hierarchy member permissions are applied only periodically. In the MDS database, in tblSystemSetting, the SecurityMemberProcessInterval setting determines how often these permissions are applied. The default setting is 3600 seconds, or 60 minutes, but you can update this to be more frequent. Note that even if you set it to every 10 seconds, you must wait 60 minutes for the 10-second intervals to start. Be aware that 10 seconds may not be enough time to fully apply permissions to all of your members.

Hierarchy member permissions are based on a version of a model and are copied forward on subsequent models. So if you set permissions on a hierarchy in Version 3, those permissions don't exist in Version 2, but they will exist in copies of Version 3. Be sure to consider that your users might have unintended access to data in earlier versions of your model if you set hierarchy member permissions in later models.

Quick Facts About Hierarchy Member Permissions

Things to remember about hierarchy member permissions include the following:

▶ They are optional.

▶ They determine which members (as opposed to which attributes) a user can view or update.

▶ They apply to all lower-level members unless another permission is explicitly assigned.

▶ They are not applied immediately, unlike model object permissions. You must wait until a specific interval of time has passed. This interval is based on SecurityMemberProcessInterval in tblSystemSetting.

▶ You can run a stored procedure to force them to be applied immediately.

▶ They are version specific. You set them for a specific version and they apply to that version and all future copies of that version. (They do not apply to any previous versions.)

▶ You should not set permissions on explicit cap or recursive hierarchies. Security for these hierarchies is not supported.

Procedure: How to Assign Hierarchy Member Permissions

To assign hierarchy member permissions to a group, complete the following steps:

1. On the Master Data Manager home page, click User and Group Permissions.
2. On the menu bar, click Manage Groups.
3. To the left of the group you want to edit, click the down arrow.
4. On the submenu, click Edit | Hierarchy Members.
5. From the lists, choose the model, version, and hierarchy you need. Keep in mind that permissions will apply to the version you select and later copies of that version after the permissions are created.
6. At the top of the page, click the Edit button.
7. Expand and collapse nodes of the hierarchy as needed, or search for a specific node. Notice that individual members are not displayed. You are setting permissions for all members that are in one or more specific nodes.
8. Right-click the hierarchy node you want to give permission to, and from the menu that's displayed, click Update, Read-only, or Deny.
9. Click Save.

Because the Main Street Clothing Company's models are fairly limited, the following example may not necessarily have real-world use, but it should help you understand how these permissions work.

In this example, the user has Update permission to two attributes for the Product entity: Color and Design.

On the Hierarchy Members tab, the user is assigned Update permission to the Female node. Permission to access all other nodes at the same level or higher is implicitly denied.

After the hierarchy member permissions interval has passed and permissions are applied, the user can update only the Color and Design attributes for the Female members. The Male members (those with Male as the Gender) are not displayed.

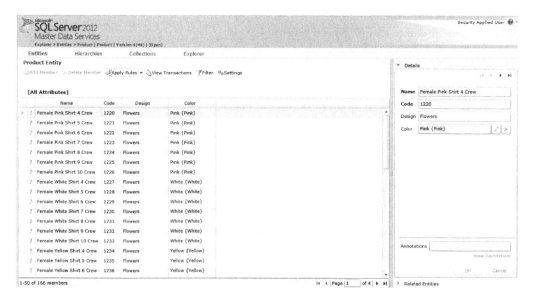

In this example, you can start to see the intersection of model object and hierarchy member permissions. (You can also think of this as the intersection of attribute and member permissions.) If you were to keep this hierarchy member security but, on the Models tab, give Update access to the Product entity, the user would be able to see these same 200 members in hierarchies and collections as well as the main grid. The other 200+ Male members would always remain hidden.

Because hierarchy member permissions must always be used with model object permissions, there are rules for how these permissions are combined. For more information, see "Determining Which Permissions Apply."

Overlapping Hierarchies

If you've assigned hierarchy member permissions to more than one hierarchy, there is a good chance that you've assigned overlapping permissions to some members. If you do assign permissions to multiple hierarchies and those hierarchies contain the same members, the following rules apply:

▶ If one hierarchy node is assigned Update permission and another is assigned Read-only permission, then the members in the node are Read-only.

▶ If one hierarchy node is assigned Update or Read-only permission and another node is assigned Deny permission, then the members in the node are not displayed.

Determining Which Permissions Apply

Permissions are applied in the following order of operations:

▶ **Permissions for each attribute are determined (model object permissions)** Permissions assigned on the Models tab cascade down the tree structure and are applied to all objects. In this way, permissions for every attribute in the model are determined.

▶ **Permissions for each member are determined (hierarchy member permissions)** Permissions assigned on the Hierarchy Members tab also cascade down the tree. In this way, permissions for all members in the model are determined.

▶ **Attribute and member permissions are combined** Permissions are combined and access to each individual attribute value is determined.

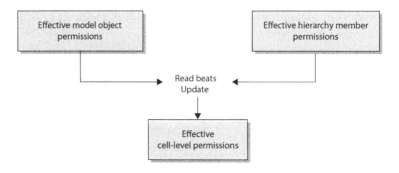

Figure 11-2 *Permissions workflow, showing the combination of model object and hierarchy member permissions*

This workflow is shown in Figure 11-2.

Combining Permissions

When attribute permissions (assigned on the Models tab) are combined with member permissions (assigned on the Hierarchy Members tab), the following rules are applied:

▶ Read-only overrides Update.

▶ Deny overrides all other permissions.

The following example shows how this works. First, on the Models tab, assign Update to the Product entity's Color attribute. This gives the user the ability to update the Color attribute for all members.

Model Permission Summary

	Type	Name	Permission
▾	Attribute	Product:Product:Leaf:Color	Update

Then, on the Hierarchy Members tab, open the Product by Gender hierarchy and assign Update to the Female node and Read-only to the Male node.

If you apply the rules, all attributes for all members in the Male node should be Read-only. Because Read-only overrides Update, the user cannot update the Color attribute for the Male members.

Read-only was applied to the members. Because Read beats Update, Read is applied to the individual attribute value.   Update was applied to the color attribute.

Combining Users and Groups

We've mentioned many times that life gets confusing when you assign permissions both to a user and to the groups the user is a member of. But if you decide you really need to do this, the web UI helps you determine which permissions are applied.

Whenever you open a user account, on both the Models and the Hierarchy Members tabs, you can select Effective from the Permissions list to refresh the web UI and display the results of any overlapping user and group permissions.

User: MDSSERVER\TestUser (Test User)

General | Membership | Functions | Models | Hierarchy Members

Model: Permissions:
All   ▾   Effective   ▾

Model Permissions   ^   Model Permission Summary

⊟ Models
  ⊞ Finance
  ⊞ 🗿 Product

	Type	Name	Source Group	Permission
▾	Model	Product	MDSSERVER\Logistics	Read-only
▾	Entity	Finance:Location	MDSSERVER\Logistics	Update
▾	Entity	Product:Color	MDSSERVER\Marketing	Update
▾	Entity	Product:Neck Style	MDSSERVER\Marketing	Update
▾	Entity	Product:Raw Materials to Product		Update

Select Effective to compare user and group permissions and determine which take effect.

This same list is not available when you're viewing groups; it's available only when you're viewing users.

If you want to understand how the combination of user and group permissions works in more detail, read on and we will attempt to clarify it for you.

The rules that apply when combining user and group permissions are

▶ Deny overrides all other permissions.

▶ Update overrides Read-only.

This means that if the user is assigned Read-only permission but the group is assigned Update permission, the applied permission is Update. MDS makes the assumption that if there is an overlap, the least restrictive permission should win. For example, if Bob is covering for a coworker while that person is out, and you add Bob to the other group temporarily, Bob keeps his existing permissions but also gains those of his coworker.

Figure 11-3 shows the additional complexity that occurs when you have overlapping users and groups as part of the security workflow.

A Matter of Distance

Unfortunately, overlapping users and groups is slightly more complex than these simple rules and Figure 11-3 can show. The cascading inheritance in the tree also plays a part. If two or more objects have permissions assigned to them, the "Update beats Read" rule applies. However, if an object has a different permission assigned and it's closer than the permission from the other user or group, then the closer permission applies instead.

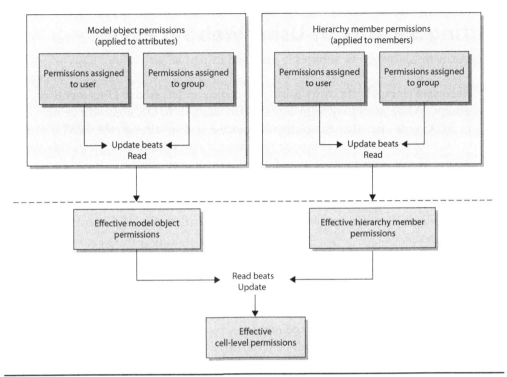

Figure 11-3   *The addition of overlapping users and groups to the security workflow*

For example, if a user has Read and a group has Update to the same model object, then Update is applied. However, if a user is assigned Update to an entity and a group is assigned Read-only to an attribute (a lower level than entity), then Update applies for the entity but the attribute is Read-only.

These same rules apply to the Hierarchy Members tab.

Thankfully, the UI does this calculation for you. On both the Models and Hierarchy Members tabs, click Effective in the Permissions list to display a user's effective permissions.

Overlapping Functional Areas

Users and groups can also have overlapping permissions to functional areas. Functional area permissions are additive: if a user has permission to Explorer and a group has permission to Version Management, then the user has permission for both areas.

Setting Security by Using Web Services

All security in Master Data Services is managed using two web service objects:

► **SecurityPrincipal** Security principals correspond to Active Directory users or groups. While users may be in a group that exists in MDS, users will be managed in MDS only after they have logged on to the system through the web UI or web service (or some custom component built on the web service). To explicitly set permission on a user who is a member of a group, you will need to add the user from Active Directory explicitly.

► **SecurityPrivilege** All distinct permissions within MDS are stored and managed as privileges. In most cases, only explicitly set permissions will be returned from the web service.

Retrieving Users and Groups

The GetSecurityPrincipals operation, shown next, returns all current users and groups that match the criteria passed into the request. Only users that have used MDS through either the web service or web UI will be returned, even if they are members of an Active Directory group with access to MDS.

NOTE

You must be a model administrator to perform this operation.

```
public OperationResult GetSecurityPrincipals()
{    //Create Request, Response, and Criteria Objects
    SecurityPrincipalsGetRequest Request =
    new SecurityPrincipalsGetRequest();
    SecurityPrincipalsGetResponse Response =
    new SecurityPrincipalsGetResponse();
    Request.Criteria = new SecurityPrincipalsCriteria();

    //Sets the type of principals to return either Group or User
    Request.Criteria.Type = PrincipalType.UserAccount;
    Request.Criteria.ResultType = ResultType.Details;
    Request.Criteria.All = true;
```

```
    //This sets the result type for each type of security
    //Three Options (Details, Identifiers, and None)
    Request.Criteria.FunctionPrivilege = ResultType.Details;
    Request.Criteria.ModelPrivilege = ResultType.Details;
    Request.Criteria.HierarchyMemberPrivilege = ResultType.Details;
    Response = mds_Proxy.SecurityPrincipalsGet(Request);
     OperationResult operationResult = Response.OperationResult;
    if (operationResult.Errors != null && operationResult.Errors.Count > 0)
        return null;
    return Response.Principals;
}
```

Retrieving User or Group Permissions

The GetSecurityPrivilege operation returns privileges matching the criteria provided.
These privileges will be related to the user or group that the permission is provided to.

```
public OperationResult GetSecurityPrivilege(
Identifier PrincipalID, PrincipalType PType)
{

    //Create Request, Response, and Criteria Objects
    SecurityPrivilegesGetRequest Request =
    new SecurityPrivilegesGetRequest();
    SecurityPrivilegesGetResponse Response =
    new SecurityPrivilegesGetResponse();
    Request.Criteria = new SecurityPrivilegesGetCriteria();

    //Set PrincipalID and Type passed into the procedure
    Request.Criteria.FunctionPrivilegesCriteria =
    new FunctionPrivilegesCriteria();
    Request.Criteria.FunctionPrivilegesCriteria.PrincipalId =
    PrincipalID;
    Request.Criteria.FunctionPrivilegesCriteria.PrincipalType =
    PType;
 Request.Criteria.FunctionPrivilegesCriteria.ResultType = ResultType.Details;
    Response = mds_Proxy.SecurityPrivilegesGet(Request);
    OperationResult operationResult = Response.OperationResult;
    if (operationResult.Errors != null && operationResult.Errors.Count > 0)
        return null;
    return Response.Privileges;
}
```

Adding Users and Groups

While the CreateSecurityPrincipals operation includes "Create" in its name, it is really used to load preexisting Active Directory users or groups into MDS. This operation will also be used to update some user-specific properties that are stored directly in MDS.

```
public OperationResult CreateSecurityPrincipals()
{
    SecurityPrincipalsRequest Request =
    new SecurityPrincipalsRequest();
    Request.Principals = new SecurityPrincipals();

    // Create some user objects
    Collection<User> users = new Collection<User>();

    // Add each new AD user to the user or group collection
    users.Add(new User());

    //Create new Identifier for each user
    users[0].Identifier = new Identifier();
    users[0].Identifier.Name = "JDoe";
    users[0].DisplayName = "John Doe";
    users[0].EmailAddress = "Jdoe@someurl.com";
    users[0].EmailFormat = EmailFormat.HTML;
    users[0].SID = Guid.NewGuid().ToString();
    //Replace this Guid with the security ID from AD

    // Add each new AD user to the user or group collection
    users.Add(new User());

    //Create new Identifier for each user
    users[1].Identifier = new Identifier();
    users[1].Identifier.Name = "PPiper";
    users[1].DisplayName = "Peter Piper";
    users[1].EmailAddress = "PPiper@someurl.com";
    users[1].EmailFormat = EmailFormat.Text;
    users[1].SID = Guid.NewGuid().ToString();
    //Replace this Guid with the security ID from AD
```

```
    //Add user collections to request object
    Request.Principals.Users = users;
    SecurityCreateResponse Response =
    mds_Proxy.SecurityPrincipalsCreate(Request);
    return Response.OperationResult;
}
```

Assigning Permissions

All types of security privileges for users and groups can be created simultaneously with the CreateSecurityPrivileges operation. Multiple users or groups can be secured within the same operation as well.

```
public OperationResult CreateSecurityPrivileges
(User user, MemberIdentifier hierParentMemberID)
{
    SecurityPrivilegesRequest request =
    new SecurityPrivilegesRequest();
    request.Privileges = new SecurityPrivileges();

    // Create a functional privilege
    FunctionPrivilege fp = new FunctionPrivilege();
    fp.Function = FunctionalArea.Explorer;
    fp.Identifier = new Identifier();

    //Functional privileges only support boolean authorization
    fp.IsAuthorized = true;

    //Set the PrincipalType and ID for the principal assigned the
    //privilege
    fp.PrincipalType = PrincipalType.UserAccount;
    fp.PrincipalId = user.Identifier;

    //Add the function privilege to the privilege collection
    Collection<FunctionPrivilege> FunctionPrivileges = new
    Collection<FunctionPrivilege>();
    FunctionPrivileges.Add(fp);
```

```
//Add collection to privilege request
request.Privileges.FunctionPrivileges = FunctionPrivileges;

//Create a model privilege
ModelPrivilege mp = new ModelPrivilege();

//Set the model permission object type,
//support any type of object in MDS
mp.ObjectType = ModelObjectType.Model;
mp.ModelId = new Identifier { Name = "Product" };
mp.ObjectId = mp.ModelId;

//Model permissions support Update, ReadOnly, Deny, and None
mp.Permission = Permission.Update;

//Set the PrincipalType and ID for the principal assigned the
//privilege
mp.PrincipalType = PrincipalType.UserAccount;
mp.PrincipalId = user.Identifier;

//Add the model privilege to the privilege collection
Collection<ModelPrivilege> ModelPrivileges = new
Collection<ModelPrivilege>();
ModelPrivileges.Add(mp);

//Add collection to privilege request
request.Privileges.ModelPrivileges = ModelPrivileges;

//Create a hierarchy member privilege
HierarchyMemberPrivilege hmp = new HierarchyMemberPrivilege();

//Set the HierarchyType and ID
hmp.HierarchyType = HierarchyType.Derived;
hmp.HierarchyId = new Identifier { Name = "Product"};

//Model permissions support Update, ReadOnly, Deny, and None
hmp.Permission = Permission.Update;
hmp.PrincipalId = user.Identifier;
hmp.PrincipalType = PrincipalType.UserAccount;
hmp.ModelId = new Identifier { Name = "Product" };
hmp.VersionId = new Identifier { Name = "Version_1" };
hmp.EntityId = new Identifier { Name = "Product" };
hmp.MemberId = hierParentMemberID;
```

```
//Set an identifier for the new permission
hmp.Identifier = new Identifier();

//Add hierarchy member privilege to the privilege collection
Collection<HierarchyMemberPrivilege> HierarchyMemberPrivileges =
new Collection<HierarchyMemberPrivilege>();
HierarchyMemberPrivileges.Add(hmp);

//Add collection to privilege request
request.Privileges.HierarchyMemberPrivileges =
HierarchyMemberPrivileges;
SecurityCreateResponse response =
mds_Proxy.SecurityPrivilegesCreate(request);
return response.OperationResult;
}
```

Summary

In this chapter, we explained the details of configuring security in MDS. We showed the process for assigning model object and hierarchy member security, and how the combination of the two determines cell-level security. We discussed model administrators and how to create and update them. We gave best practices for assigning security and talked about what happens when users belong to groups and security is assigned to both. Finally, we showed how to use the web service to view and assign permissions.

Chapter 12

Publishing Data to External Systems

In This Chapter

- ▶ Exporting Data to Subscribing Systems
- ▶ Subscription View Formats
- ▶ Common View Architecture
- ▶ Subscription Views and Model Deployment
- ▶ Creating a Subscription View with Web Services
- ▶ How Main Street Clothing Company Uses Subscription Views

Although the ability to manage data is an important feature of Master Data Services, the ability to export data to other systems in the enterprise is equally if not more important. MDS has simplified the export process by providing subscription views that you can create on any entity or derived hierarchy object within the MDS system.

In this chapter, we describe the different types of the export views that can be created and the format of each of these views. We discuss some tips and tricks for creating a proper view depending on the type of downstream system that will consume the data in MDS. We also provide an example of loading a downstream system from an export view we create. While Master Data Services provides no direct extract, transform, and load (ETL) features of any kind, the Integration Management functional area of the Master Data Manager web application (or "web UI") can facilitate your integration processes by providing a wide variety of views to assist in the loading of downstream systems.

Exporting Data to Subscribing Systems

Master Data Services can provide value for a project that keeps the data locked in its entities by providing process around the data management; however, to meet the operational or analytical needs of a master data management project, organizations need to transport stored data downstream to subscribing systems. To insulate organizations from the complex object model necessary to manage performance and the customization necessary within MDS, the developers created a subscription view layer.

You can create subscription views within the Integration Management functional area of the web UI, or by using the web service. The web service refers to these views as export views, but we'll use "subscription views" and "export views" interchangeably.

Subscription View Formats

The following table shows the available subscription view formats. When you create a subscription view, you have to choose which format you want to use. There are two major types of subscription views within MDS: attribute views and hierarchy views. Attribute views display the data stored for leaf, consolidated, or collection members in an easily consumable tabular view. Hierarchy views provide relationship data for all types of relationships in MDS, whether explicit or derived hierarchies or collection members. Collection member relationships can only be displayed in a parent-child format. An additional view is available for derived and explicit hierarchies. It contains a row for each member and the parentage all the way to the top consolidation in the hierarchy; this view is considered level-based.

View Format	Description of View
Leaf attributes	Shows leaf members and their associated attribute values
Consolidated attributes	Shows consolidated members and their associated attribute values
Collection attributes	Shows collection members and their associated attribute values
Collections	Shows collections and their members in a parent-child format
Explicit parent child	Shows explicit hierarchy structures for an entity in a parent-child format
Explicit levels	For the entity, shows all members in all explicit hierarchies in a level-based format
Derived parent child	Shows all derived hierarchy members in a parent-child format
Derived levels	Shows all derived hierarchy members in a level-based format

Common View Architecture

Many of the columns in Master Data Services' subscription views are identical across view types. The columns provide either context for the data displayed in the view or additional system information for the records contained in the view. Subscribing systems can use this information to update a subset of records based on validation status or last updated statistics.

Column	Description
VersionName	The version name for the current version being displayed. If this is a view based on the version name, this value will never change.
VersionNumber	The version number for the current version being displayed. If this is a view built on the version name, this value will never change.
VersionFlag	The current version flag for the displayed version. If a view is based on a version flag, then this column will remain constant and the VersionName and VersionNumber column values will change as the version flag is moved between versions.
EnterDateTime	The date and time the member was first entered into MDS.
EnterUserName	The user who initially entered the member into MDS.
EnterVersionNumber	The initial version this member was created in.
LastChgUserName	The user who last updated this member in MDS.
LastChgVersionNumber	The number of the version this member was last changed in.
ValidationStatus	The current validation status for the member. Validation status is discussed further in Chapter 9. Validation status only exists for leaf, consolidated, and collection attribute views, because there is no validation stored for relationship members.

Procedure: How to Create a Subscription View

To create a subscription view in Master Data Manager, complete the following steps:

1. On the Master Data Management home page, click Integration Management.
2. On the menu bar, click Create Views.
3. On the Subscription Views page, click the "Add subscription view" button.

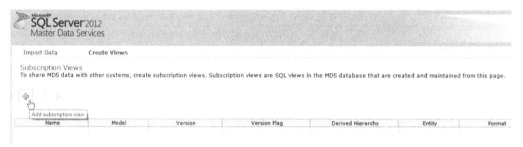

4. In the Create Subscription View pane that is displayed at the bottom of the page, enter a name for the view and select a model from the Model list. In this example, select Product and call the view **ProductsForPOS**.

   This UI can be a bit confusing. There are three columns here and the radio buttons apply to the two options shown in each column.

| In this column, choose a version or flag. | In this column, decide if you want your view to display the contents of an entity, the contents of a hierarchy, or the structure of a hierarchy. | In this column, choose a format for the view. If showing a hierarchy, choose the number of levels. |

5. In the first column of choices, select either Version or Version flag and then select from the corresponding list. As a best practice, you should create a subscription view based on a version flag. Then, as you create new versions, you can move the flag to the latest version and you don't have to update your subscription view. If you created a version flag in Chapter 9, you can select it here. Otherwise, select the version that contains the data you want to export.

6. In the next column of choices, select either Entity or Derived hierarchy and then select from the corresponding list. Your subscription view can show the contents of an entity or the structure of a hierarchy. For this example, select Entity and choose the Product entity from this list.

7. In the third column of choices, from the Format list, select Leaf attributes. This determines the format of your view. If you were creating a view of a hierarchy, you would be prompted to select a format for the view and to choose the number of levels you want to show.

8. Click Save.

The subscription view is now displayed in the top pane of the Subscription Views page. If you decide you want to change it, click the row and then the Edit button. You can also delete it if it's no longer necessary.

Scroll to the far right to view the Changed column. This column is important to note. If objects in the model structure change, this column changes to True. At that point, you need to edit the subscription view and save it again (you don't need to make changes to it; just edit and then save). This ensures that the view will still return accurate results based on the latest changes to the model.

Viewing a Subscription View in SQL Server

Now you can open SQL Server Management Studio and take a look at the view. As shown in Figure 12-1, all of the members and their attributes are shown in a format that is easy for subscribing systems to consume.

Figure 12-1   *Opening a subscription view in SQL Server Management Studio*

For each domain-based attribute that is displayed in a subscription view, three columns are displayed. The "_Code" and "_Name" columns display the name and code. The "_ID" column displays the system key for the member. This is an internal key and should not be used in subscribing systems.

Subscription Views and Model Deployment

In the SQL Server 2008 R2 release of MDS, a shortcoming of model deployment was its lack of support for subscription views. If you create subscription views for an entity or derived hierarchy, these views will not be re-created when moving model deployment packages between development, test, and production servers. Subscription views are now supported in model deployment with SQL Server 2012.

Creating a Subscription View with Web Services

All subscription views in MDS are created using the ExportViewCreate operation. Depending on the type of view being created and whether you create the view based on version or version flag, different parameters are required.

Creating Entity Views

This operation creates an entity-centric subscription view for a specified model and entity. This operation can support explicit hierarchy leveling and either method of version management.

```
//Create any type of subscription view
public OperationResult EntityExportViewCreation(string ModelName,
     string EntityName, string ViewName, ExportViewFormat ViewFormat,
     VersionFlag Flag, string VersionName, int NumofLevels)
{

    //Initialize the new request object
    ExportViewCreateRequest request = new ExportViewCreateRequest();
    request.ExportView = new ExportView();

    //Set Model, Entity, and view name
    request.ExportView.ModelId = new Identifier { Name = ModelName };
    request.ExportView.EntityId = new Identifier { Name = EntityName };
    request.ExportView.Identifier = new Identifier { Name = ViewName };

    //If VersionID is 0, then use the flag identifier
    if (VersionName == null)
        request.ExportView.VersionFlagId = Flag.Identifier;
```

```
else
    request.ExportView.VersionId = new Identifier {
    Name = VersionName };

request.ExportView.ViewFormat = ViewFormat;

//if ExportViewFormat supports levels you can restrict
//the number of displayed levels
if (ViewFormat == ExportViewFormat.ExplicitLevels &&
NumofLevels > 0)
    request.ExportView.Levels = NumofLevels;
ExportViewCreateResponse response =
mds_Proxy.ExportViewCreate(request);
return response.OperationResult;
}
```

Creating Derived Hierarchy Views

This operation encapsulates the creation of derived hierarchy subscription views. Because the level setting is only valid when the chosen format is "derived levels," this parameter is ignored for other view types.

```
//Create any type of derived hierarchy subscription view
    public OperationResult DerivedHierarchyViewCreation(
    string ModelName, string DerivedHierarchyName, string ViewName,
    ExportViewFormat ViewFormat, VersionFlag Flag, string VersionName,
    int NumofLevels)
    {
        ExportViewCreateRequest request = new ExportViewCreateRequest();
        request.ExportView = new ExportView();

        //Set model, derived hierarchy, and view name

        request.ExportView.ModelId = new Identifier { Name = ModelName };
        request.ExportView.DerivedHierarchyId = new Identifier {
        Name = DerivedHierarchyName };
        request.ExportView.Identifier = new Identifier { Name = ViewName };

        //if  VersionName is null then use the flag identifier
        if (VersionName == null)
            request.ExportView.VersionFlagId = Flag.Identifier;
        else
            request.ExportView.VersionId = new Identifier {
            Name = VersionName };
```

```
request.ExportView.ViewFormat = ViewFormat;

if (ViewFormat == ExportViewFormat.DerivedLevels && NumofLevels > 0)
    request.ExportView.Levels = NumofLevels;
ExportViewCreateResponse response =
mds_Proxy.ExportViewCreate(request);
return response.OperationResult;
}
```

Deleting Views

The following code deletes a subscription view from Master Data Services no matter what the format of the subscription view. No data within the entity related to the export view will be changed in any way by this process. This call returns an operation result that will contain any errors that occurred in the deletion process, although these will be rare in this simple process.

```
//Delete a subscription view by name
 public OperationResult ExportViewDelete(string ViewName)
 {
ExportViewListGetRequest getViewsRequest = new ExportViewListGetRequest();
        ExportViewListGetResponse getViewsResponse = mdsProxy.ExportViewList
Get(getViewsRequest);
        ExportView view = getViewsResponse.ExportViews.Where((v) =>
v.Identifier.Name == ViewName).FirstOrDefault();
        if (view == null)
            return null;

        ExportViewDeleteRequest request = new
        ExportViewDeleteRequest();
        request.Identifier = view.Identifier;
        ExportViewDeleteResponse response =
        mds_Proxy.ExportViewDelete(request);
        return response.OperationResult;
 }
```

How Main Street Clothing Company Uses Subscription Views

With all of the processes around maintaining location, product, employee, and account data now in place, Anthony must build the integration plan for passing and synchronizing data from MDS into all downstream systems.

The first step in building this plan is to determine the accuracy and accountability required for each subscribing system. Some systems require data that has been validated and version information that has been rigorously tracked. Other systems need data that is more recent and may still contain minor errors. MDS can provide this data for either purpose based on the type of version that is consumed. Version flags, as discussed in Chapter 9, also support this important distinction.

For each downstream system, Anthony must decide what type of subscription view provides the best format for consumption. Does this system require consolidation information? Does this system need attributes related to consolidated members? Anthony determines the best subscription view for each downstream system. As you can see from the following table, systems vary widely on the quality level required.

System	Data Needed	Quality Level
Online Retail System	Product (pricing and stock levels), Customer (contact information, orders)	Highly accurate (valid and committed)
Point of Sales Systems	Product (pricing)	Highly accurate (valid and committed)
Warehouse Management System	Product (stock levels), Suppliers (contact information)	Valid
Data Warehouse (Test)	All domains	Latest data
Data Warehouse (Production)	All domains	Highly accurate (valid and committed)
Finance	Products and Accounts	Approved, committed not required

The point of sale (POS) systems in each of the stores must be updated nightly with the latest product lists and prices. Anthony decides the best way to do this is to use the data presented in his subscription views to export the data he needs. He uses SQL Server Integration Services to create a package that runs on a nightly schedule. Each morning when the managers come to work, their POS systems are already updated with the latest product information.

Procedure: How to Export Subscription View Data

To export data from a Master Data Services subscription view to another data source, complete the following steps:

NOTE

This procedure is just one example of how to get data out of MDS and into a subscribing system. Your process may differ.

1. Open SQL Server Management Studio.
2. Right-click the MDS database.
3. From the submenu, select Tasks | Export Data.
4. On the Welcome page, click Next.
5. On the Choose a Data Source page, leave the defaults (it should be pointing to your MDS database) and click Next.
6. On the Choose a Destination page, in the Destination field, select Flat File Destination.
7. Browse to a text file name, select the "Column names in the first data row" check box, and click Next.

8. On the Specify Table Copy or Query page, select the "Copy data from one or more tables or views" radio button and click Next.

9. On the Configure Flat File Destination page, in the "Source table or view" list, select the view. In our case, it's the view: [mdm].[ProductsForPOS].

10. Click the Edit Mappings button. In the Column Mappings dialog box, ignore all of the Destination columns except: Name, Code, Retail Price, Discontinued_ Code, Type_Code, Gender_Code, and Manufacturer.

11. Click OK to close the dialog box. Then click Next.

12. On the Save and Run Package page, leave the Run immediately check box selected and select the Save SSIS Package check box.

13. Click Next.

14. On the Save SSIS Package page, type a name and description for your package, leave all other defaults, and click Next.

15. On the Complete the Wizard page, click Finish.

The SSIS package is saved and Main Street Clothing Company can schedule the package to run nightly. When the package runs, the contents of the view are saved as a flat file to a file share. A separate batch system transfers the file to each of the 14 stores. The POS systems retrieve the data from the file, and each morning when the stores open, the POS systems have the latest prices and information.

Summary

Consuming data from the Master Data Services system requires analysis of the subscribing system's needs. These needs should be evaluated against the supported export formats. Subscription views provide a number of columns that can help filter and manage ETL processes into subscribing systems at an individual record level. Model deployment does not deploy subscription views from packages. If an organization has a lot of subscription views, it can programmatically manage these views through the MDS web service.

Chapter 13

Extending MDS
with Web Services

In This Chapter

- ▶ Exposing the Web Service
- ▶ Exposing the WSDL
- ▶ Creating an MDS Project in Visual Studio
- ▶ Creating an Abstraction Layer
- ▶ MDS Web Service Operations
- ▶ The Most Frequently Used Operations
- ▶ Handling Errors in the Web Service

I n this chapter, we explore in more depth the web services layer provided by Master Data Services. Every operation in MDS is exposed within the web service. Despite the large number of operations, any developer can be productive working against the web service by focusing on a few high-value operations. These operations can be used to create a customized UI tailored to your solution or to integrate existing applications with MDS.

In SQL Server 2012, most of the changes are beneath the interfaces. A number of the processes in the web service have been deprecated, while most of the new calls have been marked as private, meaning Microsoft will not support external use of the call. In this chapter, we will give you an overview of the new calls and let you know which ones might be worth taking the support risk for.

Exposing the Web Service

In the 2008 R2 release, for security purposes, MDS did not publicly implement the web service when you first installed MDS. In SQL Server 2012, the web service is always exposed because Silverlight is used for the Explorer screen. If you are using MDS with prebuilt applications, then everything you need is already done. If you are going to build your own solutions or use the samples listed in this book, then you must also expose the Web Services Description Language (WSDL) in order to compile against the service interface.

Exposing the WSDL

To expose the WSDL, you must modify the web.config file directly. This file is in the WebApplication directory where MDS is installed. If you installed MDS in the default location, the full path is C:\Program Files\Microsoft SQL Server\Master Data Services\WebApplication\web.config.

Procedure: How to Enable the WSDL

Open the web.config file with either Notepad or Visual Studio 2010. Find the following section:

```
<serviceMetadata httpGetEnabled="false" httpsGetEnabled="false"/>
<!-- Enable to allow clients to see service exception details -->
<serviceDebug includeExceptionDetailInFaults="false"/>
```

Change the setting for httpGetEnabled and includeExceptionDetailInFaults to **true**. Then save the file. This enables the web service to expose the WSDL. If you have configured SSL, as described in Chapter 2, change httpsGetEnabled to **true**.

If you receive an "Access is denied" error when you save, check the security on the file. When you install MDS, permissions are set on this file so that only the users in the local Administrators group have full control.

You may also have User Account Control (UAC) running. You can disable UAC temporarily; unfortunately, you will have to restart your computer when you do this. To disable UAC, open Control Panel and click "System and Security." Under Action Center, click "Change User Account Control settings." In the User Account Control Settings dialog box, slide the bar to the bottom so that you are never notified. Click OK to save. In the confirmation dialog box, click Yes. Restart your computer, and you should be able to edit the web.config file.

Creating an MDS Project in Visual Studio

Now that the web service is exposed, you can create your first project in Visual Studio. All of the code examples in this book use Visual Studio 2010.

Procedure: How to Create an MDS Web Service Application

To create an application that uses the MDS web service, you must first create a project and then add the web service as a reference in the project. Depending on your needs, you can create any type of application you choose. In this book, we've created wrapper classes that can be used in any type of application.

Create a Project

To create a project in Visual Studio, complete the following steps:

1. Open Microsoft Visual Studio.
2. Click File | New | Project.
3. In the New Project dialog box, in the Project types section, under Visual C#, click Windows.
4. In the Templates section, choose the application type. In this example, we chose Class Library.
5. In the Name box, type a name for your application.

6. Click OK.

Add a Service Reference

To add a service reference to the project, complete the following steps:

1. In Visual Studio, with your project open, click View | Solution Explorer.
2. In the Solution Explorer pane, right-click References and click "Add Service Reference."

3. The Add Service Reference dialog box is displayed. In the Address box, type the URL for the MDS service. This is usually your URL followed by "/service/service .svc." For example:

   http://mdsserver/mds/service/service.svc

4. Click Go. The service is displayed in the Services section.

5. In the Namespace box, type a name for the service namespace. This can be anything you want.

6. Click OK.

Creating an Abstraction Layer

The MDS web service is built on Windows Communication Foundation (WCF). Many of the initial calls may seem daunting or overly complicated if you are a first-time user. The web service operations may seem complicated because they must be generic in order to port all the model types and data schemas created in disparate implementations. The operations have been built to support all possible configurations and uses of the application.

Most people, however, are interested in only a small subset of configurations and a small subset of the application features exposed to the web service. As you are getting used to the MDS web service, there are a few tips and practices that can help you more quickly integrate your organization with MDS. One of these is to create an abstraction layer.

An abstraction layer can do a number of things:

▶ Provide other developers with only those calls that you wish them to program against

▶ Ensure that everyone uses a similar standard when writing code against the web service

▶ Enable you to provide complex calls in a far more consumable fashion

MDS Web Service Operations

While more than 50 operations are supported by the MDS web service, most people need to focus on only a few of those operations to handle the majority of their routines. MDS operations can be grouped by the MDS objects they control. These groupings are listed in order of importance in the following sections.

Members

Retrieving and updating master data is by far the most frequent procedure you will want to automate. Many of these calls were optimized in SQL Server 2012 to support the MDS Add-in for Microsoft Excel. The EntityMembersUpdate and EntityMembersMerge calls can now support large datasets. When using these calls, the MDS team found that breaking extremely large sets into sets of 50,000 attribute updates is most effective on average systems. All of the operations for working with members are listed in the following table. For examples of these operations, see Chapter 7 and Chapter 11.

Operation	Description
EntityMemberAttributesGet	Retrieves a specified set of attribute values from a specified list of members. This call must be used to return the File attribute type; files cannot be returned in an EntityMembersGet response.
EntityMembersCopy	Copies selected members and their attribute values to new target members.
EntityMembersCreate	Used to create new members only. Existing members are not updated.
EntityMembersDelete	Soft deletes selected members in a specified version.
EntityMembersGet	Retrieves a set of members and their attribute values from an entity. These results can be filtered by search terms.
EntityMembersMerge	Creates new members and updates existing members. We recommend using this operation when managing most members programmatically.
EntityMembersUpdate	Updates existing members. New members are not created.
HierarchyMembersGet	Retrieves parent-child members from a hierarchy relative to a parent node. To filter results, this operation allows the use of a more advanced hierarchy location as well as search terms.

Bulk Operations

Although many of these operations are called ModelMembers, that is a misnomer. The major distinction for these operations is that they leverage staging to bulk load records into MDS. In SQL Server 2012 these operations have been marked for deprecation. When loading more than a few thousand values (members times attributes), you can now use the EntityMembersMerge and EntityMembersUpdate. For examples of staging operations, see Chapter 5.

Operation	Description
ModelMembersBulkDelete	Uses staging to bulk delete members from MDS.
ModelMembersBulkMerge	Uses staging to asynchronously create and/or update member data across one or more entities.
ModelMembersBulkUpdate	Uses staging to asynchronously update member data across one or more entities.
ModelMembersGet	Retrieves entire models, entities, and/or hierarchies. This can be used for bulk data output.
StagingClear	Clears batches from the three staging tables. This is an artifact of the original staging.
StagingGet	Retrieves the contents of the three staging tables. This is an artifact of the original staging.
StagingProcess	Sweeps existing unbatched records in the staging tables into a batch and triggers the batch to process.

Validation

In this release of MDS, a large portion of the data quality proposition is working with validation results from business rules created in the application. While there are a number of operations necessary to create business rules, only two operations manage the results of these rules. Examples of these operations are provided in the section "The Most Frequently Used Operations," later in this chapter.

Operation	Description
ValidationGet	Retrieves filtered validation results and summary information from a model in MDS.
ValidationProcess	Can trigger validation processes (applying business rules) for selected members within a model.

Transactions

All data changes made through the web service or the web application UI are saved in the transaction table. Since the Add-in for Excel is built on the MDS web service, these transactions will also show in the transaction table. These transactions can be retrieved or reversed by using the following operations. Examples of these operations are also provided in the section "The Most Frequently Used Operations."

Operation	Description
TransactionsGet	Retrieves a filtered list of transactions from a model.
TransactionsReverse	Reverses one or more existing transactions by transaction ID.

Annotations

Either members or transactions on those members can be given further explanation through annotations. Annotations are useful in providing further detail in workflow processes.

Operation	Description
AnnotationsDelete	Deletes an existing annotation by ID.
AnnotationsUpdate	Updates an existing annotation by ID.
EntityMemberAnnotationsCreate	Creates new annotations attached to a member record.
EntityMemberAnnotationsGet	Retrieves annotations that are attached to a member.
TransactionAnnotationsCreate	Creates new annotations that are attached to an existing transaction made within MDS.
TransactionAnnotationsGet	Retrieves a filtered list of transactions from a model based on transaction ID.

Subscription Views

External access to MDS managed data is enabled through views that are based on versions and view type. The following export operations manage these views. For examples of some of these operations, see Chapter 12.

Operation	Description
ExportViewCreate	Generates or regenerates provided export views.
ExportViewDelete	Removes an existing export view by ID.
ExportViewListGet	Retrieves a list of existing export views and their IDs.
ExportViewUpdate	Updates existing export view settings and regenerates the view.

Metadata Structures

Because MDS contains descriptive metadata, the naming convention for the following operations is confusing. These operations will create any of the model objects supported by MDS. For examples of some of these operations, see Chapter 4.

Operation	Description
MetadataClone	Creates an exact copy of metadata components from another MDS source, retaining the GUIDs of the original objects.
MetadataCreate	Creates new objects in MDS (attributes, attribute groups, entities, collections, hierarchies, and models).
MetadataDelete	Deletes metadata objects passed in the request object.

Security

While MDS security relies on Active Directory, MDS authorization requires that users be added as principals either by their username or an Active Directory group they are a member of. Users and groups must be assigned both functional and member privileges to have access to MDS. For examples of some of these operations, see Chapter 11.

Operation	Description
SecurityPrincipalsClone	Replicates users, groups, permissions, and their GUIDS within the security model from another external source.
SecurityPrincipalsCreate	Adds Active Directory users and groups to the MDS security model.
SecurityPrincipalsDelete	Deletes user and group associations from MDS.
SecurityPrincipalsGet	Retrieves the security principals associated with MDS.

Operation	Description
SecurityPrivilegesClone	Replicates permissions and their GUIDS within the security model from another external source.
SecurityPrivilegesDelete	Deletes permissions from MDS.
SecurityPrivilegesGet	Retrieves functional, model, and hierarchy member security permissions for selected principals and/or models.

Business Rules

The management of business rules in MDS is best left to the Master Data Manager web UI. The following operations are complex in their object model and not well documented. For examples of some of these operations, see Chapter 8.

Operation	Description
BusinessRulesClone	Re-creates new business rules that are exact copies of business rules from another MDS source, while retaining the GUIDs of the original objects.
BusinessRulesCreate	Creates new business rules with both conditions (optional) and actions.
BusinessRulesDelete	Deletes a business rule or the components of rules.
BusinessRulesGet	Retrieves business rules for specific context provided in the request.
BusinessRulesPaletteGet	Retrieves available business rule components with which to build business rules (the component palette).
BusinessRulesPublish	Publishes business rules for a model type, entity type, or member type.
BusinessRulesUpdate	Updates preexisting business rules by identifier.

System Settings

There are a number of system-wide settings that allow system administrators to customize their MDS implementation. These settings are stored in tblSystemSetting and managed in MDS Configuration Manager.

Operation	Description
SystemDomainListGet	Returns a localized fixed list of choices based on a list code.
SystemPropertiesGet	Retrieves immutable properties about the system.
SystemSettingsGet	Retrieves a list of MDS system settings.
SystemSettingsUpdate	Updates system setting values.

User Preferences

These user preference calls support the MDS web application and have limited value for external systems. Leveraging these calls in your own custom UI work is not suggested.

Operation	Description
UserPreferencesDelete	Deletes the current user's preferences for the MDS web UI.
UserPreferencesGet	Retrieves the current user's preferences for the MDS web UI.
UserPreferencesUpdate	Updates the current user's preferences for the MDS web UI.

Miscellaneous Operations

The remaining operations are not easily grouped into categories.

Operation	Description
EntityMemberKeyLookup	Retrieves either a member code or an internal ID based on the other member code or internal ID and the provided context.
ServiceCheck	Checks the availability of the web service.
VersionCopy	Creates a copy of the data within the model version.

Entity-Based Staging Operations

These operations were added in SQL Server 2012 to allow the MDS web UI to manage the new entity-based staging process. These operations are marked as internal only. Microsoft will not support custom code that calls these APIs. The thinking is that users will use the new SQL stored procedures and SSIS to move data into the tables. Please refer to Chapter 5 for more information on entity-based staging.

Operation	Description
EntityStagingClear	Clears the members associated with the batch provided in the request. There is some risk in using this API to remove batch data.
EntityStagingGet	Returns information on the batches currently in the MDS system. There is very little risk in using this API if a business system requires this information.
EntityStagingLoad	Loads relationship and member data into the entity-based staging tables. There is no real benefit in using this API over loading data with an SSIS package. An error occurs when loading data into an entity that is not hierarchy enabled.
EntityStagingProcess	Triggers the staging process for the given batch and version information. Users should use the stored procedure to trigger the same process.

Data Quality Operations

In SQL Server 2012, Microsoft shipped Data Quality Services. While DQS ships with SSIS plug-ins, it does not have an exposed API. To integrate DQS into the MDS Add-in for Excel, the Master Data Services team created these API calls linked to the DQS server. All of these calls are marked as internal only, so Microsoft does not support any use of these APIs. They are included here for the adventurous…

Operation	Description
DataQualityCleansingOperationCreate	Creates an operation request for the DQS cleansing operation. This functionality is not currently implemented in the MDS Add-in for Excel.
DataQualtityInstalledState	Returns a positive result if DQS is correctly installed and configured to work with MDS.
DataQualityKnowledgeBasesGet	KnowledgeBases in DQS store the Cleansing and Matching patterns that have been previously developed. These KnowledgeBases include defined attributes provided to the Add-in for Excel to map against existing columns from MDS.
DataQualityMatchingOperationsCreate	Triggers matching operation in DQS. Can use a pre-existing KnowledgeBase or the default KnowledgeBase.
DataQualityOperationPurgeOperation	Removes the results of a previously run DQS operation.
DataQualityOperationResultsGet	Returns matching results from DQS process.
DataQualityOperationStart	Triggers the DQS operation to begin.
DataQualityOperationStatus	Returns the status of a DQS operation. DQS operations can run for a significant amount of time.
DataQualityStoreInputData	Sets the Data Quality Store data for a DQS operation.

The Most Frequently Used Operations

The examples in this section show you how to build an abstraction layer for the most frequently used operations that are needed to integrate with MDS. We highly recommend that when you build applications against MDS, you focus on the operations provided in this section.

The operations that we do not address tend to be more complex and less useful to everyday consumers. For instance, triggering validation programmatically may be very useful for end users. Business rules, on the other hand, are complex to build in a user interface and difficult to manipulate programmatically. Because of this, creating business rules outside of the MDS application holds less value. Security is another area where most of you will not need to build additional UIs. Ignoring these two areas can greatly reduce the time to implement a customized solution.

Searching for Members

To return data from an MDS entity, you must provide a valid identifier for the model, version, and entity. To further limit and refine the results that are returned from an EntityMembersGet operation, you can provide search terms.

All filter types that are available in Explorer when you're viewing members in the Master Data Manager web UI are supported by the search term parameter in the EntityMembersGet operation. The following table lists all of the filter operators, the corresponding search term syntax, and an example of each. In the Search Term Syntax column of the following table:

▶   A stands for attribute.

▶   V stands for generic value.

▶   S stands for similarity.

▶   T stands for match type.

▶   C stands for containment bias.

Most of the examples in this table come from the Product entity in the Main Street Clothing Company example.

UI Operator	Search Term Syntax	Example
Is equal to	A = V	[Code] = '1005'
Is not equal to	A <> V	[Color] <> 'RED'
Is like	A LIKE V	[Name] LIKE 'M Red Shirt*'
Is not like	A NOT LIKE V	[Name] NOT LIKE 'M Red*'
Is greater than	A > V	[Size] > 5
Is less than	A < V	[Size] < 3
Is greater than or equal to	A >= V	[Cost] >= 2
Is less than or equal to	A <= V	[Price] <= 10
Matches	A MATCH V S T C	Examples are provided in the section "Using Matching in Search Terms" later in this chapter.
Does not match	A NOT MATCH V S T C	See "Using Matching in Search Terms."
Contains pattern	A REGEX V	[Email] REGEX '@MSTClothing.com'
Does not contain pattern	A NOT REGEX V	Email NOT REGEX '@MSTClothing.com'
Is NULL	A IS NULL	[Color] IS NULL
Is not NULL	A IS NOT NULL	[Name] IS NOT NULL

Getting Members by Using the SearchTerm Property

The following code provides an EntityMembersGet example that uses the SearchTerm property. In subsequent examples, we show only the highlighted SearchTerm portion.

```
public EntityMembers GetEntityMembers(string modelName,
string entityName, string versionName)
{
    EntityMembersGetRequest Request = new EntityMembersGetRequest();
    EntityMembersGetResponse Response = new EntityMembersGetResponse();
    Request.MembersGetCriteria = new EntityMembersGetCriteria();

    //Set the MembersGetCriteria identifiers
    Request.MembersGetCriteria.ModelId = new Identifier { Name = modelName };
    Request.MembersGetCriteria.EntityId = new Identifier
        { Name = entityName };
    Request.MembersGetCriteria.VersionId = new Identifier
        { Name = versionName };

    //This is the single search term string for the request
    //Combine terms here
    Request.MembersGetCriteria.SearchTerm =
        "[Name] = 'M Red Shirt 5 V Neck'";

    //Select the member return option. This determines whether
    //EntityMemberInformation, EntityMembers, or both are populated
    Request.MembersGetCriteria.MemberReturnOption =
    MemberReturnOption.Data;
    Response = mds_Proxy.EntityMembersGet(Request);
    EntityMembersInformation tEMI = Response.EntityMembersInformation;
    return Response.EntityMembers;
}
```

Combining Multiple Search Terms

Multiple search terms can be combined with the use of the AND operator between each search criteria term, as shown next. Like the UI, search terms in MDS do not support complex conditions like OR or grouping.

```
    Request.MembersGetCriteria.SearchTerm =
        "[Color] = 'Red' AND [Size] = 5";
```

Using Matching in Search Terms

In the Explorer functional area of the Master Data Manager web UI, you can use the Similarity operator to find matches similar to your search terms. However, you can use the MDS web service to create a much more robust process.

The following table shows the four types of similarity matches you can do programmatically. In each of these cases, 1 indicates an exact match and 0 indicates no match.

ID	Match Type	Description
0	Levenshtein	The Levenshtein distance is based on the number of edits (for example, adds or deletions) that it takes for one string to match another. This is the default match for MDS.
1	Jaccard	The Jaccard index works best when trying to match multiple strings.
2	Jaro-Winkler	The Jaro-Winkler distance is best used for finding duplicate person names.
3	Longest common subsequence	A *subsequence* is when the letters in a pattern appear in order, although they can be separated. For example, MDS is a subsequence of MaDneSs.

Levenshtein Search Term Example   The Levenshtein distance is the default type of match and does not require any additional parameters. Only Minimum Similarity and Type are supported.

```
Request.MembersGetCriteria.SearchTerm =
   [Name] MATCH 'M Red Shirt 5 V Neck' 0.8 0";
```

Jaccard Search Term Example   The Jaccard search supports an additional parameter of containment bias.

```
Request.MembersGetCriteria.SearchTerm =
   " M Red Shirt 5 V Neck' 0.8 1 0.32";
```

Jaro-Winkler Search Term Example   The Jaro-Winkler match results are the least restrictive with our sample data. This method returns more results than any other method. The Jaro-Winkler type does not support containment bias.

```
Request.MembersGetCriteria.SearchTerm =
   " [Name] MATCH 'M Red Shirt 5 V Neck' 0.8 2";
```

Longest Common Subsequence Search Term Example   Longest common subsequence does support an extra parameter of length threshold. This is provided in a decimal percentage between 0 and 1. The default is .62, and a lower threshold will increase the number of possible matches returned.

```
Request.MembersGetCriteria.SearchTerm =
    " [Name] MATCH 'M Red Shirt 5 V Neck' 0.8 3 .35";
```

Understanding the EntityMembers Object

The EntityMember class centers on a collection of members. If retrieving EntityMembers using the EntityMembersGet operation, a number of additional objects will be populated depending on the type of criteria supplied. This same EntityMembers class needs to be created and populated by the call when creating new members in MDS.

Figure 13-1 shows the EntityMembers class object and all possible members. In these class diagrams, the type of relationship between classes is denoted by 0, 1, and *. If a 1 is stated, the object is required or always provided. 0 means the class is optional, and * means multiple items can be added to the class collection.

Summarizing Member Data

When you use the web service to select data by using the EntityMembers object, you do not get summary data that is useful for pagination or for otherwise showing record counts. To get this type of information, you can use the EntityMemberInformation object. This object contains the following attributes:

- ▶ **MemberCount**   The member count of the records returned in the current request. This will be based on the paging information provided.

- ▶ **PageNumber**   The current page number returned in this request.

- ▶ **TotalMemberCount**   The total member count for the current request. The MembersGetCriteria must remain constant for this total member count to stay consistent.

- ▶ **TotalPages**   The total number of pages for the current request. The MembersGetCriteria must remain constant for this page count to stay consistent.

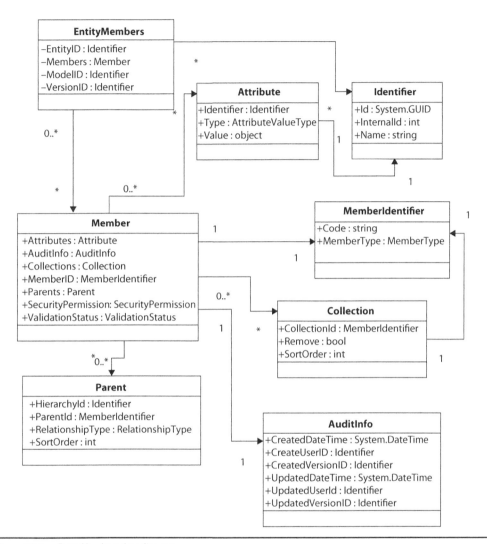

Figure 13-1 *EntityMembers class diagram*

Working with Metadata

All of the objects within MDS are created using the same operation: MetadataCreate. This operation creates models, entities, attributes, attribute groups, collections, and hierarchies. Throughout the book, there are examples of how to create these metadata objects.

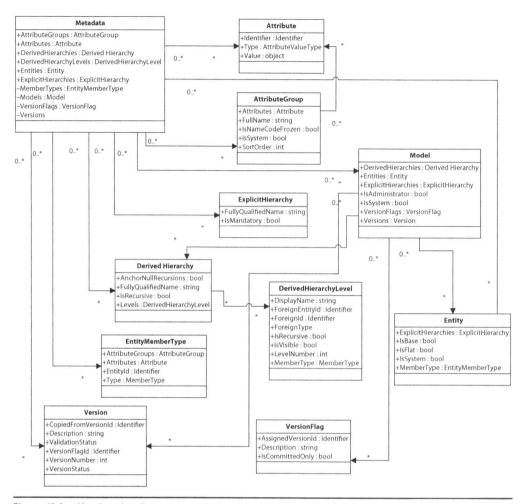

Figure 13-2   *Metadata class diagram*

As discussed in earlier chapters, MetadataCreate and MetadataClone are overloaded operations that allow you to create models, entities, and attributes within the MDS system. To create or return these objects, you must navigate the Metadata class and its child classes. Figure 13-2 shows a map of the Metadata class.

Validating Records in MDS

As an organization begins to interact programmatically with MDS, it may become necessary to trigger validation on specific members or an entire entity. Once validation has completed, users may need to retrieve validation issues that have been discovered.

We have not had a chance to discuss these web service operations earlier in the book, so we'll provide some examples here.

ValidationGet operations can be tricky because they seem to support a wide variety of parameters, but only a few combinations will return results. These combinations seem to align with the UI controls for validation issues. Four validation examples are explained next.

ValidationGetByVersion Example

This operation gets all validation issues for a model and version combination. This would be used as part of the commitment process for a version.

```
public Collection<ValidationIssue> ValidationGetByVersion(string
ModelName, string VersionName)
{
    ValidationGetRequest Request = new ValidationGetRequest();
    ValidationGetResponse Response = new ValidationGetResponse();

    //Instantiate the ValidationSearchCriteria and add the
    //identifiers for Model and Version
    Request.ValidationSearchCriteria = new ValidationSearchCriteria();
    Request.ValidationSearchCriteria.ModelId =
      new Identifier { Name = ModelName };
    Request.ValidationSearchCriteria.VersionId =
      new Identifier { Name = VersionName };
    Response = mds_Proxy.ValidationGet(Request);

    //Return the collection of current validation issues
    return Response.ValidationIssueList;
}
```

ValidationGetByUser Example

This operation returns the results that correspond to notifications that were sent to a user.

```
public Collection<ValidationIssue> ValidationGetByUser(string ModelName,
string VersionName,string EntityName, int UserId)
{
    ValidationGetRequest Request = new ValidationGetRequest();
    ValidationGetResponse Response = new ValidationGetResponse();

    //Instantiate the ValidationSearchCriteria and add the internal
    // UserId who is a member of the notification group for the issues
```

```
    Request.ValidationSearchCriteria = new ValidationSearchCriteria();
    Request.ValidationSearchCriteria.ModelId =
      new Identifier { Name = ModelName };
    Request.ValidationSearchCriteria.VersionId =
     new Identifier { Name = VersionName };
    Request.ValidationSearchCriteria.UserId =
     new Identifier { InternalId = UserId };
    Response = mds_Proxy.ValidationGet(Request);

    //Return the list of current validation issues for the specified user.
    return Response.ValidationIssueList;
}
```

You have two good options to get a valid user_id. You can find your correct user_id from the securityprincipleget web service call. If the application does not care about the user initiating the action and you want to ensure you get the most access, code using user_id = 1.

ValidationGetByMember Example

This operation returns results related to a member or set of members. In this example we pass in a single member.

```
public Collection<ValidationIssue> ValidationGetByMember(
string ModelName, string VersionName, string EntityName, string MemCode)
{
    ValidationGetRequest Request = new ValidationGetRequest();
    ValidationGetResponse Response = new ValidationGetResponse();

    //Instantiate the ValidationSearchCriteria and add
    //all relevant identifiers
    Request.ValidationSearchCriteria = new ValidationSearchCriteria();
    Request.ValidationSearchCriteria.ModelId =
      new Identifier { Name = ModelName };
    Request.ValidationSearchCriteria.EntityId =
      new Identifier { Name = EntityName };
    Request.ValidationSearchCriteria.VersionId =
      new Identifier { Name = VersionName };
    Request.ValidationSearchCriteria.MemberTypeId = MemberType.Leaf;

    //Create a member identifier for each member
    MemberIdentifier newMem = new MemberIdentifier { Code = MemCode };
```

```
    //Add Members to the members collection for which you
    // want to see validation issues
    Request.ValidationSearchCriteria.Members =
      new Collection<MemberIdentifier>();
    Request.ValidationSearchCriteria.Members.Add(newMem);

    //Return the collection of current validation issues
    Response = mds_Proxy.ValidationGet(Request);

    return Response.ValidationIssueList;
}
```

ValidationProcess Example

ValidationProcess validates a model and version combination or validates a set of
members passed into the operation. You can use an EntityMembersGet operation to
retrieve a set of members related to a group of search terms and then loop through
those members. In this simple example, we validate only a single member and pass back
all validation issues found.

```
public Collection<ValidationIssue> ValidationProcess(string ModelName,
string verName, string EntityName, string memCode)
{
    //Instantiate all request and response objects
    ValidationProcessRequest Request = new ValidationProcessRequest();
    ValidationProcessResponse Response =
      new ValidationProcessResponse();

    //Instantiate the Criteria and Options objects
    Request.ValidationProcessCriteria =
     new ValidationProcessCriteria();
    Request.ValidationProcessOptions = new ValidationProcessOptions();

    //Set Model and Version Identifiers - these will be
    //required in all instances
    Request.ValidationProcessCriteria.ModelId =
      new Identifier { Name = ModelName };
    Request.ValidationProcessCriteria.VersionId =
      new Identifier { Name = verName };
    Request.ValidationProcessCriteria.EntityId =
      new Identifier { Name = EntityName };
```

```
Request.ValidationProcessCriteria.Members =
  new Collection<MemberIdentifier>();
Request.ValidationProcessCriteria.Members.Add
(new MemberIdentifier { Code = memCode });

//Options can return validation results or trigger the commit
//of a version (when validation is already successful)
Request.ValidationProcessOptions.ReturnValidationResults = true;

Response = mds_Proxy.ValidationProcess(Request);
return Response.ValidationIssueList;

}
```

Managing Transactions

Transactions can provide users and managers with a complete record of all changes that have been made in the system. Model administrators will be able to see all transactions made within a model, while each user will have access to their own changes. These transactions also support reversal.

TransactionsGet Example

TransactionsGet operations return a list of transactions that meet the provided search criteria. Transaction search criteria only support values that are equal, so these criteria are exposed as identifiers attached to the criteria.

```
public Collection<Transaction> TransactionsGet(string ModelName, string
EntityName, string verName)
{
    TransactionsGetRequest Request = new TransactionsGetRequest();
    TransactionsGetResponse Response = new TransactionsGetResponse();

    //Instantiate the TransactionSearchCriteria class and add the
    //criteria to filter your results
    Request.TransactionSearchCriteria = new TransactionSearchCriteria();

    //TransactionSearchCriteria can consist of any of the
    //attributes of transaction management
    Request.TransactionSearchCriteria.ModelId =
      new Identifier { Name = ModelName };
    Request.TransactionSearchCriteria.EntityId =
```

```
    new Identifier { Name = EntityName };
  Request.TransactionSearchCriteria.VersionId =
    new Identifier { Name = verName };
  Response = mds_Proxy.TransactionsGet(Request);

  return Response.TransactionList;
}
```

TransactionsReverse Example

While there may be many programmatic uses for TransactionsGet, TransactionsReverse should be used with caution. TransactionsReverse does not actually reverse the transaction, but rather reverts the current value from MDS to the prior value stored in the transaction log. This procedure can be very valuable when you need to reverse a change after triggering an external action. Make sure that you reverse the most recent transaction.

The following procedure is a simple example of how to reverse a single transaction based on the ID of the transaction. This procedure will throw an error if an invalid transaction ID is provided. You could add a conditional statement around the TransactionsReversed return statement to handle this case.

```
public int TransactionReversal(int TranId)
{
    TransactionsReverseRequest Request = new
    TransactionsReverseRequest();
    TransactionsReverseResponse Response = new
    TransactionsReverseResponse();

    //Instantiate the transactions object and
    //add the integer ID for the transaction to reverse
    Request.Transactions = new Collection<int>();
    Request.Transactions.Add(TranId);
    Response = mds_Proxy.TransactionsReverse(Request);
    return Response.TransactionsReversed[0].NewId;
}
```

Handling Errors in the Web Service

All MDS web service calls return an OperationResult object within their response messages. This OperationResult object contains a Request_ID to manage long-running requests and any errors that occurred as a result of the request. These errors can provide immediate feedback to client-side developers who need to find problems with their requests. These errors can range from useful to baffling, and sometimes it will take some trial and error to determine what is wrong. Each error will populate a portion of the following properties:

▶ **Code**   Error number specific to the type of error encountered. A general classification for web service errors is provided in the following table.

▶ **Description**   Localized text describing the error.

▶ **Context.FullyQualifiedName**   The fully qualified name of the object involved in the error. Some names are only unique within their context. An entity would be qualified with a model name prefix such as *ModelName : EntityName*.

▶ **Context.Type**   The type of object related to the error.

▶ **Context.Identifier**   The identifier of the object involved in the error.

▶ **Context.Identifier.Id**   The unique GUID of the object, if specified or available.

▶ **Context.Identifier.Name**   The name of the object, if specified or available.

▶ **Context.Identifier.InternalId**   The internal key from the MDS system tables.

Area	Error Number Range
Common	100000–199999
Metadata Operations	200000–299999
Master Data Operations	300000–399999
Business Rule Operations	400000–499999
Security Operations	500000–599999

Summary

The MDS web service provides complete access to all of the functions that are found in the product. While many of the operations are detailed in other chapters of this book, this chapter acts as a reference to help you find the operations you need, and provides more detailed examples. After reading this chapter, you should be familiar with the main groupings available so you can programmatically access all that MDS has to offer. You should also be familiar with the changes made to the MDS web service in SQL Server 2012.

Chapter 14

Advanced Modeling

In This Chapter

▶ **Common Modeling Mistakes**

▶ **Rapid Model Development**

▶ **Managing Slowly Changing Dimensions**

▶ **Limiting Unneeded Complexity**

Modeling is more art than science. You need to understand not only your datasets and how they interact, but also the related systems. You also need to understand people and their processes. In this chapter, we will attempt to tackle some common complex modeling issues found in MDS projects.

Master Data Services is not a data warehouse or a reporting tool. It is a data management tool. This is a difficult distinction for many to understand. Master Data Services should be used to manage and store lists for the business. Security can create boundaries for multiple users. Business rules notify users of issues with the data, while the web UI, Add-in for Excel, and Services API give the entire organization access to work on the same datasets. All of these features are designed around managing data changes.

Once data is being managed correctly in MDS, extract, transform, and load (ETL) processes can send this data into data marts and warehouses to provide the reports demanded by the business. These systems can focus on the reporting structures, disseminating the information without concern for the data editing and quality processes. In this chapter we will try to provide insight into some of the more common complex problems that we have seen.

Common Modeling Mistakes

MDS is best built from the top down, not the bottom up. As discussed in Chapter 3, the first step in managing data is to determine the major entities that need to be managed. Unfortunately, many modelers then move directly to the downstream systems to build their models, deriving all columns from these preexisting systems. This section discusses some significant pitfalls with this approach that you should be aware of.

Building Outside Limitations into MDS

Whether a system is purchased or created, the data model of that system was developed through a series of compromises. If you were building a system to manage payroll, how many attributes would you add for each employee? Would you add information about certifications they hold? Each system is built to solve a business need. Some of these systems attempt to solve multiple needs or allow for minimal customization. If you focus on a single system, you run the risk of bringing these compromises into MDS.

A couple of common compromises seen in the field are perpetuating overloaded fields into your MDM system and propagating system column names. Either of these issues can blunt the effectiveness of your MDS implementation, limiting usability for business users.

Manage Overloaded Fields

Many systems have tables that need to have a single column to use as the primary key. To ensure this column is always unique, values in this column may be a combination of three or more distinct values that have been pasted together, typically as a fixed-length combination. Do not bring this as a single column into MDS. Allow users to manage these distinct values separately. If visibility of this value is required, use business rules to concatenate the obscure codes into this overloaded value for the external systems.

Provide Easily Recognizable Names

Most systems try to use standard naming conventions and technical shorthand to name tables and fields within the database. Ensure that you adapt these names to be easily readable by your end users. This might apply to allowable values within some fields as well. Create an entity and provide useful names to each of these unique values.

Trouble Identifying Common Attributes

Each system within your enterprise comes preconfigured with some built-in nomenclature and culture. If you look at these systems at the database level, where table and column names have been abbreviated, determining meaning and use can be difficult. This can lead to confusion about how different systems or departments manage similar attributes. While these architecture diagrams can help lead the conversation, working directly with the business users is the best way to ensure you accurately model your business.

Engineering Dead Scenarios

When we rely on the existing structures of systems within the organization, we may find ourselves modeling scenarios the business does not require. This can be due to changes in the business structure over time or an incomplete understanding of the problem when the system was implemented. It is important to take advantage of the current mindshare of the business users to build your MDS model as the business wants it.

Rapid Model Development

With the advent of the MDS Add-in for Excel, Master Data Services has revolutionized the modeling process. In the past, there was a gulf between modelers who read and create data models and the rest of the business. The best way to bridge this gulf is to design a model, review it with the users, receive feedback, and repeat the process. With competing products, this process usually takes weeks or months for each iteration, whereas with the Add-in for Excel, a team can create a fully populated model in a couple of days.

Excel is a great intermediate location for data from any source. Many of the datasets currently managed in your organization already exist within Excel. For any data that does not exist in an Excel sheet, you can use the existing data features in Excel to load the data into a workbook. Once the data is loaded into Excel, you can create a new entity by using the Create Entity wizard.

Managing Slowly Changing Dimensions

One of the most common concerns that we deal with when helping data stewards model data in MDS is how to handle history within the system. In most cases these concerns are not drawn from operational systems as these systems typically focus on the processing of the current state. Analytic systems such as data warehouses or data marts need to store or report information based on changes over time. Most modeling discussions quickly turn to managing these dimension changes in MDS. This is the wrong way to look at it. The role of MDS is to create the changes, not to store them for reporting purposes. We need to look at how to leverage the existing tools in MDS to send these changes to the reporting systems that require them.

Ralph Kimball has spent much of his lifetime documenting techniques for analytic systems. One of his most discussed concepts is the handling of slowly changing dimensions. Mr. Kimball identified three types of dimensions that we will discuss here.

Overwriting Rows (Type 1)

The simplest form of storage is in those dimensions that are stateless. Without any need to understand any previous values, ETL processes can simply overwrite the dimension from the subscription view without any further analysis. In a majority of companies, this should be the predominant type of data transfer, especially for supporting entities in the data warehouse.

Adding Rows (Type 2)

The most prevalent type of versioning data in data marts and warehouses stores a new row for each change in the member record. The prior member record is effectively closed using a new key. In order to determine that a change has occurred and a new record needs to be made in the warehouse, the ETL process can look at the last changed date to trigger a new record for the member to be created, each row with a new surrogate key. Natural key or MDS code columns can be used to ensure different record versions can be tracked. You do not need to store this history in MDS.

Unfortunately, the MDS system, like most systems, logs the last changed date as the date and time the change was made. In some cases, the date needs to be explicitly captured separate from the log. If the date is extremely important to the process and is part of the master record itself, create a new field or fields in MDS to store these effective dates. We will discuss the best way to manage these type 2 scenarios later in the chapter.

Adding Columns (Type 3)

Some systems or dimensions use the concept of another column per attribute change. This can be as simple as a prior and a current column for a single attribute. If your warehouse already has a table designed in the standard type 3 fashion, you can continue to populate this model using MDS. Otherwise, type 3 scenarios are tailor-made for versioning, as most users want to run reports for different periods of time.

To support original type 3 table formats, you can source current attribute values from the current version subscription views while sourcing all prior columns from a different set of subscription views linked to the prior version. These subscription views should leverage version flags to ensure they can work across multiple periods of time.

Using the Power of MDS to Simplify the Problem

We can view the loading of history into downstream data marts and data warehouses as an ETL problem or we can attempt to leverage MDS to improve the system. The reason most data marts and data warehouses traditionally used type 1, 2, and 3 storage methods was that data was flowing from one static data model into the reporting system. Information architects were unable to change the original tables that were storing managers, products, or accounts in their initial systems, so they needed to build ETL processes that attempted to pull the history into the reporting database structures.

Unfortunately, these structures all have their drawbacks in this scenario. Type 1 storage is the most efficient, eliminating all duplication from the system. Type 2 is the most robust and most costly, as each change creates another entire record. Type 3 suffers from significant column expansion and an ever-changing data model as different history is required.

MDS can change this equation. When history is required for a downstream dimension, it is rarely needed for all attributes. In fact, when working with data marts, only a few specific attributes require history, and using the time at which the change was made is extremely inaccurate. It is the effective date that matters sometimes for each report. This is where the MDS architecture can be extremely useful. In a matter of minutes, a new entity can be created that stores the important historical relationship along with two effective date columns, Start and End. We can then use subscription views to send this data from MDS. While the original type 1 dimension in MDS is unaffected by the new requirement we can populate a new dimension table to support the time-sensitive reporting requirement. Let's use Main Street Clothing Company to illustrate this problem.

Managing Dimension for Main Street Clothing Company

For the past year, Main Street Clothing Company has been paying its individual store managers a monthly bonus based on sales at that manager's store. A monthly report has been created to provide sales numbers per manager to determine these monthly bonuses. Recently a new mall being built has created an increased demand for experienced managers in the area, and manager turnover has been increasing within the area. The market has also dictated that managers' bonuses be guaranteed in their employment contracts.

Corporate must now include effective dates in the manager report to ensure accurate accounting of the bonuses. Instead of making changes in the Employee entity, making this a type 2 dimension, IT has decided to create an additional entity called Store Manager Relationship. In this entity, secured users can modify the effective management dates of each manager for each store.

Limiting Unneeded Complexity

Another common scenario that occurs in MDS modeling is over-engineering an entity. The two common scenarios I see are data stewards designing for exceptions and designing for *N*. In both of these cases, the computer scientist in us can override common sense, creating additional complexity without adding significant business value. In each of these cases, considering the design time of each scenario is not as important as considering the time needed for users to manage data.

Designing for Exceptions

In many cases, I need to manage a dataset that has a relatively stable change rate 90 percent of the time or more. At other times, this dataset or a portion of the dataset may require a significant change in granularity. The easiest maneuver would be to manage the full dataset at the finer granularity and just make the changes in this single data format. Yet MDS is not designed as an automated system; it encourages and fosters user involvement. The value of a little additional design and integration time can provide significant benefits in terms of user satisfaction and limiting mistakes once the system is live.

Let's take the common example of store hours. Suppose that you work in the corporate IT department of a company that owns a national chain of restaurants. The management of each store in the company has the option of opening and closing at any time they choose. The management of each store is given some discretion in determining their hours of operation because eating habits vary in different parts of the country. The company wants you to design a model where every store is able to do its own cost/benefit analysis of staff versus revenue to optimize its operation's profit.

While every store can select a different hour (or half-hour) at which to open and close each day, you find that certain patterns emerge. None of the restaurants opens before 5 A.M. or closes after 10 P.M. Hours of operation are different on the weekends, while weekday hours generally remain the same throughout the week. The major exception for this dataset is holidays. Every few months, a holiday significantly impacts the number of hours the restaurant is open. For reporting purposes, it is important to know the daily hours of operation when analyzing variable costs and revenue. No matter what happens, your ETL processes are going to need to translate this store operation information into usable data for reporting, and the cost for creating these processes is nominal no matter how you store the hours.

Getting the correct operating hours from each restaurant is the single most important criteria in this project. These hours will be displayed on the company's website, which drives business to the stores. All of your reports will base calculations on total open hours, to determine labor efficiency. If you can't get accurate hours of operation for all stores, nothing else matters. Let's consider three architectures you could implement to solve this problem.

Many IT professionals will like the simplicity of the design shown in Figure 14-1. A single table can store any number of days with similar hours. Now let's think through the use case for the actual table users in MDS. To correctly enter data into this format, a restaurant manager will need to add data changes into MDS as a new row. Any changes to this schedule require users to search and update many different records. Want to change the opening time on Friday for the year? You better set aside next Saturday to do so!

Figure 14-1 *One size fits all*

The model shown in Figure 14-2 gives the most flexibility, allowing users to set regular opening and closing hours each day of the week, with a separate table to break out any exceptions such as holidays. Each restaurant manager should be able to manage their standard hours in a matter of minutes. Whenever exceptions occur, the manager can quickly add them to the table. With this model, the ETL is a little more complicated because the Hours dimension needs to be generated from a combination of two subscription views, but the ease of use for the end user should quickly outweigh this extra complication.

The final example, shown in Figure 14-3, has some positives and negatives over the second option. While the second option gives each restaurant the ultimate flexibility in managing their own hours of operation, for some, this could lead to additional problems, with too much flexibility. Does corporate want to provide acceptable patterns for hours of operation?

This example also limits the chances for mistakes. In the previous example, a manager could mistakenly indicate that the restaurant will be open at 3 A.M. for dinner. Picking from a set of options can also allow new managers to leverage the wisdom of prior

Figure 14-2   *Holiday exceptions only*

Figure 14-3   *Weekday and weekend patterns*

locations, by picking an operational pattern already in use. As a negative, adding a new hours pattern can be a complicated process, and changing hours on a specific day could be complicated or misuse the exception table.

Designing for *N*

Oftentimes we find models that value flexibility over function. While there are many business cases that support flexibility, and others where it may be mandatory, often the business value is questionable at best, and the additional complexity can kill usability. There is no greater case for this than managing customer data. In today's world, any customer can have multiple addresses and multiple phone numbers. Model builders might be tempted to support a customer model that allows for multiple contacts. This could be a separate address or phone table with the customer as an attribute. While this is supported in MDS, this practice can lead to problems both in usability and data quality control.

Think about the case of running a retail establishment. You would like to get more information about your customers. Does the contact card you hand them give blanks for every phone number they are associated with? How about each address? We have found a much more usable model contains a single Customer entity with separate attributes for each phone number by type. A primary address set of attributes is also advisable unless business necessitates a separate table.

The benefits of adding attributes to a single table are not confined only to the model's general usability. A single entity can more easily support business rules, as well as better integration with matching and data quality tools.

Summary

Master Data Services is really your data model layered on the Microsoft proprietary model. To use MDS most efficiently, data stewards must embrace the system as a data management tool and not as a data warehouse. Your MDS system should not mirror every dimension table in your data mart or data warehouse any more than it mirrors list tables in your operational systems. Business needs for data management should drive the model in MDS and the ETL process to load downstream data marts.

Index

The Secure Beginner's Guides

SECURITY SMARTS FOR THE SELF-GUIDED IT PROFESSIONAL

The Secure Beginner's Guides offer trusted, hands-on coverage of current and emerging security topics. Written by experts in the field, these books make it easy to put security concepts into practice now.

Security Metrics: A Beginner's Guide
978-0-07-174400-3

Wireless Network Security: A Beginner's Guide
978-0-07-176094-2

Computer Forensics: A Beginner's Guide
978-0-07-174245-0

Web Application Security: A Beginner's Guide
978-0-07-177616-5

Available in print and e-book format.

 Follow us @MHComputing

Learn more. Do more.™
MHPROFESSIONAL.COM

Master Microsoft® SQL Server® 2012 and Microsoft's Powerful Business Intelligence Tools

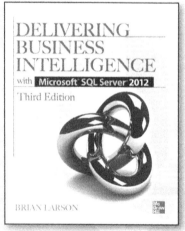

Microsoft SQL Server 2012: A Beginner's Guide, Fifth Edition
Dušan Petković
Filled with real-world examples and hands-on exercises, this book makes it easy to learn essential skills.

Microsoft SQL Server 2012 Reporting Services, Fourth Edition
Brian Larson
Create, deploy, and manage BI reports using the expert tips and best practices in this hands-on resource.

Delivering Business Intelligence with Microsoft SQL Server 2012, Third Edition
Brian Larson
Equip your organization for informed, timely decision making with the expert tips in this practical guide.

Visualizing Data with Microsoft Power View
Brian Larson, Mark Davis, Dan English, and Paul Purington
Unlock the power of Microsoft Power View and build rich BI reports with just a few clicks.

Microsoft SQL Server 2012 Master Data Services, Second Edition
Tyler Graham and Suzanne Selhorn
Learn best practices for deploying and managing Master Data Services (MDS).

Available in print and e-book format
Follow us 🐦 @MHComputing

Learn more. **McGraw Hill** Do more.
MHPROFESSIONAL.COM

CPSIA information can be obtained at www.ICGtesting.com
Printed in the USA
OW03s1123260714

980LV00001B/8/P

9 780071 797856